THE MANAGER'S
GUIDE TO
COMPETITIVE
MARKETING STRATEGIES

THE MANAGER'S GUIDE TO COMPETITIVE MARKETING STRATEGIES

Norton Paley

amacom

AMERICAN MANAGEMENT ASSOCIATION

This book is available at a special
discount when ordered in bulk quantities.
For information, contact Special Sales Department,
AMACOM, a division of American Management Association,
135 West 50th Street, New York, NY 10020.

Library of Congress Cataloging-in-Publication Data

Paley, Norton.
    The manager's guide to competitive marketing
strategies.

    Includes index.
    1. Marketing—Management. I. Title.
HF5415.13.P32   1989   658.8   88-47708
ISBN 0-8144-5910-2

Printing number

10 9 8 7 6 5 4 3 2 1

To my family
In memory of my father, **Elias Paley**
In honor of my mother, **Bessie Paley**
In love of my wife, **Annette,**
and daughters, **Julia and Susan**

Acknowledgments

Many individuals are responsible for the development of a book. My thanks to Ed Ritvo, formerly of the American Management Association, for identifying the need for a seminar on competitive marketing strategy and, specifically, for initiating action that resulted in this book. My thanks, also, to Joshua Martin of AMA for reviewing the manuscript and for providing insightful comments on its content, as well as suggestions for its use in other projects. Thanks to Julia Paley for her editing ability in turning the complex into manageable reading; and to Philip Henry, who provided valuable guidance in content and structure in his desire to make the book as practical as possible for the reader. And thanks to Ronnie Kelly of AMA for her patience and skill in typing and retyping the manuscript. Finally, general thanks to all those in the background, especially members of my family, who encouraged the development of this book.

Contents

Introduction

This book is about competitive strategy and, more precisely, its application to marketing strategy. It is a commentary on how companies are succeeding despite seemingly overwhelming obstacles—and a guide to how managers can become successful strategists in an increasingly embattled competitive marketplace.

Setting the Scene

The business scene today is one where new urgency is enveloping managers' thinking with global considerations beyond the scope of responsibility usually associated with the jobs of marketing director, product manager, and sales manager. Business publications such as *Business Week, Fortune,* and *Forbes* tell of this urgency through cover stories: "Fighting Back," "Wake Up America," "Marketing: The New Priority," "How to Beat the Japanese."

Those stories and other environmental pressures are creating new priorities and practices that are redefining the roles of managers—particularly middle managers in the larger organizations and, certainly, senior managers in smaller firms. Environmental factors include:

- Slowing of real growth worldwide
- Changing demographics
- Changing lifestyles
- Fragmented markets
- Deregulation of major industries
- Global competition
- Rapid technological change
- Shortened product life cycles
- Product proliferation

What results from these environmental pressures are new marketing priorities:

- Target marketing
- Marketing intelligence
- Strategic marketing planning
- Positioning strategies
- Accelerated new product development

Consequently, we now see the marketing manager—and all levels of middle management—taking on a scope of thinking formerly associated only with senior level management: competitive strategy.

Steve Harrell, former General Electric manager of strategic planning, said of the marketing manager[1]:

The marketing manager is the most significant functional contributor to the strategic planning process—with leadership roles in:
1. Defining the business mission
2. Analyzing the environmental, competitive, and business situations
3. Developing objectives and strategies
4. Defining product, market, distribution, and quality plans to implement the business strategies

Additional attention was focused on the manager in a landmark article published in 1980 by Harvard Business School professors Robert H. Hayes and the late William J. Abernathy, "Managing Our Way to Economic Decline."[2] The authors blame American managers for the nation's declining industrial competitiveness. Certainly, monumental environmental factors such as the Organization of Petroleum Exporting Countries (OPEC), inflation, monetary policy, labor-management problems, and trade policy contribute to the country's unresponsiveness to competitive urgencies. But Hayes and Abernathy argue that management has given in to the pressures of Wall Street for short-term gains. They lambast U.S. managers for being too cautious, for failing to invest in manufacturing technology, and for giving operations managers little prestige. They berate managers for managing by numbers and for killing the entrepreneurial spirit that made U.S. industry great.

The transition back to that entrepreneurial spirit has begun in some

[1] Steve Harrell, speech given at the Plenary Session of American Marketing Association's Educators' meeting, Chicago, August 5, 1980, quoted in David W. Cravens, *Strategic Marketing* (Homewood, Ill.: Richard D. Irwin, 1982), p. 17.

[2] R. H. Hayes and W. J. Abernathy, "Managing Our Way to Economic Decline," *Harvard Business Review,* Vol. 58, No. 4 (July–August 1980), pp. 67–77.

organizations. Managers are beginning to think like successful strategists. For example:

Smith-Corona has the distinction of still being the only U.S. manufacturer successfully turning out typewriters for the whole U.S. market in the face of severe Asian competition.

Texas Instruments is battling the Japanese head-to-head in the high-volume dynamic RAM (random-access memory) market with a competitive attitude that is infusing the company with new vitality and aggressive strategies.

Echlin Inc. maintains a competitive advantage in the intensely competitive U.S. auto and truck parts market. Managers at all levels are dedicated to product quality, speed of delivery, service, and customer satisfaction.

Hewlett-Packard Co., once a loosely run engineering-oriented organization with competitors attacking it at virtually every point along its 9,000-product line, has reorganized to become a responsive market-driven organization.

Cummins Engines, the leading U.S. manufacturer of diesel engines, is successfully using strategy to counter Komatsu Ltd. and Nissen's indirect attempts to enter the U.S. market in an unfilled niche.

Kelly-Moore Paint Co., Inc., is outperforming the giant du Pont and Sherwin-Williams Co. by producing 10 percent net on sales compared with the competitor's average of only 2.5 percent net on sales.

Russell Corp., an Alabama-based sportswear maker, is the country's largest producer of athletic uniforms with 35 to 40 percent of the market, not only surviving against low-cost Asian competition but commanding a leading share of the market as well.

Blue Bell Inc., maker of Wrangler jeans, and Wal Mart Stores, Inc., developed a strategy of cooperative distribution using a computer hook-up to fill orders in one day instead of five weeks.

Thus we see evidence of a new style of manager in the making. The paper shuffler, the analyzer, the narrow-focused type of manager is giving way to the strategist, the implementor, the innovator.

As reported in *Business Week,* a new generation of CEOs is emerging who feel that they are "strategic thinkers" and also believe that their operating managers should be as well.[3] "Those who succeed in thinking strategically are the people who are going to move ahead at this company," says Hicks B. Waldron, chairman of Avon Products,

---

[3]"The New Breed of Strategic Planner—Number Crunching Professionals Are Giving Way to Line Managers," *Business Week* (Sept. 17, 1984), p. 62.

Inc. A similar idea was expressed by CEO Donald R. Melville of the Norton Co.: "You can't get ahead just thinking in terms of operations. You won't become a top executive unless you think strategically."

Thinking strategically is filtering down to the lowest levels of successful organizations—to those line managers with responsibilities for individual products. The range of such thinking extends from long-view assumptions about the business environment to anticipating counter strategies competitors might employ to blunt a marketing manager's efforts.

Purpose and Use of This Book

The aim of this book is to awaken managers at all levels—from district sales manager to marketing director—to take responsibility for their respective divisions, departments, product lines, or individual products. The intent is to stimulate a businesslike spirit of entrepreneurship and innovation and the expression of such attitudes in the form of competitive strategies. It is also intended for upper-level executives who are running divisions or smaller organizations, to help them refocus on their role as *strategists,* while they continue to wrestle with the day-to-day problems inherent in every job.

This book can be used in several ways. First, you can read it cover-to-cover as a textbook, and acquire the basic concepts, explanations, and techniques for analyzing, planning, and developing competitive strategies. Second, you can use its workbook format and numerous checklists to develop a strategic marketing plan. Third, you can open the book to any of the more than 70 different case examples of companies that are operating as successful strategists and find mental nourishment and stimulation.

Briefly, Chapter 1 describes five key strategies derived from over 2,500 years of recorded military history and applied to business situations. It also presents basic principles of strategy to use in formulating your own competitive strategies.

In Chapter 2, you see how to develop a framework for competitive analysis by "looking out the window," that is, by using an external viewpoint reached through careful scrutiny of customer behavior and needs, competitors' capabilities, and industry trends. Equally important, Chapter 3 demonstrates how to "look in the window" to examine the capabilities of your own organization or business unit for defending or attacking markets and to help you analyze those strengths and weaknesses with precision.

Chapters 4 and 5 discuss how to develop a working model for marketing and competitor intelligence systems involving collecting, compiling, cataloging, and digesting data to be applied, through strategy development, to the marketing planning covered in Chapters 6 and 7.

Chapters 8 through 13 are devoted to developing specific strategies and tactics for target markets with emphasis on product, pricing, distribution, and promotion strategies, as well as on strategy teams.

The bottom line is to create a sustained competitive advantage by developing competitive strategies and a global marketing perspective (see the Appendix). Such a perspective means *thinking like a strategist* and encompasses the primary themes of this book, such as seeking new opportunities for targeting unserved, poorly served, or emerging markets; overcoming obstacles of market position and intense competition; and reacting quickly enough to stop aggressive competitors.

Finally, the Appendix provides checklists for actual use in outlining your strategies.

It is appropriate here to mention the distinction between the words "customer" and "consumer" as used throughout the book.

"Consumer orientation" is generally understood to mean a focus on the end user and is usually associated with a consumer packaged-goods product. The same designation can be given to the recipient of a service, or other terms can be used such as "client" or "patient." Even for a manufacturer selling direct to an end user, the term "consumer" is appropriate.

"Customer," on the other hand, is generally understood to be the intermediary in the distribution chain between manufacturer and end user, e.g., distributors, wholesalers, and retailers.

In Conclusion

The world of business is going through a period of change that reaches out in global dimensions. For some companies, such as Digital Equipment Corp., change has been evolutionary; for others, it has been revolutionary—for example, Chrysler Corp. during the period of 1981–85. For middle management in particular the upheaval is best exemplified by Procter & Gamble Co.'s aim to transform all levels of marketing managers into global strategic thinkers with aggressive entrepreneurial spirits. The executive management of P&G is pushing managers to take more risks and exploit opportunities more rapidly. Why? A tougher competitive environment, shrinking market shares, changing market behavior, and maturing of key markets are forcing a fresh look at P&G's strategies of waging marketing war. Managers are being asked to generate long-lasting, breakthrough products and ways to exploit new markets with P&G's technology.

In a departure from its paternalistic history, P&G management is phasing out mediocre performers from management ranks. Time-honored, cautious styles are rapidly changing. For example, in the past, P&G would test-market a new product, such as Bounce fabric softener, for years before finally introducing it. In contrast, P&G began selling its Duncan Hines frosting throughout the United States after just 15 months of testing. One executive reports "a new sense of urgency throughout the organization." One reason for the urgency of paying more attention to expanding product lines is that a failure to do so would enable even the smallest competitors to carve out niches in markets that P&G presently dominates. Now P&G is also adding a flood of variations to established products. The results of these activities? A new type of manager is emerging at P&G equipped to handle tough competitors and maturing markets.

The situation at Procter & Gamble shows that middle-level managers are in a threatened position unless there are changes in job performance. Here are some trends:

Global perspective: as indicated by P&G, the manager must think strategically with a total business perspective and not just a product focus.

Entrepreneurial thinking: the emerging manager must look for innovative ways of expanding existing markets, identifying new markets, and evaluating new product opportunities and innovations.

Planning capability: an effective manager must have the ability to develop a well-thought-out strategic marketing plan.

Team approach: the manager must display the leadership to gain willing participating from R&D, manufacturing, finance, sales, and other functional areas and merge that input into the strategic marketing plan.

Implementation: the manager must be able not only to shape the objectives, but to implement them through competitive strategies.

In summary, it is vital that the subject of competitive strategy and marketing be studied thoroughly. At stake are the livelihoods of employees, the survival of businesses, and the economies of towns and cities. Planning, vision, and the effective application of strategies can make the vital difference in developing a sustained competitive advantage.

ONE

Strategy
and
Its Basic Principles

Marketing strategy is the most significant planning challenge of the 1980s regardless of industry or size of company. Our goal will be to reevaluate and examine constantly our marketing position.

Our emphasis will be on market strategy, technique and product innovation.

Coopers and Lybrand and Yankelovich, Skelly and White, in their survey of 250 corporate executives, *Business Planning in the 80s: The New Competitiveness of American Corporations*

Marketing strategy has been the key planning challenge for the 1980's, and will continue to dominate the thinking and actions of executives throughout the 1990's. It encompasses such critical issues as the competitiveness of a country or individual company, changing demographics, new customer behavior patterns, globalization of companies and products, saturated markets, aggressive competitors, rapid technological change, and shortened product life cycles. The ability to develop competitive strategies and implement them is the hallmark of a good manager, but to acquire that ability you need to understand what strategy is and how to incorporate it into your planning. Chapter 1 provides just such a foundation.

1

Competitive Strategies
in Action

Objectives:
To enable you to

1. Understand what strategy means
2. See how military concepts apply to marketing techniques
3. Learn the basic strategy principles of speed, indirect approach, concentra-

   tion, alternative objectives, and unbalancing competition
4. Formulate competitive marketing strategies by applying military strategy to business situations

---

Case Example

Standard Motor Products' Pull-Through Strategy
The case of Standard Motors Products, Inc., one of the most rapidly expanding companies in today's automotive market, provides a good introduction to basic concepts in marketing strategy. Operating in a shrinking market, Standard increased its revenue at a 15 percent annual rate. In seven years the company doubled to 25 percent its market share in such products as ignitions, carburetors, and battery cable parts. Company executives believe that their $205-million company can outperform such formidable competitors as General Motors AC-Delco Division and Echlin Inc.

Despite the general downturn within the automotive parts industry, Standard has been expanding its marketing team and launching new product lines. Management encourages entrepreneurship and the taking of risks. For example, when industry sales dropped sharply in 1980, Standard kept inventories high, built a new distribution center, and expanded its sales force.

The results? In just 12 months Standard picked up its market share faster than before, profits shot up from $3.3 million

Figure 1-1. *Pull-through strategy.*

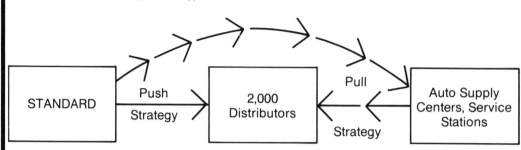

in 1980 to a record $21 million in 1984, and the price of stock doubled.

Standard's success is not based entirely on general expansion. Rather, Standard uses a specific strategy to gain a competitive edge within the industry. Ordinarily, automotive parts manufacturers sell to distributors who then sell to auto supply centers. Recognizing that small distributors usually lack adequate sales forces, however, Standard has taken on the job of influencing the auto supply centers to buy from the distributors. This is called a *pull-through strategy* (Figure 1-1). It uses a dual approach: Standard maintains ongoing contact with its 2,000 distributors, then it sweeps around and attracts the auto supply centers and service stations to the distributors.

Beyond increasing sales, the pull-through strategy has additional advantages. First, contact with retail companies gives Standard access to marketing intelligence that can be used for new product development and for developing strategies to counter competitive threats. Second, it strengthens relationships with distributors and establishes long-term relationships with auto supply centers that can lead to market share dominance.

The Standard Motor case exemplifies many elements of competitive strategy: corporate growth objectives, company competitiveness, maneuvering, competitor intelligence, market penetration, and product development.

Strategy Defined for Business

Keeping in mind the uses of strategy by Standard Motor, we can arrive at a definition of strategy suitable to our topic. *Strategy is the art of coordinating the means* (money, human resources, materials) *to achieve the ends* (profit, customer satisfaction, company growth) *as defined by company policy and objectives.* IBM's long history of extraordinary success reflects this definition of strategy, as does the 1987 turnaround of Ford Motor Company to become the most profitable company in its industry.

Strategy can be further defined at three levels. First, *higher-level corporate strategy* aims to coordinate and direct the company's resources toward the attainment of fundamental company policy without exhausting those resources. Corporate strategy must be implemented with a view toward the state of the market—the long-range potential for further development and profitable growth—and with a minimum expenditure of company resources.

Second, *middle-level operations strategy* takes place at the division, strategic business unit, department, or product-line level. While contributing to overall company policy, it is more precise than corporate strategy. It covers a period of three to five years; focuses on quantitative and nonquantitative objectives; and provides for continued growth by penetrating existing markets with existing products, expanding into new markets with existing products, developing new products for existing markets, and developing new products for new markets.

Third, *lower-level execution strategy (tactics)* requires a shorter time frame than at the two higher levels (usually one year), and may correlate with the annual marketing plan. While consistent with long-term strategies and goals, tactics are designed to achieve short-term objectives. They are precise in areas of pricing and discounts; advertising media and copy approaches; sales aids and deployment of the sales force; distributor selection and training; product packaging and service; and selection of market segments for product launch.

Human Factors in Strategy

With the computerization of marketing techniques, many managers rely exclusively on quantified data to develop a marketing plan. They consider the market to be a set of objective factors that can be predicted, analyzed, and managed with the appropriate techniques. While correct calculations and well-coordinated objectives are indispensable for marketing strategy, they are not sufficient for handling uncertain business conditions and human response.

Marketing—like the military—is a battle of mind against mind, manager against competing manager, marketing strategy against competitor's strategy. It is essentially a conflict of human wills, and its strategies must, therefore, meet and counter unpredictable human responses. Basil Liddell Hart, the foremost military historian, has written:

> Natural hazards, however formidable, are inherently less danger-
> ous and less uncertain than fighting human hazards. All condi-
> tions are more calculable, all obstacles more surmountable than
> those of human resistance. By reason, calculation, and prepara-
> tion they can be overcome almost to a timetable.[1]

To understand the role of strategy and the impact of human will, consider what happens when an existing firm enters a new market. Immediately the newcomer will encounter resistance from companies already dominating the market. Therefore, a prime purpose of strategy is to diminish resistance. The goal of strategy is not direct combat in the marketplace, which would exhaust a company's resources and increase resistance. Rather, the goal of strategy is dislocation of the competition and concentration by your own company.

Dislocation takes place at two levels: physical and psychological. At the physical level, it entails a series of moves to upset the competition's plans through a sudden attack on a market segment. For instance, a move might impair a company's ability to supply outlets or make deliveries on time by dislocating its distribution and organization. Movement depends on calculations of market conditions, competitor's resistance, timing, geography, distribution, and transportation.

At the psychological level, dislocation relies on surprise to disorient and demoralize the competing manager. When the competing manager feels trapped and unable to counter your moves quickly enough, he or she may make mistakes in judgment, and thus play the market into your hands. Surprise depends on a calculation of the conditions that are likely to affect the *will* of the competition.

Movement and surprise, the physical and psychological elements, must be used together for strategy to work. The purpose of combining physical and psychological techniques is to distract the competing manager from your own efforts, disperse his attention among many unprofitable avenues, and dislocate him from his grip on the market. Overextended and limited in his options, he will be less able to interfere with your moves.

To dislocate your competition, you may have to distribute your own efforts temporarily in order to appear being spread out. Once you have weakened your competition, however, you must *concentrate* your strength at the point of greatest market potential. The fa-

[1]B. H. Liddell Hart, *Strategy* (New York: Praeger, 1954), p. 163.

miliar marketing term given to such concentration is *segmentation* or *niche marketing*.

The best way to achieve this concentration is to have a plan with *alternative market objectives*. If the competing manager is certain of your aim, he has the best chance of blunting your efforts. By taking a line that threatens him with alternative objectives, you distract his attention, divide his efforts, and place him on the horns of a dilemma. By leaving yourself a number of options, you ensure the achievement of at least one objective, perhaps more. Therefore, your plan must be flexible enough to respond to changing circumstances.

In sum, the aim of the manager is not to battle directly with the competition, but rather to use strategy to dislocate and weaken the competitor, while concentrating his company's own strength in the market. And it all boils down to manager versus manager, one person competing against another.

Military Strategy and Marketing Approaches

Since the time that the ancient Greeks coined the word *stratēgia,* meaning to lead an army, thousands of generals have used military strategy to conquer territory and gain power. To impose their wills on others, they have had to unbalance their opponents physically and psychologically. Faced with a conflict of wills, the captains on the battlefield were forced to maximize the effectiveness of their economic and human resources in order to achieve their goals. These challenges—outwitting competing wills, gaining territory and power, and conserving resources while expanding influence—are precisely those of businesses. Military strategies of attack and defense are, therefore, an excellent resource for businesses.

Most confrontations—be they military, business, or even athletic—involve a defense protecting its ground and an offense, or attacker, trying to overtake that ground. The key to offensive strategy is the efficient use of resources to accomplish the attack and overtake the territory, or market segment. The military perspective provides five basic approaches: direct attack, indirect attack, envelopment attack, bypass attack, and guerrilla attack.

Direct Attack Figure 1-2 illustrates the *direct attack,* a head-on confrontation by the attacker against a defender. Note there is no maneuver. History dictates that in such a situation the initial advantage is always with the

Figure 1-2. *Direct attack.*

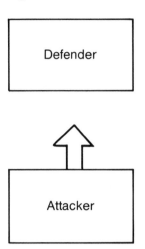

entrenched defender, who has both economic and physical strength. As a result, losses are enormous for the attacker. In a military sense, the attacker is "bloodied on the barbed wire," losing human and material resources and exhausting itself before even reaching the primary target.

In a business sense, a direct attack means exhausting budgets—using sales, advertising, manufacturing, and other resources without achieving the objectives. Even if a company does achieve some minor objective, such as minimal sales or gaining nominal market share, few or no resources will remain for breaking through or penetrating the market. Using the military analogy, no resources remain to "get off the beaches" before the counterthreat of being "pushed back into the sea" is mounted.

In his book *Strategy,* Liddell Hart presents a massive study covering 12 wars that decisively affected the course of European history in ancient times and 18 major wars of modern history up to 1914. In all, these 30 conflicts embraced more than 280 major military campaigns. The study reveals that in only 6 of those campaigns did a decisive result follow a direct frontal approach; and of those 6, most began with an indirect attack but were changed to a direct attack for a variety of battlefield circumstances. Consequently, Liddell Hart states:

> History shows that rather than resign himself to a direct approach a Great Captain will take even the most hazardous indirect approach—if necessary over mountains, deserts or swamps with only a fraction of his force even cutting loose from his commu-

Figure 1-3. *Direct attack on IBM.*

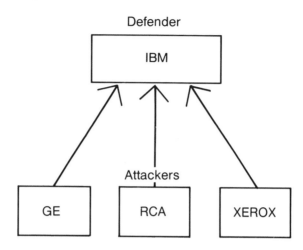

nications. He prefers to face any unfavorable condition rather than accept the risk of frustration inherent in a direct approach.[2]

Thus, reviewing the overwhelming evidence of history, we can conclude that no general is justified in launching his troops in a direct attack upon an enemy who is firmly in position.

Just how much stronger is the defense than the attacker in a direct attack? Napoleon estimated a three-to-one advantage was needed to break through a defender's line in a direct frontal attack. In Napoleon's time, a three-to-one advantage meant having three times more infantry, artillery, or cavalry, and three times more logistical support than the defender had. Thus, even if a breakthrough did occur by using a massive infusion of resources, inadequate human and material resources would remain for follow-up and penetration. In business terms, a three-to-one advantage translates into three times more salespeople, advertising expenditures, research and administrative support—a huge expenditure of resources for little, or perhaps even no, return.

A business example of a direct attack is General Electric, RCA, and Xerox launching a direct frontal attack during the 1970's against IBM, an entrenched defender (Figure 1-3). RCA alone lost $500 million on the venture. All three attackers retreated from that market.

During World War II, General Douglas MacArthur made the following statement at a strategy meeting with President Franklin D. Roosevelt: ''The use of a direct frontal attack is a sign of a mediocre

[2]*Strategy*, pp. 162–163.

Figure 1-4. *Indirect attack.*

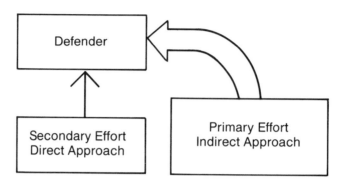

commander and there is no room in modern warfare for such a commander.'' To paraphrase MacArthur for our topic: The use of a direct
frontal attack against an entrenched competitor is a sign of a mediocre manager. And there is no room in today's competitive environment for such a manager.

Indirect If the direct attack puts the defense at an advantage, requires an enor-
Attack mous infusion of resources, deprives the attacker of strength for market penetration, and is generally likely to fail, then an alternative
approach must do the opposite. It should put the defense at a disadvantage by concentrating on its weaknesses. At the same time, the
strategy should efficiently channel the attacker's resources toward
maximizing market share rather than exhausting them in the attack.

Figure 1-4 illustrates the foremost method of accomplishing these
goals: the *indirect attack*. As shown in the diagram, the attacker
launches a primary attack against one of the competition's weaknesses, and uses a secondary direct attack to distract attention away
from the primary effort. According to Liddell Hart, this form of attack has been the most fruitful approach.[3] It has the greatest chance
of success while conserving the greatest amount of strength.

When indirect attack is applied as a business strategy, the attacker
concentrates on a weakness in the current market environment—a
market segment that is emerging, neglected, or poorly served by other
companies. This segment is the *point of entry*. It could be in product
(a cassette with the digital capabilities of a compact disc), in price (a
computer cheap enough for students to afford), in promotion (mineral
water oriented toward high-class consumers), or in distribution (video
cassettes dispensed at supermarkets). While applying its strength in

[3]*Strategy,* pp. 25, 164.

one area, the attacker distracts the competition by appearing to launch a direct attack against the competitor's stronghold. This action disorients the defender, causing it to waste effort and resources. After penetrating an underdeveloped market segment, and thus establishing a market presence, the attacker can more easily capture parts of the market previously dominated by competitors. This critical follow-up to entry is called *market expansion.*

Examples of the advantages of the indirect attack abound in business. For instance, when the Germans and Japanese first entered the U.S. automobile market, they came in with small cars, a market virtually neglected by U.S. manufacturers during the 1970's and earlier. Similarly, Miller discovered the light beer segment as an emerging market. Honeywell for years concentrated its computers on the medium- and small-size cities generally neglected by IBM. Burroughs Corporation became a dominant factor in a segment specifically serving the financial community with computer hardware and software.

With the abundance of business examples and with evidence from military history, there is never any justification for a manager to undertake a direct frontal attack in today's competitive market. Rather, it is a manager's obligation and necessity to use an indirect approach by (1) finding an unattended, poorly served, or emerging market; (2) concentrating all available resources on fulfilling the unmet needs and wants of that market in a strength-conserving manner; and (3) eventually expanding into other parts of the market.

Case Examples

Xerox Corp. The case of Xerox Corp. provides one of the most dramatic illustrations of the damage the indirect approach can cause to a defender. In the mid-1970's, Xerox had an 88 percent share of the copier market, mostly in large- and medium-size copiers. By the mid-1980's, Xerox forfeited to competitors more than half of the market for plain copiers, even though it had virtually created the plain copier machine with its classic 914 model (now displayed in the Smithsonian Institution). What happened to cause the disastrous plunge?

Japanese companies, hoping to expand in the United States during the mid-1970's, looked to the office products field and, in particular, to the copier market. Scanning the market they saw a sizable segment that was virtually unattended by Xerox: small-size copiers. Research indicated that clerks in millions of U.S. companies were making copies at coin-operated machines in local stationery shops. The owners of these companies never thought they could afford to own a copier. The Japanese com-

Figure 1-5. *Indirect attack on Xerox.*

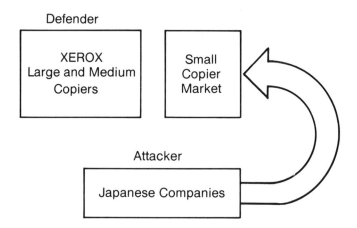

panies saw the opportunity for an indirect approach into the exposed flank (segment) of the small business market. Xerox, facing out in one direction by supplying large copiers to medium and large organizations, took no notice of competitors such as Canon, Sharp, and Ricoh coming from behind. Figure 1-5 illustrates their attack.

If the Japanese companies had tried to force their way into the U.S. market with large machines, they would have been launching a direct frontal attack against Xerox, which dominated the market. They would have expended huge amounts of time and money, exhausted their resources for future progress, and might well have failed completely. Instead, they used an indirect approach.

Having chosen their strategy, the Japanese companies developed their marketing mix:

Product: They introduced a small tabletop copier that used plain paper, no chemicals, and performed only the basic copying function. It could not copy two sides, staple, punch three holes, or collate; it simply made a copy. And that was exactly what the small business owners wanted.

Price: They entered with a low price to penetrate the market and to gain market share rapidly. Profits would come later.

Promotion: Media was targeted directly to the small business audience.

Distribution: The Japanese manufacturers could not match the huge direct sales force of Xerox. Instead they approached office supply dealers who had immediate access to the small business market, the targeted segment.

Thus, we have the *entry phase* to a market. But to remain with a minor foothold is risky. The next phase is *market expansion.* In military terms, the aim is to get off the beaches and go inland or suffer the possibility of being pushed back into the water. The Japanese companies did the next predictable thing: They expanded their product line with a full range of models and eventually pushed Xerox's share of the market down to 44 percent before leveling off.

How could Xerox have responded? If Xerox had immediately applied its resources to developing a small copier or obtaining one from outside sources, the Japanese attack would have become a direct one, which would have slowed down the penetration and could possibly have pushed the Japanese manufacturers out of the market. Xerox had the product name, the reputation, and the market presence to give it a solid hold on the market. Thus, the initial strength was with the defender, Xerox. Napoleon's ratio of three-to-one suggests that the Japanese manufacturers would have had to expend huge resources to gain a minimal share of the market in a direct attack.

However, Xerox did not respond in time. It is currently making excellent strides in coming back and is now a "lean and mean" organization with a full line of small and large copiers. But the fight back to dominate is always costlier than retaining market share already possessed.

Xerox's counterstrategy looks like this:

1. It is utilizing cost improvement strategies through quality circles, assembly line automation, and less labor-intensive product design.
2. It is changing its attitude on profitability—forgoing short-term results in favor of long-term profitability and market-share expansion.
3. It is slashing prices on certain models to recapture market share.
4. It is introducing new lines of copiers to envelop Japanese product lines.
5. It is increasing R&D and has already invested over $600 million in new product development.
6. It is attacking the Japanese home markets through its joint venture with Fuji Xerox.
7. As a total corporate strategy, it is competing against the Japanese in every market segment in order to regain market leadership.

Having lost its market dominance through inadequate defense against an indirect attack, Xerox is having to use its own strategies to recapture the market.

Black & Decker Corporation   For a similar situation with a different outcome, we can examine the case of Black & Decker. It held a strong foothold in the power tools market aimed primarily at the home hobbyist. Makita Electric Works, Ltd., of Japan, in its effort to take over Black & Decker's market, looked for an indirect approach rather than a head-on frontal attack against the established defense. Makita found a segment within the professional power tools market that was poorly served by Black & Decker. Makita's strategy was to fill that niche with improved power tools at lower prices than Black & Decker's and thus outmarket its competitor.

However, Black & Decker quickly saw Makita's impending threat and formed a counterstrategy. It realized that Makita's entry into the professional power tool market was just a preliminary step to invading Black & Decker's primary segments. In order to protect its own market segment from intrusion, it took the following steps.

First, it rapidly *closed all possible weaknesses* in its marketing and manufacturing so that Makita would not be able to find a point of entry. In order to achieve that result, it initiated marketing research to identify consumer needs and used marketing intelligence systems to close all vulnerable product gaps.

Next, Black & Decker conducted extensive *competitor analysis:* Its researchers dissected, scrutinized, and duplicated Makita's products to unravel the secrets of cost advantage and quality. Then Black & Decker cut its prices to match Makita's, and modernized its plants to achieve a manufacturing cost advantage.

Consequently, Makita's attack became a direct one in which advances slowed down and allowed Black & Decker to recapture leadership in virtually every market segment in the power tool industry. Although Makita had devised a useful indirect strategy, Black & Decker preempted Makita's moves by filling in product gaps and strengthening weaknesses. Black & Decker expanded its market share and Makita was forced to retreat and devise a new strategy.

International Mailing Systems, Inc.

We examine now a case of a small company making strong inroads against a powerful defender by using indirect strategy. At one time, Pitney Bowes Inc. owned the U.S. postage meter market with a 90 percent share of the market. Market research by competitors revealed criticisms that Pitney Bowes's meters required a high degree of service and were overpriced. During the mid-1980's, International Mailing Systems, Inc., a small mailroom equipment company, entered the market as a U.S. distributor for Hasler Ltd. Hasler is a Swiss manufacturer of a quiet, compact, and reliable postage meter that is easy to maintain and can be upgraded as mail volume increases. In the 18 months since its introduction in the United States, the Hasler meter has won more new orders than the number two supplier, Friden Alcatel Company. IMS has pushed its way into mailrooms long controlled by Pitney Bowes, including those of the American Express Company, Bank of America National Trust & Savings Assn., Aetna Life & Casualty Company, and several government agencies. For Hasler, the United States had already become its largest single market, second only to Europe as a whole.

How did IMS enter the market? Using an indirect attack, it applied the following strategies:

Product: IMS became an exclusive distributor of a quality product that emphasized performance, dependability, low maintenance, and upgrading capabilities—a clear product advantage.

Price: It penetrated the market with lower prices than Pitney Bowes, averaging a 5 to 10 percent differential. IMS also offered a five-year lease program that earned customers an extra 15 percent discount—a price advantage.

Distribution: IMS had strong penetration of mailrooms with its line of gummed tape dispensers and electronic scales, providing a clear-cut benefit by adding a complementary (postage meter) product.

Promotion: IMS's promotion strategy positioned it as an attractive alternative to Pitney Bowes by emphasizing performance, dependability, and price.

Market: In addition to larger installations, IMS attacked the market segment of smaller mailrooms (processing fewer than 100 envelopes per day) with a special product and price advantage.

As this case shows, the indirect approach gives even small companies the leverage and market presence to overtake segments once controlled by a powerful defense.

Envelopment Attack

Envelopment strategy consists of two stages. First, as in the indirect attack, the attacker focuses on a specific market segment that will provide a point of entry. Then, by identifying additional market segments and adding new products, the attacker uses an expansion strategy to *envelop* the entire market (Figure 1-6).

For example, Seiko initially entered the U.S. watch market in one segment, and then enveloped the market by offering 400 models of

Figure 1-6. *Envelopment attack.*

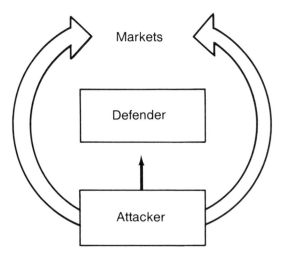

watches to penetrate every major watch outlet and overwhelm the competitors. The Timkin Company offers 26,000 shaped-ball-bearing combinations, a product line unmatched by any competitor, as a means of fulfilling customers' needs and enveloping that market segment.

Case Example

Heublein Inc. Heublein Inc. has become an almost classic example of the envelopment attack. The company produces Smirnoff vodka, a leading brand with a dominant share of the market in the U.S. During the 1960's, Smirnoff was attacked on price by another brand, Wolfschmidt, produced by The Seagram Company Ltd. Wolfschmidt was priced at $1.00 a bottle less than Smirnoff and claimed the same quality. Recognizing a real danger of customers switching to Wolfschmidt, Heublein needed a strategy to protect its market dominance. It had a number of options:

1. Lower the price of Smirnoff by $1.00 or less to hold on to its market share.
2. Maintain the price of Smirnoff but increase advertising and promotion.
3. Maintain its price and hope that current advertising and promotion would preserve the Smirnoff image and market share.

While some options were attractive, they were basically obvious, direct approaches. Heublein decided instead on envelopment (Figure 1-7). First, it raised the price of Smirnoff by $1.00 and preserved the premier image the brand already enjoyed.

Figure 1-7. *Heublein's envelopment attack on Seagram.*

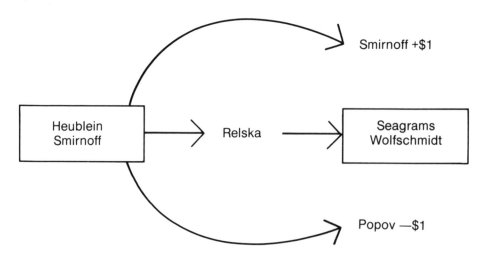

Next, Heublein introduced a new brand, Relska, and positioned it head to head as a fighting brand against Wolfschmidt's price and market segment. While that holding action was taking place, Heublein introduced still another brand, Popov, at $1.00 less than Wolfschmidt. That action had the effect of enveloping Wolfschmidt. By the mid 1980's, Smirnoff remained number one in cases of all imported and domestic vodka shipped in the United States, with Popov in the number two position.

The Heublein case is also a clear illustration of how strategy lies in the sphere of human behavior, which is in turn affected by movement and surprise. Movement was demonstrated by the physical act of repositioning Smirnoff upscale, and by introducing the threatening, fighting brand, Relska, directly at Wolfschmidt. The move also had a psychological effect on Wolfschmidt's managers, who were distracted by the threat to their market share. By dislocating Wolfschmidt in this way, the move diminished its capabilities to resist. Surprise was achieved and the envelopment completed by introducing Popov, which caused a psychological paralysis to further action by Wolfschmidt.

Bypass Attack The *bypass attack* allows the attacker to circumvent its chief competitors and diversify into unrelated products or into unrelated geographical markets for existing products (Figure 1-8). Companies will sometimes use the bypass attack to compensate for missed opportunities for expansion within their own market. For example, in 1985 the Eastman Kodak Co. began a bypass approach into such diverse areas as electronics and biotechnology, with products as diverse as electronic publishing systems, cattle feed nutrients, and anticancer drugs. This relatively sudden move into diverse fields followed an ultraconservative period in which the company dragged its feet while com-

Figure 1-8. *Bypass attack.*

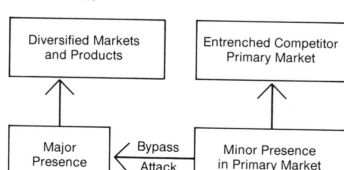

petitors grabbed such markets as instant photography, 35mm cameras, and video recorders, all natural extensions of Kodak's core business since 1880.

The bypass strategy is difficult because expansion into a range of unrelated fields can diminish a company's strength in any single area. An example of a fairly unsuccessful use of bypass strategy is the Colgate-Palmolive Company (Delaware). Although Colgate surpassed the Procter & Gamble Co. in many European markets and maintained a lead for its existing products there, in most U.S. markets Colgate remained behind Procter & Gamble. To increase its success in U.S. markets, it diversified into textiles, hospital products, cosmetics, sporting goods, and food products. However, Colgate has had to retreat from its wide variety of businesses because the diversification was too costly.

Guerrilla Attack

Guerrilla attack involves small intermittent attacks on different markets. It can be useful for a small company competing against a large corporation, or where a product with a small market share is combatting a brand leader. It can also be executed by a larger organization against its competitors. Guerrilla attacks are characterized by a number of actions: selective price cuts, supply interferences, executive raids, intensive promotional bursts, and assorted legal action. The aim is movement and surprise to create confusion and distraction, and to cause the opposing manager to make mistakes.

Case Example

International Business Machines Corporation

A dramatic example of the guerrilla attack, as well as other indirect approaches, was demonstrated by IBM during 1985. At that time, IBM noted the successful Japanese invasion of U.S. markets for cars, cameras, and consumer electronics. Determined to prevent its markets from being shattered by those awesome successes, IBM became an aggressive strategic marketer.

When Japan tried to move into IBM's markets by attacking its vulnerable underside, software, IBM dealt a powerful blow in a clear example of a guerrilla attack. After winning a lawsuit against Hitachi, Ltd. for allegedly stealing IBM software, IBM decided to stop disclosing its source codes, which are descriptions of the operating system of software needed to run all applications programs.

This single strategic move put the Japanese computer manufacturers on the defensive, forcing them to spend huge amounts of time and money rewriting old programs and developing software that would not infringe on IBM's copyright. According to some experts at the time, this put Japan five to ten years behind IBM.

While this guerrilla move took place, IBM aggressively moved into the Japanese home markets. During 1985, its sales in those markets rose 26 percent over the previous year, higher than its closest competitor, Fujitsu. These strategic moves put the Japanese computer manufacturers on the defensive, protecting their home markets and thereby temporarily distracting them from invading U.S. and other world markets.

Then, while all this movement, surprise, distraction, and dislocation were taking place through the various guerrilla actions already described, IBM moved aggressively as follows:

1. It invaded several potential growth markets. For example, IBM created a nationwide videotext service through a joint venture with Sears, Roebuck, and Co. and CBS, Inc.
2. It moved into other growth markets by introducing 600 new software products for its personal computers.
3. It moved into large, integrated information-processing systems that combined computer-aided design, automated manufacturing, and back-office operations.
4. It began to capture a segment of the huge global telecommunications market by forming a joint venture with Aetna Life & Casualty Company and Communications Satellite Corporation.
5. It moved into broader distribution patterns by utilizing mail order companies, retailers, and value-added resellers who package the computers with software written for specific industries.
6. It continued to improve its strength in after-sales service, which it viewed as one of the most important aspects of its marketing strategy.

IBM's use of guerrilla warfare in strategic marketing demonstrates that even a giant company is not invulnerable to the threats of smaller competitors and must constantly maintain a defensive/offensive posture. In cases of medium-size or smaller companies the threat from competitors is even greater.

Strategy Principles

With the discussion of attack techniques in mind, we can now bridge the vast historical perspective of military strategy and the more recent view of business. The military–marketing relationship can be summed up in the following statements:

Figure 1-9. *Strategy principles.*

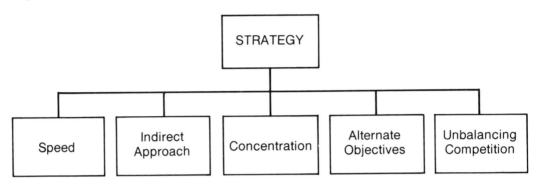

> The object of war is a better state of peace.
> Liddell Hart

> The object of business is to create a customer.
> Peter Drucker

From the 2,500 years of recorded military history we find five essential principles that are characteristic of all strategy, be it military, athletic, political, or financial—practical principles that you can apply to your business for successful competitive strategy. These principles are speed, indirect approach, concentration, alternative objectives, and unbalancing competition (Figure 1-9). An understanding of these practical principles is critical for implementing successful competitive strategy. Below, you will find descriptions of the strategy principles, examples from actual corporations, and step-by-step procedures for applying them to your firm.

Speed Speed is as essential to marketing as it is to the military. There are few cases of overlong, dragged-out campaigns that have been successful. Exhaustion—the draining of resources—has killed more companies than almost any other factor. Extended deliberation, procrastination, cumbersome committees, and long chains of command from home office to regional sales office are all detriments to success. Protracted efforts divert interest, diminish enthusiasm and depress morale. Individuals become bored and their skills lose sharpness. The gaps of time created through lack of action give competitors a greater chance to react and to blunt your efforts.

In today's competitive business environment, a manager must evaluate, maneuver, and concentrate marketing forces quickly to gain the most profit at least cost in the shortest span of time. In the cases already cited, IBM acted quickly to invade Japanese markets while bringing legal action against its Japanese competitor. Heublein worked rapidly to reposition Smirnoff and introduce two new brands before Seagram could respond. The proverb "Opportunities are fleeting" or, in the more current language, "The window of opportunity is open" has an intensified truth in today's markets. Speed is essential for gaining the advantage and exploiting the advantage gained.

Organizing for Speed and Quick Reaction

Two factors make it possible for the manager to react with speed. First, new technologies in product development, communications, and computerization challenge companies to set up organizations to react quickly and decisively, in a ratio of a short span of time to a large amount of space. However, even with new technology, gathering market intelligence entails long periods of research, experiment, and investment for each marketing situation. Therefore, the second factor for maximum speed—the essential ingredient—is *efficient organization:* simplifying the system of control and, in particular, shortening the chain of command.

In a small organization the chief executive officer or president is at the helm; he is in a unique position in that he controls both policy making and execution. Because decisions do not have to be channeled through others, they are unlikely to be misinterpreted, delayed, or contested; they can be implemented with consistency and speed.

But small, single-product businesses ruled by one person are rare these days. The pendulum has swung to multiproduct firms as well as the new breed of diversified corporations created by leveraged buyouts and other financial procedures. With these developments come problems of organization. New people, new products, new positions, and new levels of authority coming together into one organization may well result in a cumbersome, inflexible operation.

Individuals in the field often feel that there are obstructions in the decision-making process for moving into new markets. Missed opportunities are common, and "go" decisions get stuck for reasons other than the competition. Even first-line managers think that there are too many people at the staff level or in service departments and not enough on the job with revenue divisions. The large size of office staff and the shortage of efficient managers are sources of constant complaint. As a result, companies have sometimes tried to reduce their staffs to a "lean and mean" level. But often this reduction only upsets the efficient working of existing organs of control without providing compensating gain.

Your own experience may well support the obvious inference that an organization with many levels in its decision making process cannot operate with speed. This situation exists because each link in a chain of command carries four drawbacks:

1. Loss of time in getting information back.
2. Loss of time in sending orders forward.
3. Reduction of the top executive's full knowledge of the situation.
4. Reduction of the top executive's personal influence on managers.

Therefore, to make your marketing effort effective, reduce the chain of command. The fewer the intermediate levels, the more dynamic the operations tend to become. The result is improved effectiveness of the total marketing effort and increased flexibility. A more flexible organization can achieve greater market penetration because it has the capacity to adjust to varying circumstances, carry alternative objectives, and concentrate at the decisive point. Organizational flexibilit, can be enhanced by the use of strategy teams (Chapter 13) made up of junior and middle managers representing different functional areas of the organization.

Speed of Reaction at the Lower Echelons

Today, competitive business relies on the ability of organizations to adapt quickly to the unexpected. Marketing success has become a serial process composed of many local market opportunities. Exploiting these situations depends on the intelligence and initiative of *junior managers*. It is they who are first exposed to grasping the need for change, even when senior executives are reluctant to swerve at all from their accustomed paths. Long training and extended time at one job level may make managers more expert in execution, but such expertise is bound to be gained at the expense of fertility of ideas, originality, and flexibility—the essential elements for swiftly meeting market demands and opportunities. The junior manager can be an excellent source of qualities needed for speedy reaction.

Application

To increase the speed of your operations and improve your flexibility, do the following:

1. Reduce the chain of command in your company. Reorganize management for efficiency.

2. Utilize junior managers for ideas, flexibility, and initiative in identifying and taking advantage of new opportunities.
3. Use strategy teams made up of junior and middle managers representing different functional areas of the organization to increase the company's flexibility.

Indirect Approach As noted in the discussion of military strategy and marketing approaches, you should avoid the frontal attack at all costs in favor of an indirect approach, which can include any of the nondirect forms of attack: indirect, envelopment, bypass, or guerrilla. The object of the indirect approach is to circumvent the strong points of resistance and concentrate in the markets of opportunity with a competitive advantage built around product, price, promotion, or distribution. The cases of Xerox (small copy machines), Black & Decker (professional power tools), and the Japanese and German firms (small automobiles) already cited illustrate an indirect attack centered around market segment and product. Heublein, on the other hand, built an envelopment attack around product and price. In the following cases, L'eggs exemplifies a competitive advantage in promotion and distribution, and Iomega Corporation demonstrates a different type of indirect strategy—the pull-through.

Other cases have become marketing legends. Columbia Records used an indirect approach centered around distribution to start the first record club. Book-of-the-Month Club started in the late 1920's and circumvented the traditional bookstore as the "only" way to sell books. In the early 1970's Sony Corp. entered the U.S. market with a small TV, thus using the indirect approach against the U.S. giants that focused only on larger sets.

Case Examples

L'eggs Products, Inc. L'eggs provides a marketing classic in indirect approach. Begun in 1971 as a division of Hanes Companies, Inc., L'eggs climbed to first place as the largest-selling brand of women's hosiery in U.S. supermarkets and drugstores. Prior to 1971, Burlington Industries, Inc., Kayser-Roth Corporation, and Hanes led the hosiery industry by distributing through department store outlets. Only inexpensive, poor-quality foreign brands had supermarket distribution at that time.

Using an indirect approach, Hanes took an end run around the standard channels of distribution. It created the brand name L'eggs and packaged relatively high-quality hosiery in a highly visible, egg-shaped carton. It set up a network of 450 freelance "route girls" and dressed them in unique costumes to stock the freestanding store displays. Hanes also bypassed the traditional method of selling: Rather than asking stores to make an investment, it requested just two-and-a-half square feet of floor space and put L'eggs displays in the store on consignment, a form of selling whereby the stores did not have to pay for the merchandise until it was sold.

Through its indirect approach, Hanes identified an area of weakness (supermarket distribution), used differentiation (unique packaging with a quality product), diminished resistance from supermarket managers (consignment), and improved distribution (efficient inventory stocking service). As a result of this marketing assault, after only 24 months L'eggs sold in 75 percent of the major urban markets in the country.

Iomega Corporation Iomega Corporation manufactures an innovative system that packs more information on a floppy disk than competitors' systems. Back in 1983, the company was generating revenues of less than $8 million and had losses of $15 million. Upon the arrival of Gabriel Fusco as its new president and chief executive, the company saw its revenues jump to $51 million in just one year. The operation ran in the black for the first time. Revenues were expected to hit $120 million two years later.

What happened? Before Fusco's arrival, the company attempted to persuade computer makers to use its product for data storage—a direct frontal strategy. Most companies rejected the new product even though there were distinct product and cost advantages. In a bold move, Fusco decided to employ an indirect approach—the pull-through strategy—by building up a consumer following for its products through the retail stores.

He set to work building a special disk subsystem that computer owners could attach to their computers. Then he met with executives of Computerland Corporation and persuaded them to carry Iomega's disk drives. Success came quickly: In a relatively short period of time, 35,000 systems were sold for IBM PC's and IBM-compatible machines. Fusco figured that between customers needing hard-disk backup and those upgrading floppy systems, 20 to 30 percent of computer owners were prospects for Iomega products.

Application

To use an indirect approach, do the following:

1. Search for emerging, neglected, or poorly served market segments through competitive analysis (see Part Two) and fill product gaps.

2. Identify a competitive advantage centered around price, product, promotion, or distribution (see Part Four).
3. Use movement, surprise, speed, and alternative objectives to dislocate and confuse your competitor.
4. Once you have gained a point of entry, move toward market expansion.

Concentration Concentration has two uses in business terms. First, it means directing resources toward fulfilling a specific need or want of a market segment. In modern marketing practices concentration is used in target marketing, segmentation, and niche marketing. Second, in strategy, concentration means focusing the strengths of the attacker against the weaknesses of the competitor.

How do you determine the weaknesses of the competitor? You use *competitive analysis* in your strategy development to detect the strength–weakness relationship (see Part Two). Internal analysis allows you to identify what Philip Kotler in his various books on marketing calls your "distinctive competencies" or strengths.[4] External analysis allows you to identify your competitor's weaknesses.

Case Example

The U.S. Trucking Industry Nissan Motor Co., Ltd., Mitsubishi Heavy Industries, Ltd., Isuzu, and Hino began shipping medium-size trucks in volume to the United States in 1986. This effort was the beginning of a full-scale assault on U.S. medium-truck markets, which could result in the Japanese manufacturers grabbing a major share of this market. At the onset of the Japanese effort, General Motors Corp., Ford, and Navistar International Corp. (formerly International Harvester) owned 90 percent of the domestic medium-truck segment.

The Japanese spotted a weakness in this particular truck category and entered the market with a truck design known as the cab-over, rather than the bonnet type that had been manufactured in the United States. While the Japanese design did not have as much comfort for the driver, it did represent a trend because of its economy of operation, an increasingly important consideration for the hard-pressed, deregulated trucking industry.

The U.S. manufacturers recognized the Japanese concentra-

[4] P. Kotler, L. Fahey, S. Jalusripitak, *The New Competition* (Englewood Cliffs, N.J.: Prentice-Hall, 1985), p. 248.

tion of effort into a specific market segment. However, instead of fighting back, they joined their competitors; that is, instead of manufacturing the cab-over design in their own facilities, they imported it from the Japanese manufacturers.

While this medium-size category was being filled, the Japanese manufacturers started to look for other segments for concentration. They found, for example, a segment in the class 3 category, the next step up from a pickup, that had not been served by U.S. truck producers.

As long as U.S. manufacturers don't combat it, the Japanese will continue to use the strategy of concentration they initiated in 1968. The truck situation is only another example of the concentration strategy that has won the Japanese the consumer market, the automobile market, the steel market, the appliance market, and others.

Application

In order to concentrate in a market, do the following:

1. Use competitive analysis to identify your competitors' weaknesses and your company's strengths.
2. Concentrate on an unserved, poorly served, or emerging segment of the market that you have determined to be a growth segment and that will be a basis for establishing a beachhead into other market segments.
3. Introduce a product (or product modification) not already developed by existing manufacturers in the overall product category.
4. Develop multilevel distribution by privately labeling the product for the existing suppliers concurrent with establishing your own brand. Therefore, if one strategy falters the alternative strategy wins.
5. Follow up by expanding into additional market segments with the appropriate products in order to dominate the entire market category.

Alternative Objectives There are basically four reasons for having alternative, or multiple objectives. First, on a corporate scale, any business will have a variety of needs and goals to fulfill through various avenues. It thus needs a wide range of objectives.

Second, concerning strategy, the principle of concentration can be implemented successfully only through the application of alternative objectives.

Third, alternative objectives permit you to maintain enough flexibility to exploit opportunities as they arise. By designing a number of objectives, any of which can be used depending on the circumstances, you leave options open for achieving one objective when others fail.

Last, and most important, the use of alternative objectives lets you keep your competitors on the horns of a dilemma—unable to detect your real intentions. By displaying a number of possible threats, you force a competing manager to spread his resources and attention to match your action. While you have dispersed intentionally in order to *gain* control, you cause him to disperse erratically, inconveniently, and without full knowledge of the situation—thus, you cause him to *lose* control. You can then concentrate rapidly on the objective that offers the best potential for success.

Since the major incalculable is the human will (the mind of one manager against the mind of a competing manager), the intent of alternative objectives and the strategies that follow is to unbalance the opposing manager into making mistakes through inaction, distraction, wrong decision, false moves, or misinterpretation of your real intent, thereby exposing a weakness that you can exploit through concentration of effort.

This unbalancing or dislocation is achieved through movement and surprise. Refer again to the Smirnoff example: Heublein used physical movement in introducing a fighting brand, Relska, and repositioning Smirnoff upscale. Introducing the low-priced Popov created surprise, which had the psychological effect of paralyzing the Wolfschmidt management in an inability to respond to the multiple actions. In fact, concentration can be implemented successfully only through the application of alternative objectives.

These aspects of strategy, dislocation, concentration, and alternative objectives are capsulized in the following examples:

Deere & Company created a range of objectives by moving beyond its basic farm equipment business to entering the consumer lawn-tractor market, manufacturing engine blocks and diesel engines for General Motors, and making chassis for recreational vehicle manufacturers.

Apple Computer, Inc. selected additional target segments in its stronghold consumer markets, and it attacked new or poorly defended segments in the business markets held by IBM and Compaq.

Maytag Corporation set alternative objectives for defending and attacking the premium-priced segment, medium-priced mass market, and lower-end homebuilders' segment. Maytag thereby maintained flexibility as to which segment it would defend and where it would be more aggressive in increasing market share.

While the actions described may appear to be simply moves for expansion, they actually serve as strategies to keep competitors guessing as to which objective the concentration of efforts will be focused upon. The alternative market and product objectives and strategies illustrated cut across a wide spectrum of opportunities that send confusing signals to competitors, thereby permitting maximum flexibility in selecting areas for concentration.

Case Example

American President Companies, Ltd. American President has been an aggressive company in the shipping industry by employing a variety of innovative objectives and strategies to fight its way out of an industry slump. Its battle rages while the total industry has been going through a decline: Price wars have whittled the number of U.S. operators from 13 in 1975 to 7 during the mid-1980's.

American President's major weapons are alternative objectives. The company used the following techniques, illustrating a variety of applications.

1. Establishment of a market position and image as a premium service shipper.
2. Installation of a computer system to aid its customers by linking up with U.S. Customs, thereby speeding shipments through potential bottlenecks.
3. Institution of intermodal services, that is, transporting goods in single containers from trucks to trains to ships.
4. Redeployment of its worldwide fleet to the Pacific to cut costs and focus on high-volume market niches.
5. Establishment of a ten-year contract with Union Pacific RR. to ensure adequate rail service to meet customer shipping requirements over the next growth period.

Application

To use alternative objectives, do the following:

1. Consider such areas as customer service, improved delivery time, extended warranties, sales terms, after-sales support, packaging, and management training as alternative objectives.

2. Identify alternative niches in the initial stages of attack to cause distraction among your competing managers.

3. Exploit your competitors' confusion through later concentration.

Unbalancing Victory in many situations is not necessarily due to the brilliance of
Competition the attacking or defending, but to the mistakes of the competing manager. If there is any brilliance at all it is the manager's deliberately developing situations that unbalance the competition as a result of the psychological and physical effects created through speed, indirect approach, concentration, and alternative objectives. Unbalancing creates dislocation—a change in the equilibrium of things, which has a psychological effect. And dislocation fulfills strategy's ultimate purpose: the reduction of resistance.

The practice of unbalancing competition is epitomized in the announcement of a new product that would make the competing manager's product line obsolete. Even a press release about a yet-to-be-released product line can "make them sweat" and create panic and, therefore, mistakes. This unbalancing is practiced continuously in day-to-day activities that range from the threat of legal action to the effects of mergers and acquisitions.

Case Example

The IBM–Digital The full impact of these strategy principles was expressed in
Equipment the opening salvos of the 1986–87 IBM–Digital Equipment Cor-
Corporation poration (DEC) War. DEC decided to wage an all-out war
(DEC) War against IBM. Prior to this aggressive action, DEC had stuck to its strong position of serving factories and science laboratories with its midsize computer systems. The Massachusetts-based company moved out by using its new line of Vax minicomputers to attack IBM's stronghold in the large financial service companies and corporate data processing centers. One factor that contributed to the solid revenue and market share gains for DEC was the industry shift from centralized mainframes to networks of smaller computers—a direction in which DEC had taken the initial lead.

The counterattack from IBM came soon after it sighted the first breach in its stronghold. It introduced a new minicomputer called the 9370 (nicknamed by some industry observers as the Vax killer) that ran the same software as its mainframe. Using aggressive pricing, new discount options, better warranty, and new programming assistance, IBM claimed 10,000 orders on the books before shipments were made.

But that was only a minor skirmish. The big battles were yet to come, with each company trying to outmaneuver its competitor. DEC then attempted to unbalance IBM's attack by providing the free service of a DEC programmer for one year with the purchase of its largest Vax systems. It also cut prices, expanded discount options, and extended one-year warranties to all hardware. Further, DEC rapidly challenged IBM with a new Vax that competed directly with the IBM 9370.

By mid-1987, IBM sent the word out to the industry that its next counterblow would be an indirect approach by introducing a long-awaited standard called Systems Application Architecture that would permit the same software to run on all IBM equipment.

The corporate commitment to total warfare took over. IBM redeployed 5,000 employees from staff positions to field marketing—along with a potential 6,000 marketing employees from the Rolm Corp., IBM's telephone equipment subsidiary, to boost its marketing army to 34,000. DEC, on the other hand, which had been short on marketing know-how by its own admission, put greater emphasis on bolstering its ability to market. Where it was common to never have a sales rep call on some accounts, DEC fielded 6,000 salespeople by 1987, a 30 percent increase from the previous year. It concentrated its marketing efforts on commercial data processing and office automation, invading those IBM markets with a full complement of new products.

After the smoke cleared from the initial battles, DEC won a substantial victory in market share gains and in profitable revenue increases.

Application

To unbalance competition, do the following:

1. Identify the areas in which the competition is not able (or willing) to respond to your actions. (Use the competitor analysis checklists in Part Two for this purpose.)

2. Make a conscious effort to create an unbalancing effect through surprise announcements of new services, for example, just-in-time delivery or technical on-site assistance. The unbalancing effect will have the greatest impact to the extent that you are able to maintain secrecy until the last possible moment.

3. Utilize new technology to unbalance competitors and make them scramble to catch up. Technologies applied to marketing, such as electronic data interchange (EDI), to speed delivery from manufacturer to customer, and interactive video systems, to enhance the selling approach, are described in Chapter 13 (under Opportunities 2 and 3, respectively).

A Focus on Business Strategy

The five strategy principles—speed, indirect approach, concentration, alternative objectives, and unbalancing the competition— derived from military history, characterize all types of strategies.[5] This section focuses those strategy principles into three fundamental components of *business* strategy: *indirect approach, differentiation, and concentration.* An understanding of these fundamentals will help you incorporate the strategy principles into a useful business form, and thus help you to succeed through the use of competitive strategies.

Indirect Approach Avoid a direct approach against an entrenched competitor. The odds are totally against you. Instead, distract your competitor. Create confusion as to your real intentions. Search for emerging, neglected, or poorly served market segments and fill product gaps. Tie up the output of common suppliers. Gain access to channels of distribution through add-on services or special inducements. Use legal actions to dislodge a competitor, if appropriate. In all activities use speed to create surprise, which in turn will cause confusion among your competitors. Then use alternative objectives to further reinforce the dilemma in your competitor's mind about your intentions.

Differentiation The most effective means of applying the indirect approach is to seek differentiation in the areas of the marketing mix (product, price, promotion, distribution). It is important to remember that, although your product may seem like an undistinguishable commodity, there are always ways to differentiate it. Writes Levitt: "There is no such thing as a commodity."[6] His suggestions for differentiating products and services are summarized as follows: *Consider differentiation in such areas as* customer service, improved delivery time, extended warranties, sales terms, after-sales support, packaging, management training (your own staff and that of your distributors), knowledgeable sales-

---

[5]These strategy principles are based on my thoughts, first formed in the 1960's, about the military–marketing relationship expressed in my article "Corporate Objectives and Marketing Aim: What Is the Relationship?" *California Management Review,* Winter 1968. Only in the 1980's, because of the urgency and struggle to maintain competitive advantage, have such respected authors as Philip Kotler, Michael Porter, William Cohen, Al Ries, and Jack Trout published similar parallels in the military–marketing relationship as historical pathways to understanding the application of strategy to marketing practice.

[6]Theodore Levitt, *The Marketing Imagination* (New York: The Free Press, 1983), p. 72.

people. *Try differentiation with such intangibles as* reliability, image, nice-to-do-business-with reputation, credibility, prestige, convenience, value, responsiveness to problems, and access to key individuals in your firm.

While the competitive products may be identical, the suggested areas of differentiation add up to a total product package that moves you away from the commodity status and can give you a competitive edge.

Concentration The ability to concentrate is predicated on the effective applications of the indirect approach and differentiation. Concentration is successful to the extent that you can distract the competitor and seek out an opportunity in an unserved, emerging, or neglected segment. Concentration is also effective only to the extent that you can differentiate yourself from the competitor.

This particular component is so vital to successful strategies that Liddell Hart indicated that if all of strategy could be summed up into one word, it would be *concentration*.[7]

Competitive Analysis These three fundamentals of strategy can be successfully applied only if adequate competitive analysis (see Part Two) is used. For example, identifying emerging, neglected, or poorly served markets is useful to the extent that you can preempt your competition and satisfy the needs and wants of those markets. Employing areas of differentiation is advantageous to the extent that the competitors cannot or are not willing to respond to your action. The confidence level of your strategy is strengthened by your diligent effort in using competitor analysis to shape an indirect approach.

Strategy Lessons

From the principles and strategies of military history applied to competitive marketing strategy, four major lessons stand out.

1. While the tools of marketing (advertising, sales promotion, field selling, marketing research, distribution, pricing) are physical acts, they are directed by a mental process. The better-thought-out your strategy, the more easily you will gain the upper hand, and the less it will cost.

[7] *Strategy*, p. 347.

2. The tougher you make your marketing practices, the more your competitors will consolidate against you. You will thus harden the resistance you are trying to overcome. Even if you succeed in winning the market, you will have fewer resources with which to profit from the victory.

3. The more intent you are in securing a market entirely of your own choosing and terms, the stiffer the obstacles you will raise in our path; and the more cause you will provide for competitors to try to reverse what you have achieved.

4. When you are trying to dislodge your competitor from a strong market position that will be costly to forfeit, leave that competitor a quick way to retreat from the market.

In a broad application, the lessons are evident in the current position some Japanese companies have created against the United States, as well as against some European countries and companies. Such companies as Sony, Nissan, Komatsu, and Toshiba Corporation have been monumentally successful in focusing human and material resources into shaping a strategy to attack and overwhelm their respective markets. However, in many instances, the toughness of their competitive practices has had the countereffect of consolidating the efforts of surviving companies in seeking retaliation through trade barriers, union resistance, and legal action for patent infringement, as well as through the new movement of companies initiating cooperative relationships by establishing R&D facilities to service member companies in countering the efforts of their adversaries.

In Conclusion

With the military–marketing perspective, and with the five basic strategy principles condensed into indirect approach, differentiation, and concentration, you have the foundations for developing successful competitive strategies. It should be apparent from the discussion, however, that a good deal of work must precede the formulation of competitive strategies. That work includes conducting a competitive analysis; developing a marketing intelligence system and employing marketing research to gather market and competitive intelligence; and organizing and sorting the data you have gathered into a usable form via a strategic marketing plan. All of those areas will be covered in the following chapters.

TWO

The Framework
for
Competitive Analysis

Conducting a competitive analysis is the first step in developing competitive strategy. The purpose of the analysis is to systematically view all those factors, both external (Chapter 2) and internal (Chapter 3), that can affect your decisions in selecting a strategy. By using sound analysis as the basis of strategy development, you will be able to overcome pressures from competitors when entering a new market or when defending an existing one. You will be able to develop indirect approaches, identify areas for differentiation, and concentrate resources in a way that achieves your objectives in a strength-conserving manner.

Figure 2-1. *A framework for competitive analysis.*

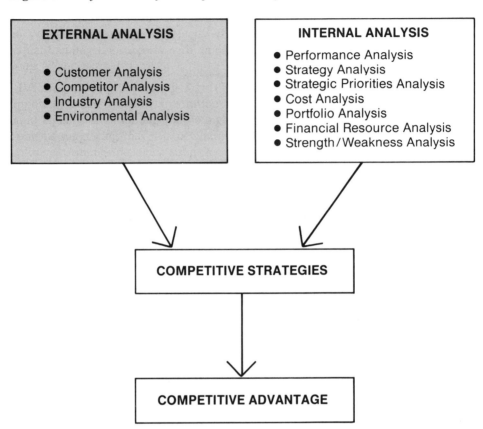

2

External Analysis

Objectives:
To enable you to

1. Identify the factors related to a *customer analysis* by segment, behavior, and wants and needs
2. Conduct a *competitor analysis* by products, dealer, and distributor, communications and promotional mix, operations, R&D, overall costs, financial strength, organization, managerial capabilities, and market–product portfolio

3. Design an *industry analysis* by size, dimension, cost structure, distribution systems, industry trends, technology developments, and stage in the industry life cycle
4. Develop an *environmental analysis* by technologies, governments, economics, demographics, and cultural and behavioral changes

Figure 2-1 illustrates the two major components of competitive analysis: external analysis and internal analysis (see Chapter 3).[1] Companies use external analysis to get a strong grasp on the condition of the market. The object of external analysis is to uncover opportunities and threats that result in alternative strategies and, ultimately, in a competitive advantage. External analysis thus concentrates on four market spheres: customers, competitors, industry, and environment. Let's look at each type of external analysis in turn to see how it contributes to shaping competitive strategies.

---

[1] The overall frameworks for external and internal analyses are modified versions of those used by David Aaker, *Developing Business Strategies* (New York: Wiley, 1984) and Michael E. Porter, *Competitive Strategy* (New York: The Free Press, 1980).

Customer Analysis

> Marketing is a total system of interacting business activities designed to plan, price, promote, and distribute want-satisfying products and services to organizational and household users at a profit.

It is obvious from this definition that the customer is the center of marketing's attention. To produce "want-satisfying products and services," you must know what the customers want, where they find what they want, and how to communicate to them that you are able to meet their needs. The case of Smith-Corona dramatizes how customer analysis helped to develop a competitive strategy.

Case Example

Smith-Corona Smith-Corona, the typewriter manufacturer, had the distinction of being the only manufacturer in the United States turning out typewriters for the whole U.S. market during the mid-1980's. After five years of losses it made a complete financial turnaround, and for the first half of its fiscal 1986 year it made $12 million in operating income on revenues of $116 million. Productivity had quadrupled in two years.

How did the company achieve this remarkable success in the face of severe Asian competition? Smith-Corona used customer analysis to identify market segments of opportunity. As a result of the analysis, the company changed its *product mix* and developed a new line of electronic typewriters that matched the increasingly sophisticated Japanese models. It also pushed forward in *technical innovation* to lead the market in that area. For example, it introduced the first spelling correction option for home typewriters and was also the first to bring out a word processing computer as an add-on for home use.

Because of these innovations, revenues during 1986 ran 25 percent ahead of the preceding year and boosted Smith-Corona's market share in North America for computers and portable typewriters from 30 percent to 40 percent.

To fully understand customer analysis, you should be familiar with its components: market and product segments, patterns of customer behavior, and unfilled wants and needs.

Market and Product Segments Segmentation can be defined as splitting the overall market into smaller submarkets or segments that have more in common with one another than with the total market. Subdividing your market is a means of identifying and satisfying the specific needs of individuals within your chosen segments and thereby gaining competitive strength. Segmentation permits the concentration of your strength against the weakness of your competitor, and the concentration of your efforts in satisfying a specific unfilled want or need.

Examples abound of companies concentrating on segments: Snap-On Tools Corp. serves professional mechanics only; White Rock Corp. Products concentrates on small niches that are of no interest to Coca-Cola or Pepsi Cola; Measurex Corporation initially built a strong foundation for computer-based process control equipment in a single industry; Godiva Chocolates, priced at over $18.00 a pound, is aimed at an affluent "me" generation; Women's Health Centers of America, Inc. is an organization serving female patients only; Honda Motor Co., Ltd. originally focused on selling high-quality, small motorcycles to an entirely new type of customer, the suburban middle class male.

Case Example

Zayre Corp. Zayre Corp., an 845 store retail chain, progressed from a condition of deep trouble to prosperity. In 1986, profits climbed from $12 million to $70 million. One major factor in Zayre's remarkable turnaround in just a few years was the company's effective use of market segmentation within the framework of customer analysis.

When Zayre's competitors moved toward the trendy upscale market, Zayre astutely cultivated a lucrative niche for itself among blue collar workers who made under $20 thousand annually and who were located mostly in the East and Midwest. Maurice Segall, its president and the individual responsible for turnaround, says, "We are one of the few large retailers still actively catering to low-income groups and we've proved we can do it profitably."

For example, Segall recognized that low-income shoppers appreciate being treated with care, just as high-income customers do. He ran big advertisements in newspapers promising to open a cash register any time the checkout line grew to three people. He promised a 10 percent discount if an advertised item was out of stock and had to be ordered. He realized that low-income people appreciate attractive surroundings as much as affluent people do.

Clearly, market segmentation was one of the strategic factors moving Zayre's sales volume from $1.2 billion in 1978 to over $3 billion in 1986.

Choosing Market Segments

Segmentation is obviously an essential part of customer analysis, and concentration in a segment is the essence of a competitive strategy. Therefore, in doing your own customer analysis, you're going to need to know what criteria to use in choosing market and product segments, as well as what factors to use in identifying a market segment and how to develop a segmentation analysis.

Use the following criteria to guide you in selecting market segments.

Measurability. Can you quantify the segment? For example, you should be able to assign a number to how many plants, how many farm acres, or how many people are within the market segment.

Accessibility. Do you have access to the market through sales force, distributors, transportation, or warehousing?

Substantiality. Is the segment of sufficient size to warrant attention as a segment? Further, is the segment declining, is it mature, or is it a growing segment?

Profitability. Does the segment provide sufficient profitability to make concentration in it worthwhile? Use your organization's stan-

Figure 2-2. *Bases for market segmentation.*

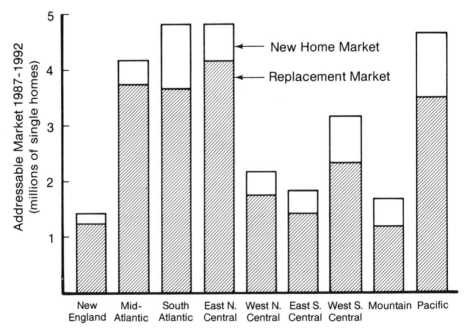

Source: Jack Z. Sissors, "What Is a Market?" *Journal of Marketing* (July 1986), p. 21. Published by the American Marketing Association.

dard measurement for profitability, such as return on investment, return on equity, gross margin, or profits.

Compatibility with Competition. To what extent do your major competitors have an interest in the segment? Is it of active interest or of negligible concern to your competitors?

Effectiveness. Does your organization have sufficient skills and resources to serve the segment effectively?

Defendability. Does your firm have the capabilities to defend itself against the attacker of a major competitor?

Using your answers to those questions, you will be able to select a market segment with good potential for concentration and with sufficient information for customer analysis. These criteria can also be used as tests for the viability of a market segment once you have chosen it. But how do you select one? You can identify market segments by dividing a market into groups of customers with common characteristics.

Categories for Segmenting Markets

Figure 2-2 and Table 2-1 illustrate some of the many approaches to market segmentation. Figure 2-3 displays the four most common ways

Table 2-1. *Major Segmentation Variables for Consumer Markets.*

Variable	Typical Breakdowns
Geographic	
Region	Pacific, Mountain, West North Central, West South Central, East North Central, East South Central, South Atlantic, Middle Atlantic, New England
County size	A, B, C, D
City or SMSA size	Under 5,000; 5,000–20,000; 20,000–50,000; 50,000–100,000; 100,000–250,000; 250,000–500,000; 500,000–1,000,000; 1,000,000–4,000,000; 4,000,000 or over
Density	Urban, suburban, rural
Climate	Northern, southern

(continued)

Source: P. Kotler, *Marketing Management: Analysis, Planning, and Control,* 6th edition (Englewood Cliffs, N.J.: Prentice-Hall, 1988), pp. 90–92.

Table 2-1. *Continued.*

Variable	Typical Breakdowns
Demographic	
Age	Under 6, 6–11, 12–19, 20–34, 35–49, 50–64, 65+
Sex	Male, female
Family size	1–2, 3–4, 5+
Family life cycle	Young, single; young, married, no children; young, married, youngest child under 6; young, married, youngest child 6 or over; older, married, with children; older, married, no children under 18; older, single; other
Income	Under $2,500; $2,500–$5,000; $5,000–$7,500; $7,500–$10,000; $10,000–$15,000; $15,000–$20,000; $20,000–$30,000; $30,000–$50,000; $50,000 and over
Occupation	Professional and technical; managers, officials, and proprietors; clerical, sales; craftsmen, foremen; operatives; farmers; retired; students; housewives; unemployed
Education	Grade school or less; some high school; high school graduate; some college; college graduate
Religion	Catholic, Protestant, Jewish, other
Race	White, black, Oriental
Nationality	American, British, French, German, Scandinavian, Italian, Latin American, Middle Eastern, Japanese
Psychographic	
Social class	Lower lowers, upper lowers, lower middles, upper middles, lower uppers, upper uppers
Lifestyles	Straights, swingers, longhairs
Personality	Compulsive, gregarious, authoritarian, ambitious
Behavioral	
Use occasion	Regular occasion, special occasion
Benefits sought	Quality, service, economy
User status	Nonuser, ex-user, potential user, first-time user, regular user
Usage rate	Light user, medium user, heavy user
Loyalty status	None, medium, strong, absolute
Readiness stage	Unaware, aware, informed, interested, desirous, intending to buy
Attitude toward product	Enthusiastic, positive, indifferent, negative, hostile

Figure 2-3. *A bar graph presentation of the addressable market for consumer appliances.*

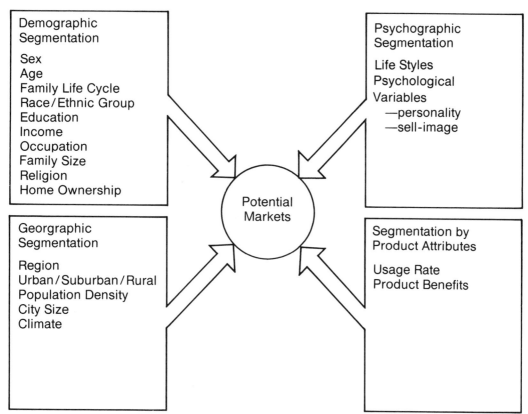

to segment a market: by demographic, geographic, psychographic, and product attribute (or behavioral) factors. Each of these factors, particularly when used in combination with the others, represents an opportunity or identifies a need that can be satisfied with a product. Table 2-1 gives specific examples for each of the categories shown in Figure 2-2.

To demonstrate the use of these figures in identifying market segments, let's look at the example of a job matching agency looking at the temporary office services field to differentiate from secretarial work to professional consulting. By using the information in these figures, it might come up with two new market segments to test:

1. Older retired (demographic/age, occupation) professionals interested in occasional light work (product attributes or behavioral/usage rate).

2. Middle-aged educated women with young children (demographic/family life cycle, sex, age, education), women who want

regular but flexible work in their careers (product attributes or behavioral/benefits sought, use occasion, usage rate) during their child-rearing years.

You can use these figures as guides to define segments in your own markets. You can see that there is virtually no limit to the ways in which you can segment your market for opportunities. And to increase your understanding of market segments, geographic, demographic, psychographic, and, the relatively new form, geodemographic segmentation are discussed in greater detail.

Geographic Segmentation

Geographic segmentation is relatively easy to perform because the individual segments can be clearly delineated on a map. It is a sensible strategy to employ when there are distinct differences in climatic conditions or cultural patterns.

Geographic segmentation even extends to facial features used in advertising. When Kodak introduced its Instamatic camera worldwide, the company quickly learned that potential consumers in many countries around the globe, from the Philippines to India and from Hong Kong to South Africa, could not relate to the American girl portrayed in the advertising. The advertising was quickly modified with the use of local models that contributed to a phenomenal success story. Internationally, blocks or clusters of countries, called *regional markets,* can often be approached in a similar fashion, particularly if they share the same language and cultural heritage. For instance, in most of Latin America the same advertising media are often appropriate for several countries.

Domestically, you can segment by region; by state, county, or county size; by city size, by population density, or by other geopolitical criteria. However, such segmentation is effective only if it reflects differences in need and motivation patterns. Many firms, for example, adjust their advertising efforts to as small an area as a county.

Demographic Segmentation

Along with geographic information, demographic variables are among the longest-used segmentation factors. They owe their popularity to two facts: (1) they are easier to observe and/or measure than most other characteristics and (2) their breakdown is often closely linked to differences in behavioral patterns. As noted in Table 2-1, demographic factors include age, sex, family size, stage in the family life cycle, income, occupation, education, religion, race, nationality, and social class.

In many instances, demographic variables can be combined to produce a more meaningful breakdown than a single criterion could. For example, it is common to combine the age of the head of the household with the family size and the level of household income. If four age levels, three family sizes, and three income levels are distinguished, a total of 36 segments results. Using a combination of primary data, secondary data, and judgment, you can then determine the value of each segment and thus arrive at a well-thought-out conclusion about which segments warrant clearly targeted efforts.

Unrelated demographic characteristics can prove unreliable at times: Sex makes little difference in the consumption of toothpaste and soft drinks. Chronological age is often a poor indicator of behavior patterns. Income level is only fairly relevant; it becomes more so only in relation to other variables such as social class, family life cycle, and occupation.

Psychographic Segmentation

The most exciting form of segmentation results from the application of psychographic variables, such as life style, personality, user status, usage rate, spending behavior, and marketing factor sensitivity. Banks, car manufacturers, and liquor producers, to name a few, have availed themselves of the advantages of psychographic segmentation. It is a branch of market segmentation that is still evolving and promises great vitality in the future.

Department stores use *lifestyle* departments that they vary according to neighborhood. However, *personality* as an isolated psychographic variable—although attractive to marketers—has not proved to be a valid criterion for segmentation.

User status refers to a breakdown according to nonuser, ex-user, potential user, first-time user, and regular user groups that might respond favorably to different kinds of stimulation. Companies with high market share are especially eager to attract potential users, while smaller competitors with lower market share are better off trying to convert existing users.

The *usage rate* is of practical importance in segment marketing. Marketers typically distinguish among nonusers and light, medium, and heavy users of their product. Heavy users often represent a relatively small share of total households or industrial buying and yet account for the major portion of the sales volume in the market. For example, with regard to beer consumption, 17 percent of the households in the United States account for 50 percent of the users and 88 percent of the beer consumed. In contrast, the usage of such an item as toilet tissue is far less concentrated; 50 percent of the households account for 75 percent of the total consumption.

The term *spending behavior* covers a variety of patterns from emotional to practical, from brand loyalty to price- and deal-conscious. *Market factor sensitivity* refers to the responsiveness of buyers to the various elements of the marketing mix: quality, price, service, advertising, product design, sales promotion, and channel availability.

Geodemographic Segmentation

One of the newer techniques for segmenting the market is known as geodemography. It has been developed to combine many of the advantages of geographic and demographic segmentation. It is based on census data obtained from the 256,000 census "block" groups or neighborhoods in the United States. People having similar life styles tend to cluster in neighborhoods. Some market analysts believe that geodemography can give businesses more precise information about their target markets and how best to reach them.

For example, consider a block group with a high concentration of families having annual incomes over $50,000 and made up of business managers and professionals who are college educated and over age 50. This group likes to watch television programs similar to the popular *60 Minutes* and also has four times the nation's usage of vodka. Another block group is categorized by watching *Happy Days,* a television situation comedy popular in the mid-1980's, and drinks almost no vodka. Members of this group tend to be rural and elderly; housing is low-value and owner-occupied. It is obvious, then, that individual approaches would be required for two such differing targets.

Potential users of geodemography are banks, which need to determine where to install automatic teller machines, and baby food manufacturers, which want to test-market a new product on the basis of clusters with large numbers of first-time mothers. The technique also is of particular interest to catalogers, credit card companies, and other businesses that have large direct-mail programs.

Graphic Techniques for Segmenting Markets

Figures 2-3, 2-4, and 2-5 show some of the different graphic techniques you can use to define market segments. Figure 2-3 is a bar

Figure 2-4. *A matrix format of market segments for natural gas services.*

	Gas Availability	Gas Equipment Operational Cost	Gas Equipment First Cost	Gas Equipment Features
Residential Space Heating				
Residential Appliances				
Commercial Space Conditioning				
Commercial Cooking				
Co-Generation				
Industrial Process Markets				
Industrial Boiler Markets				
Utility Boiler Markets				

graph used by a *consumer* appliances company. The company divided the United States into nine regions and each region into two types of markets for appliances: new home and replacement. Using this technique, the company can see which geographic regions have the greatest market potential and which type of market (replacement or new) predominates in each. By analyzing competitors' sales records, the company can identify niches that are underserved within these segments. The graph shows the company where to distribute its sales force according to volume of business and location, and at the same time displays the need to tailor advertising to the region and markets.

Figure 2-4 shows a matrix format for segmenting a *service* market. The vertical axis displays market segments that use natural gas and related services. The horizontal axis shows features that influence

Figure 2-5. *A matrix format of market segmentation for computer-aided design systems.*

DESIGN ENGINEERS

Business and Industry	Technical or Engineering Management	Equipment Design Engineer	Circuit Design Engineer	System Design Engineer
Computers, Data Processing Equipment Manufacturing				
Test Measurement and Instrumentation Manufacturing				
Communications Systems and Equipment Manufacturing				
Industrial Controls and Equipment Manufacturing				

customers' choice of energy product. A manager reviewing this matrix can look closely at the boxes to identify which have the greatest potential for market concentration. For instance, the industrial boiler markets would probably be most concerned with gas availability. Making gas more readily available for that segment or designing gas-conserving parts for industrial boilers would be two ways to concentrate on that market segment.

A similar matrix, Figure 2-5, is example of *industry* segmentation in which types of design engineers are displayed on the horizontal axis and the industries in which they work are designated on the vertical axis. A company could focus on the needs of one type of engineer in one type of business, or on all businesses for one type of engineer, or on all engineers in one type of business.

Patterns of Customer Behavior In addition to market and product segments, another component of customer analysis examines customer behavior patterns. That is, how is a customer likely to think, behave, and make decisions regarding your products and services? Then, how can you use that information to reach and attract potential customers? What impact does behavior analysis have on customer analysis and, therefore, on the selection of strategies? The case example involving medical services illustrates the relevance of these questions to customer analysis and, thus, to the larger issue of strategy.

Case Example

Women's Health Centers of America, Inc. Women's Health Centers of America, Inc., a San Diego-based company, operates full-service women's clinics. The business is centered on the customer behavior of a particular segment of the health care industry: female patients who were unhappy with conventional health care. The management of this organization discovered that women felt their doctors rushed them through appointments, told them little, and often were patronizing.

Additional research on the behavioral patterns of women indicated that after the age of 14 women visit the doctor 25 percent more often and are hospitalized 50 percent more often than men. Operations unique to women, such as hysterectomies and cesarean sections, account for 11 of the 20 most frequently performed surgeries. The research showed women to be health care consumers.

It was also determined that 60 percent of the time women decided where their families would go for health care. As a result, many hospitals are finding that operating a successful women's clinic can draw family members to other services. Still further research and observation of customer behavior showed that women were demanding that the clinics address more than just reproductive care—that they provide more information from medical professionals and supply health reference material.

Understanding the Behavioral Cycle

Because it can be universally applied, a model (Figure 2-6) provides a useful framework for the analysis of customer behavior. While the examples given refer to individual customers, groups of consumers or industrial buyers also fit the patterns described. The figure highlights the major elements of behavior analysis: stimulus, sensation, need and predisposition, perception, motives, and consumer behavior.

Stimulus

Consumer behavior is shown in the model as being triggered by a stimulus. A stimulus is any external or internal force or event that arouses one or more senses. An example of an internal stimulus is a

Figure 2-6. *Basic consumer behavior model.*

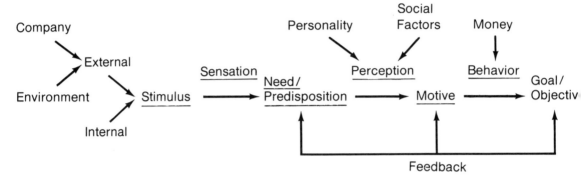

Source: Marketing Update, Issue 5 (1977), p. 1. Published by Alexander-
Norton Publishers, Inc.

grumbling stomach, while external stimuli can come from any element of the environment outside the body. Whatever its nature, a stimulus is relevant only if it reaches at least one sense and brings about a sensation.

Sensation

A sensation, or sensory impression, is the arousal of a sense and is a prerequisite for perception. It is important to note that sensations are involuntary and thus not under the control of the consumer but, rather, controlled by the stimulus and its source. Once a shopper is exposed to a given stimulus situation, such as walking down a supermarket aisle, a variety of stimuli activate the senses. Short of closing your eyes, you cannot prevent packages from making a visual impression. Sensory discrimination is based on the ability of the stimulus to stand out and attract attention. The ability to attract attention is dependent on (1) the level of stimulation present (for example, some viewers charge that TV commercials are louder than the programs they interrupt) and (2) the consumer's ability—or inability—to distinguish among similar stimuli (studies show that most consumers cannot identify their favorite brand of beer, cigarettes, or cola drink in unlabeled tests).

Need and Predisposition

Once a sensation has been created, it has to evoke a response from a need or predisposition before it can produce perceptions and, ultimately, conscious consumer behavior. A need can be described as an inactive condition within an individual that will be expressed by active behavior when properly stimulated. One example is an increased appetite in response to a need for food. Because needs are often both dormant and vague, it is a challenge to every marketer to awaken and focus them. The process leading to a desire for a particular product or service is called motivation.

A predisposition is an attitude, a tendency to react in a particular way to a stimulus. It can be favorable or unfavorable and it reflects a consumer's receptiveness to a certain type of stimulation. For example, some consumers are reluctant to buy presweetened cereals because they are thought to hasten tooth decay. Taken together, needs and predispositions are filters for selecting favorable stimuli to be acted upon or for discriminating against unfavorable stimuli, which, under normal circumstances, would not even reach the level of consciousness.

Perception

If a stimulus passes through the filters of need and predisposition, perception will occur. Perception is the interpretation of sensations. It involves conscious mental processing relating sensory impressions to an individual's frame of reference and, therefore, varies from one person to another. Because perception is subject to personality influences and to social factors, it can result in a considerable distortion of reality. Apart from any defects a product may have, the way in which a consumer views your product or service will determine whether it will be bought. More than any other element in the model, consumer perception warrants careful study and constant attention.

Motives

A stimulus that is perceived may result in a motive. A motive is a state of tension (want, desire, urge, drive) that causes an individual to act to reduce or eliminate the tension. The case example of the women's clinics indicated that there was a clear-cut motive on the part of women to eliminate the tension that existed in their feelings about their health care. As such, a motive represents an activated and focused need that is now oriented toward the achievement of a goal.

The problem for the marketer is that consumers act rarely, if ever, from a single motive. Rather, multiple and, at times, even conflicting motives govern most behavioral acts. The purchase of a car, for instance, may be influenced by the motives of prestige, comfort, safety, and economy. It is unlikely that all these motives will point to the same choice. Consumers, therefore, have to assign priorities to their motives to decide which ones are more important. As a marketer, you should try to determine consumers' motives, as well as their priorities, to be able to address and trigger them properly with your stimuli in the form of advertising and other elements of the marketing mix.

Consumer Behavior

Consumer behavior toward a product is an attempt to decrease or eliminate tension. It is goal oriented and may take three major directions: (1) a consumer may decide to purchase and use your product, (2) a consumer may determine that he or she needs more information and so begins a search effort, or (3) a consumer may decide to drop the whole matter and take no action.

Once a purchase has been made, the consumer compares expectations and fulfillment in a process called *feedback*. The outcome of this comparison affects future behavior. A single positive experience produces satisfaction that leads to reinforcement. Continued reinforcement results in the formation of a habit, which is an ideal situation because it means repeat purchase of your product and brand loyalty. A negative experience, on the other hand, may result in the consumer changing brands, avoiding an entire product category, or, as in the health care case example, not returning to the clinic.

Using the Behavior Model

One of the major benefits of the basic behavior model is that it is highly adaptable to specific situations. Individual components can be substituted or added to fit special conditions. It applies, for instance, equally well to selective behavior (where a choice is made when a product is first considered) and to repetitive behavior (where successful actions are habitually repeated). In the case of selective behavior, motive turns into a more or less decision-making stage. Although the model is based on the behavior of the individual consumer, it can, nevertheless, be used to explain the behavior of entire market segments. If your customers are industrial buyers, the model is equally applicable to their behavior as individuals or as group decision makers.

Two tables have been designed to help you apply the information produced by analyzing consumer behavior. Table 2-2 shows you how

Table 2-2. *Experience Patterns and Marketing Action.*

| Type of Experience | Consumer | | Company | |
	Nature	Result	Appropriate Marketing Action	Reasoning
Single positive	Satisfaction	Reinforcement	Free samples, direct-mail couponing	Build loyalty
Repeated positive	Continued satisfaction	Habit formation	Cents-off campaign, advertising other uses	Strengthen loyalty
Single negative	Dissatisfaction	Adjustment	Explain, repair, replace	Convert to loyalty
Repeated negative	Continued dissatisfaction	Avoidance	Refund, substitute, cross-coupon	Convert to other product

to respond to selective and repetitive forms of consumer behavior. It outlines the nature and result of the consumer's experience, and then gives you the appropriate marketing action to take in order to gain or retain consumer loyalty. For instance, in the case of repeated positive experiences on the part of the consumer, you can strengthen that loyalty with a cents-off campaign.

Table 2-3 reviews the different factors in behavior analysis and tells you how to influence consumers in each of these areas. For example, regarding motives, the chart counsels you to investigate how consumers choose the brand they will use, and then to use this information in designing your product and advertising.

Unfilled Wants and Needs The third component of consumer analysis is determining the unfilled wants and needs of various customer segments. The analysis, however, goes beyond simply identifying these wants; it specifies ways to fulfill them by examining how consumers adopt a new product and how you can communicate your offerings to them.

Case Example

Intel Corporation A product becomes a commodity when it is relatively easy to duplicate and there is little perceived differentiation among available brands. This development frequently occurs because of offshore, low-cost manufacturing that undercuts more specialized versions. This scenario has been duplicated throughout the battle-torn U.S. economy in such industries as steel, machine tools, automobiles, and consumer appliances, and in a score of

Table 2-3. *Applying the Behavioral Model.*

Factor	What You Should Do to Influence Consumers
Stimuli	Test, in a competitive environment, how much attention your stimuli create (e.g., product design, advertising, packaging).
Sensations	Unless you can create sensory impressions, no action is likely to follow; stimuli must stand out from their environment to be distinguishable.
Needs/predispositions	Address yourself (e.g., in product design and/or advertising) to the most pressing or powerful current need(s) and/or most positive predispositions.
Perception	Ask consumers what your advertising and packaging tell them about your product.
Personality	Consumers try to match personality profiles of the products they buy with their own; make sure that yours has a clear-cut profile—it cannot be all things to all people.
Social factors	Include acceptance by others in your advertising.
Image	Unless you can create a positive image for your product, consumers are unlikely to buy; ask them how they view your product and adjust image, if necessary.
Information search	Provide informative and persuasive booklets— free for the asking.
Motive	Investigate what ultimately makes consumers choose one product over another; build this argument into your product and advertising.
Decision making	Offer financing. Make the decision atmosphere easy and pleasant; offer special incentives for making a decision before the specified date.
Behavior	At this point, your product's package is probably the most powerful influence on consumer behavior, the "silent salesman" on the store and pantry shelf; make sure that it encourages purchase *and* consumption.
Goal orientation	Explain how your product gives desired results.
Feedback	Find out who is repurchasing or abandoning product and why.

other products within the consumer, industrial, and service industries.

INTEL Corporation faced this situation in that its microchips were virtually indistinguishable from those produced by its competitors; INTEL could neither match its foreign competitors' prices nor offer customers any special features. Thus, it suffered severe market losses in its industry. In looking for a solution to its dilemma, INTEL chose to apply elements of marketing theory to its problem.

Marketing theory suggests that businesses should display a customer-driven orientation. Managers need to determine the wants and needs of customers and then satisfy those needs using the resources of the organization. In researching the needs of its customers—manufacturers of electronic products such as calculators and televisions—INTEL discovered that their problems were exactly the same as its own. The inexpensive reproduction of microchips, and of electronic appliances generally, had made it difficult, if not impossible, for INTEL's customers to produce electronic appliances that could compete with producers from abroad. Both INTEL and its customers desperately needed to solve the cloning problem that was causing disastrous losses and threatening their survival.

Consequently, INTEL opted to *differentiate*. It decided to give up its high-volume, integrated circuits business, and transformed itself into a leading manufacturer of custom and semi-custom chips. That is, the company custom-designed microchips for each of its customers in order to let these companies specialize and grow.

Further, to make the strategy workable, it formed a strategic alliance with IBM, the nation's largest user of chips. Under a five-year technology-exchange agreement, IBM provided the designs that were the foundation for many of the 15,000 chips it made for its own use. Then INTEL customized those designs for others. In return, INTEL got to use the proprietary computer system that IBM employed to design its own chips.

As part of their strategic alliance, INTEL and IBM will continue to pool their chip designs, resulting in an extensive library of predesigned circuit modules that can be assembled like building blocks to produce chips for specific applications. The library will also contain special chips with generic logic devices that are connected to perform particular jobs.

For INTEL, the custom chip business is its best hope for staying solvent. Users, in turn, are relying on these chips to make their products more difficult to copy and thereby solve part of the cloning problem. The urgency to shape the strategy for attacking the cloning problem and to fill the wants and needs of its customers has also changed the mentality of the INTEL organization. Once a large-volume producer, INTEL is now gearing up to handle many custom designs that can be produced in a matter of weeks and in small quantities.

The significance of the INTEL case is that customer analysis involves the efforts of all managers and the commitment of an entire organization. Customer satisfaction and a customer-driven mentality are the foundations for developing competitive strategies. By meeting customer needs, INTEL was able to revitalize an entire industry as well as stimulate its own success in the marketplace.

How Customers Adopt a New Product

Identifying needs and wants is one step toward fulfilling those needs with products and services. The INTEL case example shows how one company met the overall need of the electronics industry by identifying need areas, and then fulfilled the individual needs of companies through differentiation, alliance, and customer analysis. (Figure 2-8 on pages 77–78 gives you a fertile list of ideas for differentiation and innovation in the market so that you can fulfill customers' wants and needs in your business area.) Once needs and wants have been identified and a solution has been created, however, the new innovation must be *communicated* to and *adopted* by the customer.[2]

When a new product is introduced to the marketplace, two interrelated processes are brought into play: diffusion and adoption. Diffusion is the spread of a new idea from your company to its ultimate users or adopters. Adoption, on the other hand, is the decision-making process that prospective users go through after they learn about an innovation. In the final stage of the adoption process the consumer decides whether or not to purchase your new product on a regular basis.

Because innovations are vital to the growth of your firm, it is essential for you to understand the processes by which information and opinions about your product are communicated and then either accepted or rejected. In order to achieve the maximum flow of communication about your innovation, you need to be knowledgeable about the processes and factors involved in the diffusion of innovations. You also have to know what decision-making stages individual customers go through in making up their minds about your new product, and what possibilities you have to influence their decisions in your favor.

Diffusion: Communication of Innovation

Diffusion—spreading the word about your new product—is initiated by you, but it is only partially under your control because a great deal of it occurs in face-to-face encounters and exchanges between customers, over which you have no direct influence. Thus, it is important to give them every reason to think and speak favorably about your innovation. In this context, it is particularly crucial to understand the nature of innovation and communication.

---

[2]Portions of this section have appeared in *Marketing Update,* a publication of Alexander-Norton, Inc., New York, of which Norton Paley is president.

An *innovation* is an idea perceived as new by customers. This fact has far-reaching implications. First of all, *ideas,* not products, are spread in the diffusion process. Only if you can convince customers to accept the new idea underlying your product will they consider the product itself. Some examples will underscore this point:

The idea of family planning is alien to the culture of India, in spite of vigorous government efforts to promote it. Thus, it makes absolutely no difference how safe, convenient, or inexpensive a particular birth control product is. Indians, by and large, will not even consider it, much less buy it.

Closer to home, a brief look into fashion history offers interesting insights. When miniskirts first appeared, many women hesitated to wear them. They wondered whether this was just a passing fad or a genuinely new way of dressing and expressing oneself. Once it became clear that the mini was widely accepted, it became old-fashioned even for grandmothers to cling to the longer hemline. By contrast, the midi length that followed never took off. Prodded by *Women's Wear Daily,* the respected trade newspaper, manufacturers and retailers went heavily into the midi. But Ms. America quietly resisted the dictates of Seventh Avenue. She felt that this new style made her look unattractive, and she was not about to wear it. When the disaster hit, retailers literally could not give midis away. It mattered little how good the name, the fabric, the workmanship, or the price—the idea had been rejected.

Second, customers will talk about your product if they *perceive* it to be new or different; it need not actually be new. For example, commercially prepared baby food was invented in the United States in 1928 by David Gerber. Straining fresh peas for his infant daughter one night, this executive of a family-owned canning company spoke the classic words: "There has to be a better way,"[3] and a new U.S. industry was born. Thirty years later, in 1958, an executive of a German manufacturer of infant formula visited the United States to learn about the baby food business. His company later pioneered baby food in the German market. The point is: Although baby food was by then an institution in the United States, in 1958 it was decidedly new to German mothers.

Conversely, if customers view your new product as being the same as all the others, they will not consider it worth a try. Again, it makes very little difference whether or not your product represents a sub-

[3] *Marketing Update* (New York: Alexander-Norton Publishers, Inc.), Vol. 1, Issue 8 (1977), p. 1.

stantial departure from other products on the market. The only thing that counts is what customers *think* your product is.

What customers perceive is, to a large degree, the outcome of what and how you *communicate* to them. When introducing a new product or service, you must expose your target market to messages that are both informative and persuasive. While these contacts between your firm and its ultimate buyers can be termed controllable communication (because your company determines the nature of its promotional efforts), there is a considerable amount of uncontrollable communication going on in the diffusion process. Advertising and sales personnel of competitors and middlemen, independent professional evaluation through testing laboratories, and the exchange of personal opinions among customers cannot be directly influenced by your firm.

Given this situation, it will prove helpful to identify the types of *communication sources* that are active in the diffusion and adoption processes. Depending on whether or not they have a commercial interest in promoting the product, sources can be classified as either advocate or independent. It is also helpful to distinguish a personal source, such as a face-to-face contact, from an impersonal one that involves an object or medium communicating with the customer. Combining these source types results in four distinctly different types of communication sources:

1. **Advocate impersonal** sources are primarily represented by the mass media. These sources are advocates because they get paid for the advertising messages they carry, and they are impersonal because they address vast audiences in print or broadcast form.

2. **Advocate personal** sources, in contrast, impart the human touch to the promotional effort because they involve face-to-face encounters. They are advocate sources if they are paid to persuade prospects to buy from your company. In other words, advocate personal sources are your firm's sales people.

3. **Independent impersonal** sources are typified by test magazines, government reports, and articles in professional journals reporting the results of studies involving the use of your product. For example, the professional journal is of great importance in the pharmaceuticals field, where an endorsement by a prominent physician can make a decided difference in how a new drug is received.

4. **Independent personal** sources include friends, neighbors, colleagues, relatives, and peers. Their advice and opinion are sought because they may have had prior experience with the product or their acceptance of the new idea is essential to the particular

customer. In conversations with this type of source, the customer is much more relaxed and casual than with advocate personal sources, since independent personal sources are people trusted and known. A product recommendation by a friend can very well trigger a purchase decision.

Because of the obvious partiality of advocate sources, independent sources are considerably more credible and influential. They do not have self-interest at heart and derive no financial benefit from promoting your product. However, the results of many studies indicate that advocate impersonal and independent personal sources interact in an important sequence that has been described as the ''two-step flow hypothesis'': Innovations are spread first from your company through the mass media to *opinion leaders,* and from them to their *followers.*

Mass media, by their very nature, make both opinion leaders and followers aware of your product at roughly the same time. But these two customer groups react differently to this information. People who turn out to be opinion leaders quickly make up their minds and try your new product. People in the follower category, however, do not respond immediately to mass media messages. To be stimulated to try your new product, they need reinforcement from opinion leaders.

Opinion leaders are those customers to whom others turn for information and advice. They, therefore, influence the decisions of these others with regard to the adoption of innovations. Contrary to popular myth, opinion leaders usually are not members of a higher social class but are on the same rung of the social ladder as their followers. So, opinion leadership is exerted not vertically but horizontally among peers.

Finally, it is obvious that diffusion takes time. The members of your target market are likely to be geographically dispersed. Since many of them need double exposure (mass media and opinion leaders), simply reaching them via advertising is frequently not enough. In addition, the speed of diffusion depends on the degree of newness involved. If yours is only a minor modification, buyers and prospects may not find it worth talking about. If, on the other hand, a dramatic change is involved, there may be much talk about the new product but greater reluctance to adopt it. A careful balance must be struck.

Adoption: A Multistage Decision-Making Process

Diffusion of your new idea is a prerequisite for adoption. Only after a customer has learned about the existence, availability, and desirability of your innovation can he or she decide about its adoption.

Figure 2-7. *How consumers adopt a new product.*

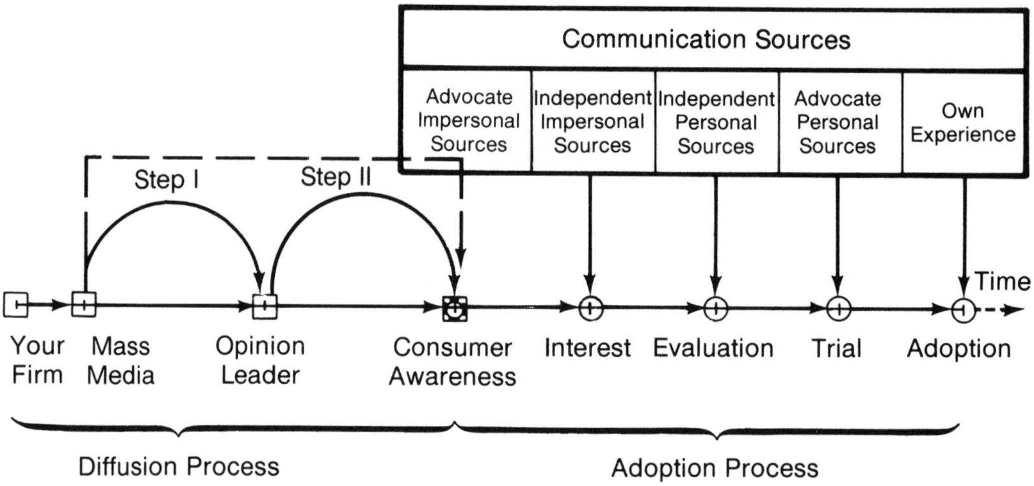

Note: The term "Step I" and "Step II" refer to the "two-step flow hypothesis" mentioned in the text.

Key: ☐ = Sources/recipients of information ○ = Stages of the adoption process

Source: Marketing Update, Issue 8 (1977), p. 3. Published by Alexander-Norton Publishers, Inc.

Information and persuasion are passed on from your firm via the mass media and opinion leaders to individual consumers who, in turn, go through several phases of decision making (see Figure 2-7). Besides that mainstream of information and influence through which consumers first become aware of and interested in your innovation, other sources of communication come into play at different stages of the adoption process. Therefore, although the diffusion process reaches into every stage of the adoption process by means of communication flow, adoption is essentially an individual matter. In the end, it is the consumer alone who must make the decision after giving due consideration to outside factors.

As is evident from Figure 2-7, a consumer adopting your innovation passes through five distinct phases: awareness, interest, evaluation, trial, and adoption.

1. *Awareness.* At the awareness stage, product information flows to the customer with no initiative on his part. He receives it passively but experiences little emotional response. His information at this point is incomplete in that he may not yet be sufficiently informed about your innovation's availability, price, and features. As indicated in Figure 2-7, the efforts of the mass media—amplified, it is hoped, by the impact of opinion lead-

ers—are particularly well suited to the purpose of creating widespread awareness because they can establish contact at a relatively low cost considering the size of the audience.

2. *Interest.* As the information received in the awareness stage is absorbed, a customer may say to himself, "That sounds good. Let me find out more about it." Thus, the interest stage is initiated. It represents a 180-degree turnaround from the nonchalance of the awareness phase. The customer is now "turned on," at least sufficiently to investigate the matter further. He conducts an active search for more information. The purpose of this effort is to obtain a comprehensive picture of your innovation. While folders and brochures from your company will be helpful, and other sources may be consulted, particular emphasis and confidence are likely to be given to independent impersonal sources such as *Consumer Reports,* professional journals, and government studies.

3. *Evaluation.* Having collected as much additional information as possible, the customer examines the evidence and ponders whether or not to try the product. In the evaluation stage, after weighing the pros and cons of a purchase, the prospect solicits the advice of relevant individuals who are trusted personal sources. Two groups of people are involved here: "experts," that is, friends who possess some degree of knowledge in the subject and can be consulted from a functional and financial point of view; and members of the social system (for example, family) who will be affected by a purchase decision and whose acceptance therefore becomes crucial, even though they may not have any expertise.

   Since the customer perceives both a financial risk (that your product may not perform to his satisfaction, thus resulting in a loss of money) and a social risk (that the innovation will not be accepted by his reference group, bringing about a "loss of face"), he will be strongly influenced by these two factors, which override any influence on your part at this point.

4. *Trial.* During the trial stage, a prospect will test your new product, often by purchasing it on a small scale. Since this usually forces consumers to enter a store, it is the salesperson who potentially becomes the most powerful source of information, sometimes influential even to the point of altering the prospect's original purchasing intention. While many items can be sampled in small quantities, difficulties arise in the case of durable goods that require trial under conditions of normal use, which is all but impossible unless the product is rented or purchased. Because test-driving a car around the block can hardly be con-

sidered an adequate trial, some consumers lease the model of their choice for a week, driving it to work or for a weekend ride to get the feel of it. In many instances, however, this procedure is not practical. Trial will then typically come after the purchase, significantly increasing the customer's perceived risk.

You can reduce the customer's apprehensiveness by building up a strong brand name and by offering a liberal return privilege plan, thus decreasing the fear of "getting stuck" with a less than satisfactory product.

5. *Adoption.*   When he completes his personal trial of your innovation, your buyer will determine whether or not it has proved to be useful and desirable in his particular situation. If his decision is positive, the customer will adopt—that is, he will decide to continue using or consuming your product. Besides his own trial experience, your company and product image as well as his social environment will influence this final decision.

Needless to say, your target market can reject your innovation at any stage. A customer can eliminate your product idea even at the awareness stage as being of no interest to him. This dismissal may well be due to a misunderstanding if your advertising message was not strong enough. During the course of his information gathering, he can decide your product is inappropriate or unaffordable. His evaluation of benefits and drawbacks may cause him to reject it. He may discard it as unsatisfactory after the trial period.

A rejection after adoption, however, represents a *discontinuance* because it follows an earlier commitment. An understanding of the interplay between adoption and discontinuance is of great importance for the design of a successful market strategy. Many firms restrict their analysis to a study of the adoption rate, which is simply the ratio between the number of actual and potential adoptions. An increasing adoption rate can, however, be misleading, because it suggests growing popularity of your product, which may not be the case. If, instead, you investigate the interplay of adoption, discontinuance, and readoption, you may well find that, even though more and more of the original nonadopters convert to adoption, a certain percentage (large or small) of your former adopters discontinue using your innovation.

How Social Systems Influence Diffusion and Adoption

While volumes have been written about social systems, it suffices for our purposes to say that a social system is your target market or the group of customers that you are trying to address. Social systems play a major role not only in diffusion, but also in the adoption of your innovation.

- Some innovations will be adopted by customers regardless of the decisions of other individuals in the social system. In such cases, the items involved are typically inconspicuous or ubiquitous, such as toothpaste, bar soap, canned vegetables, and refrigerators.
- In many instances, new products will be purchased by a consumer because other members of his or her social set acquired them. The keep-up-with-the-Jones syndrome explains this tendency for conspicuous items such as swimming pools.
- A certain type of innovation requires prior acceptance by the majority of a social system's members before individual adoption decisions can be made. A charter flight is a good example; the individual still has a choice, but can adopt only if the group supports the idea.
- Another type of innovation is adopted by the majority of a social system and is subsequently forced on those who opposed it—local zoning laws, for example.

These few illustrations make it clear that the diffusion and adoption of innovations are shaped, and often initiated, by the interaction of the people belonging to the social system that you are trying to penetrate. The perceptions, motives, values, habits, attitudes, and beliefs that are prevalent in this social system may make or break your new product. The adoption of innovations is often governed by behavioral patterns of the consumer, with the functional characteristics of the product taken for granted and playing only a minor role. Of necessity, then, psychology, social psychology, sociology, and other behavioral sciences have become important tools for marketing executives.

Application The picture of customer reaction to the introduction of your new product is now complete. You can see that potential buyers react differently, though somewhat predictably, in accordance with their psychological makeup, financial situation, and interaction patterns. The spread of new ideas via various communications channels is closely related to individual adoption decisions.

The customer analysis will indicate how you can manipulate the information input at each stage of the adoption process, how you can differentiate between adopter categories, and finally, and most important, how the acceptance of your innovation can be speeded up.

For example, if your product addresses itself to a large audience, you should definitely include mass media in your communications package, because no other vehicle can deliver consumer awareness as quickly and inexpensively. In spite of the commercial noise and clutter out there, your message can get through if it is unique and presented frequently enough. Be aware that the informational content of any mass media advertisement is necessarily limited. So you may want to suggest to your audience that they request a free booklet in which you can present your message more thoroughly. Such a request is, at the very least, an expression of interest on the part of a prospect that, depending on the nature of your product, could be followed up by a sales call. However, since independent sources carry more weight at the interest stage, it is wise to use press releases and press kits to initiate such potentially favorable coverage.

If your product is truly news, you may even want to think about a press conference with appropriate fringe benefits for the attendees. To trigger adoption in medical circles, pharmaceuticals manufacturers frequently encourage an outstanding authority in a particular field to conduct research with a new drug and report his or her findings in a prestigious professional journal, a procedure akin to independent personal endorsement.

While you, of course, cannot directly control independent personal sources, you can attempt to either simulate or stimulate personal influence. One way to simulate personal influence is to use in your advertising a celebrity with high credibility as a substitute for the influence of friends. Stimulating personal influence is the approach that suggests, "Ask somebody who knows"—namely, a user of your product.

Winning over your dealers' sales personnel is a further crucial step in your game plan. You can motivate them to sell your product more aggressively if you conduct a contest or even, with their principal's permission, pay them a commission. Improving your prospect's own experience with your innovation can provide the ultimate push. It is common practice among car manufacturers to welcome new car buyers in their owner's manual to the "happy family of purchasers of one of the finest cars on the road today." If you believe in your product, you may also want to think about a liberal satisfaction-guaranteed offer or marketing research feedback program.

It would give a great boost to the adoption of your product if you could identify and persuade likely opinion leaders—no easy task. Because opinion leadership and mobility are correlated, some firms avail themselves of lists of American Express cardholders who have used their cards for travel purposes within the past twelve months, and communicate with them via direct mail. A more promising, though more cumbersome, approach is to identify community leaders such as school board and Democratic and Republican committee chairmen, presidents of church councils, and so forth. Obtaining their support for your innovation in their respective communities could be most fruitful.

Finally, there is a proven tactic for speeding up the acceptance of your new product by your target market. You can bypass the first three stages of the adoption process and move consumers right into the trial phase by presenting them with free samples of your innovation. They will have positive attitudes about something that they received without charge and may well continue to buy your product after a satisfactory trial. Colgate-Palmolive has successfully employed this tactic on a nationwide scale in the introduction of Ultra-Brite toothpaste and Irish Spring bar soap. If you do not want to, or cannot be as generous, you can achieve somewhat lesser results by making cents-off offers, couponing, or selling trial sizes.

Summary of Customer Analysis

In conducting your customer analysis, focus on the following three major components:

Market and product segments: Categorize by geographics, demographics, psychographics (life style and social class), geodemographics, product attributes, market size or customer size, common buying factors, common distribution channels, and any other segments that protect your position against competitor inroads.

Patterns of customer behavior: Examine purchase patterns by regular use or by special occasion; review benefits related to economy, convenience, or prestige; review product usage ranked by light, medium, or heavy user; analyze customer loyalty ranked as none, medium, strong, or absolute; examine readiness to buy a product related to unaware, aware, informed, interested, or intending to buy; and review buyers' sensitivity related to quality, price, service, or advertising.

Unfilled wants and needs: Identify wants and needs and consider differentiation related to *product* quality, features, options, packaging, sizes, services, or warranties; *price* as it relates to discounts, allowances, payment periods, credit terms, or special financing; *distribution* coverage, inventory control, transportation, or availability of your product; and *promotional* incentives, advertising, personal selling, and other forms of customer assistance.

Competitor Analysis

While customer analysis lets you examine how to attract and satisfy customers, competitor analysis gives you a picture of your competitors' positions in the market. You can use this information for concentrating on their weak spots, differentiating your product line, preempting their attacks, and creating your own competitive strategies. Competitor analysis should be viewed from a variety of perspectives. First, competitors are analyzed by how customers select the product or company from which they purchase; second, by how competitors segment the market; third, by how behavioral purchase patterns of wants and needs are displayed; and fourth, by how competitors develop their competitive strategies against you. In short, competitor analysis can be categorized by *customer selection, competitor segmentation, behavioral purchase patterns,* and *competitor strategies.*

Case Example

The Dun & Bradstreet Corp. The Dun & Bradstreet Corp. runs what may be ranked as one of the most consistently well-run business information companies in the world. Even in its worst year, 1980, earnings grew by 15 percent. The essence of the company's strategy is to exploit its most valuable asset: a huge data base. Using its millions of electronic records on everything from corporate credit reports to airline departures (through its *Official Airline Guide*), D&B managers diligently search for ways to repackage its information for new customers. For example, D&B delivers the same credit report via computer, telephone, and mail.

D&B's strategy concentrates on searching for opportunities and new product lines through cross-pollination of products among the various divisions within the organization. It is an effort to meet the needs of a variety of customers and to enter a number of different markets. Not all of its products are new to the world; some are modifications or line extensions. For example, in the case of its *Official Airline Guide,* travelers can refer to the large book-size version of airline schedules, use the pocket-size version, or access the electronic version. As an additional spin-off, users of the electronic version can make their reservations via computer through another D&B company, Thomas Cook Travel.

This immensely successful operation doesn't just happen. It's the constant infusion of a customer-oriented attitude that reaches every level of the organization that makes it work. The intensity of the effort continues at a tremendous pace to maintain D&B's competitive edge. The $2.8 billion organization in-

troduced 200 new products in 1986 alone. And with all that
success, there are bound to be competitors anxious to share in
the wealth. Competitors are assembling in every part of the
business; they are attracted by the high profits D&B shows and
the seemingly unending opportunities for growth in business
information. Most important to Dun and Bradstreet are the
types of competitors: For each different product type D&B produces, it encounters a different set of competitors. It thus requires multiple competitor analyses.

In order to maintain its market stronghold against these attacks, D&B has conducted competitor analyses from a number of
of viewpoints.

1. D&B looked at how customers chose to fulfill their wants
   and needs, that is, which competitors they bought from.
   For instance, customers for D&B's products, such as the
   Official Airline Guide, can refer to similar guides published
   by competitors; they can call travel agents or use other
   published listings. Thus, by observing *purchasing activities of customers,* D&B could identify its competitors.

2. It analyzed which groups of *market segments its competitors served* and how they delivered their services to those
   markets. Although D&B filled many markets, some of its
   competitors provided only directories. Thus, by concentrating in the directory market, D&B could force some of its
   competitors to differentiate or suffer significant losses.

3. It looked at new *behavior purchase patterns* in order to
   fulfill wants and needs. For instance, D&B identified one
   growing market segment: business executives and salespeople who make such frequent changes in their travel
   plans that they need travel information in an easily accessible form, such as a timetable of plane flights to carry in
   their briefcase. In order to gauge its success in fulfilling
   behavioral purchase patterns, D&B compared its services
   with its competitors' along such lines as warranty, reliability, and prestige (see Figure 2-8 for checklist).

4. D&B recognized that existing and emerging competitors
   were searching its performance for exposed niches of opportunity—areas of differentiation in product, price, promotion, and distribution that could represent areas of attack on D&B. Dun & Bradstreet *analyzed these strategies*
   in order to preempt them (refer to Figure 2-10 on page 84
   for checklist).

Customer   As discussed in the Dun & Bradstreet example, the category of cus-
Selection tomer selection is made up of traditional and new entrants to the
field. Customers for D&B's products, such as the *Official Airline
Guide,* can use competitors' guides, call travel agents, or use other
published listings. Thus, when you branch into new markets, competitors are, in effect, preselected for you. By observing purchasing

activities of customers, you can identify your competitors and then group them so that you can conduct a competitor analysis on the basis of such factors as quality, versatility, accuracy, reliability, speed of access of information, cost, and types of additional information.

As further evidenced by customer selection, there are direct and indirect competitors. Looking to other industries, for example, bankers find their traditional depositor customers are placing their savings in a variety of channels that are now competitors to banks. Insurance plans, such as Universal Life, have an investment component that serves as a savings vehicle. Brokerage houses, mutual funds consisting of stocks and bonds, and government securities are also competitors of banks. In other fields, Pepsi and Coke battle between themselves as well as with noncola drinks. Airlines also have indirect competitors when their customers select teleconferencing and electronic transmission of detailed information as alternatives to expensive and time-consuming travel. The filtering-down process continues when airport limousines, hotels, and restaurants feel the effect of such indirect competition.

Competitor Segmentation

Market segmentation has already been discussed in connection with customer analysis, but now we can examine it from another vantage point: how competitors might segment their markets. Your interest is in knowing the various possibilities through which you can be attacked by an existing or new competitor. In addition, such an examination provides insights from which you can develop a counter-strategy.

You should be aware that, in addition to segmenting to protect their own positions against competitive inroads, competitors can segment by a set of common buying factors (performance, quality, service, delivery, and price); by range of measurable characteristics (customer size, growth rate, and location); by common sales and distribution channels; and by application of new technology. They can use these segments singly or in any combination. Philip Kotler discusses a variety of market niche possibilities:[4]

- *End-use specialist:* Serves one type of end-use customer; for example, a law firm may specialize in the criminal, civil, or business law market.
- *Vertical-level specialist:* Specializes at some vertical level of the production–distribution cycle; for example, a copper firm may

[4]Philip Kotler, *Marketing Management,* 6th edition (Englewood Cliffs, N.J.: Prentice-Hall, Inc., 1988), p. 342.

concentrate on producing raw copper, copper components, or finished copper products.

- *Customer-size specialist:* Concentrates on selling to either small, medium-size, or large customers; many "nichers" specialize in serving small customers that are neglected by the major suppliers.
- *Specific-customer specialist:* Limits itself to selling to one or only a few major customers; many firms sell their entire output to a single company, such as Sears or General Motors.
- *Geographic specialist:* Sells only in a certain locality, region, or area of the world.
- *Product-line specialist:* Produces only one product line or product; for example, within the laboratory equipment industry there are firms that produce only microscopes, or, even more specifically, only lenses for microscopes.
- *Product-feature specialist:* Specializes in producing a certain type of product or product feature; Rent-A-Wreck, for example, is a car rental agency that rents only heavily used cars.
- *Job-shop specialist:* Manufactures customized products as ordered by the customer.
- *Quality-price specialist:* Operates at the low or high end of the market; for example, Hewlett-Packard specializes in the high-quality, high-priced end of the hand calculator market.
- *Service specialist:* Offers one or more services not available from other firms; for example, a bank may take loan requests over the phone and hand-deliver the money to the customer.

Case Example

Progresso Quality Foods Company Progresso Quality Foods Company, marketer of everything from olive oil and soups to pasta and spaghetti sauce, sells its products in 30 metropolitan markets mostly on the East and West Coasts. During the mid-1980's, it rolled out nationwide with new product lines into new market segments against its major competitor, Campbell Soup Company.

The management of Progresso realized that Campbell had a record of clamping down on challengers. Therefore, Progresso utilized a strategy of niche marketing, a form of indirect approach that avoided a direct confrontation against Campbell. For example, it zeroed in on high-margin segments where the company believed it could dominate yet not compete frontally with Campbell. Such areas included ready-to-serve soups, sauces other than tomato, and such expensive exotics as arti-chokes and pignoli nuts.

In addition, Progresso's strategy stressed ethnic authenticity and premium quality at a price comparable to that of Camp-bell's Chunky line of soups; but its soup line never aimed di-rectly at Chunky's markets. The strategy was summed up by Progresso's president, Gasper F. Taormina, who said, "We are not undertaking a frontal assault." Instead, the president chose to carve out a niche that was not strictly competitive. In 1986, Progresso introduced its products into five to ten new markets on a six-month basis, and the company estimated that its local television ads reached 60 percent of all U.S. households, up from 40 percent the year before.

The case illustrates how one company, Progresso, analyzed its market and its competition and positioned itself accordingly to avoid a frontal attack. On the other hand, Campbell Soup Company, in protecting its major markets, had to look at how Progresso segmented its market to determine what counter-strategy to employ. Such segmentation analysis is critical to any attack or counterattack that may need to be developed.

Behavioral Purchase Patterns Why do prospects buy from your competitor rather than from you? What are the behavioral patterns most noticeable in customer behavior? What are the trends as they relate to such factors as product, price, promotion, distribution, research and development, service, and courtesy of salespeople? It is useful within the context of competitor analysis to categorize these trend areas so you can consciously look to the behavioral patterns that cause a prospect to purchase from your competitor rather than from you, or vice versa.

Figure 2-8 is an evaluation tool. Using your major competitors in the evaluation, it provides a side-by-side analysis of the key factors that affect purchase considerations. Score each applicable factor on a scale of 0 to 5. Place the evaluation number 0 (low) to 5 (high) in each column. If any factor doesn't apply, skip over it and proceed to the next factor. In actual use, the number can represent the consensus of a planning group, the average of each member of a group scoring a factor separately, or a single individual's assessment. The factors listed in the form are stated briefly, so you should be certain that the meaning is precise among those individuals doing the evaluation. It is important to have accurate interpretation if meaningful information is going to come out of the analysis. The total of the scores for each competitor, when compared with those of your own company, provides useful input for the full analysis of competitors.

Competitor Strategies Of the four components of competitor analysis, competitor strategies should be singled out as being of major importance. Every other part

Figure 2-8. *Competitive evaluation sheet.*

Factors	Your Company (or Product Line)	Competitor A	Competitor B
Product			
Quality			
Features			
Options			
Style			
Brand name			
Packaging			
Sizes			
Services			
Warranties			
Returns			
Versatility			
Uniqueness			
Utility			
Reliability			
Durability			
Patent protection			
Guarantees			
Price			
List price			
Discounts			
Allowances			
Payment period			
Credit terms			
Financing			
Distribution			
Channels			
Direct sales force			
Manufacturers' reps			
Distributors			
Jobbers			
Dealers			
Market coverage			
Warehouse locations			
Inventory control systems			
Physical transport			

(*continued*)

Figure 2-8. *Continued.*

Factors	Your Company (or Product Line)	Competitor A	Competitor B
Promotion			
Advertising			
Customer			
Trade			
Personal selling			
Incentives			
Sales aids			
Samples			
Training			
Sales promotion			
Demonstrations			
Contests			
Premiums			
Coupons			
Manuals			
Telemarketing			
Publicity			
Total Scores:			

of the analysis is subordinate to the strategies that your competitors will use against you.

Case Example

Cummins Engines Company, Inc. The drama and excitement of competitor strategies were displayed in a 1986 encounter between Cummins Engines and the Japanese manufacturers Komatsu and Nissan. Cummins Engines, the heavy diesel engine manufacturer, had been fighting uphill against aggressive Japanese competitors, particularly Komatsu and Nissan. The first word of the impending problem came from Cummins' customers, Navistar and Freightliner Corp., which reported that they were testing Japanese medium-truck engines.

Knowing the Japanese strategy of using an indirect approach into a market, Cummins recognized the medium-engine entry into the market as a strategic move that would lead to the next step of penetrating Cummins' dominant 58 percent share of the U.S. market for heavy-duty diesel truck engines. It saw the strategy evolve:

The Japanese competitors entered the market with prices as much as 40 percent below prevailing levels to quickly gain market share.

They found a poorly served and an emerging market segment in medium-size engines.

They developed a quality product, and they were prepared to expand their product lines.

Faced with the dilemma, Cummins took the following action:

1. Launched into the medium-size truck engine market with four new engine models. The timing, however, was coincidental because Cummins had been planning this market entry for five years through a joint venture with the J. I. Case Company.

2. Immediately cut prices of the new engines to the Japanese level. As Chairman Henry Schacht observed, "If you don't give the Japanese a major price advantage, they can't get in."

3. Cut costs by one-third. This action was the toughest job in what was perceived to be a bare-bones, efficient manufacturing operation. Schacht reduced overhead by using more flexible machinery to cut down on setup time for different engine models. He eliminated the need for excess inventory, which was cut from a 60-day supply to a 4-day supply.

4. Gained participation from suppliers on suggestions about cost cutting. An impressive 18 percent reduction in material costs was the result of changing the traditional adversarial attitude toward suppliers to one of fostering cooperative relationships.

In its implementation, the strategy worked as an effective defense against the competitor inroads.

Application Strategy involves the mobilization of every human and functional part of a company, and focuses the sum of those resources to achieve corporate, divisional, or product-line objectives. Therefore, to analyze competitors you have to analyze the total competitor organization and compare it with your own. However, in realistic terms, the extent of the analysis may focus only within the responsibility of a division vice-president of marketing, product manager, marketing manager, or sales manager, and only on selected competitors within a target market. If the competitor's total organization must be analyzed, what are the areas for analysis?

Noted authors such as D. Aaker, D. Abell, J. Hammond, P. Kotler, M. E. Porter, and G. Steiner have dealt with the subject of analysis in recent years. The intent here is to condense the various approaches into formats for everyday use by a manager who has responsibility for a specific product or market. All the approaches found in the literature essentially aim to answer similar questions, such as:

- What are the competitors' objectives as to size, growth, profitability, and market share?
- What are the competitors' current strategies?
- How are they performing?
- What are their strengths and weaknesses?
- What actions can be expected from existing and emerging competitors in the future?

Developing a strengths/weaknesses checklist is one format for analysis. This approach was used in a narrower perspective in the previous section on behavioral purchase patterns. A second approach is to determine how competitors fit into strategic groups, and a third framework creates an operating profile to analyze marketing strategies and tactics employed by competitors.

Strengths/Weaknesses

Of the various formats and checklists available to analyze strengths and weaknesses of competitors, Figure 2-9 stands out as one of the most effective. To expand on its application, the form can be modified to fit a particular firm's needs. It can be used to evaluate how your firm measures up to a competitor's organization. It can be used to match one division against another or to compare key competitors within a product line or market segment. The evaluation is intended to determine where your firm is weak or where it is strong as compared with the competition.

Strategic Groups

Another approach to analyzing competitor strategies is to categorize your competitors by strategic groups.[5] This system is another approach to organizing groups of competitors by similarities of the strategies they pursue. The strategic groups, which Porter refers to as generic strategies, are identified as follows:

---

[5] Hall and Porter are the leading commentators on the use of strategic groups. See William K. Hall, "Survival Strategies in a Hostile Environment," *Harvard Business Review* (Sept.–Oct. 1980), p. 80, and Michael E. Porter, *Competitive Strategy* (New York: The Free Press, 1980), Chapter 2.

Figure 2-9. *Checklist for analyzing strengths and weaknesses.*

Check off in each category how you evaluate your organization according to:

Column I	Better than anyone else. Substantially in excess of present needs. Definitely a leader.
Column II	Better than average. Good, strong performance. No problems.
Column III	Average. Adequate. Competitive. Solid.
Column IV	Should be better. Deteriorating. Cause for concern.
Column V	Definitely worrisome. Must be improved. Bad. Crisis. "We are being clobbered."

Category	I	II	III	IV	V
Finance					
Debt–equity structure	—	—	—	—	—
Inventory turnover	—	—	—	—	—
Customer credit	—	—	—	—	—
Capital resources	—	—	—	—	—
Available cash flow	—	—	—	—	—
Break-even points	—	—	—	—	—
Sales per assets employed	—	—	—	—	—
Ratio fixed to liquid assets	—	—	—	—	—
Performance versus budget	—	—	—	—	—
Return on new investments	—	—	—	—	—
Ownership	—	—	—	—	—
Dividend history	—	—	—	—	—
Production					
Capacity	—	—	—	—	—
Production processes	—	—	—	—	—
Conversion efficiency	—	—	—	—	—
Labor supply	—	—	—	—	—
Labor productivity	—	—	—	—	—
Raw material supply	—	—	—	—	—
Sales per employee	—	—	—	—	—
Sales per fixed investment	—	—	—	—	—
Age of plant equipment	—	—	—	—	—
Quality control	—	—	—	—	—
On-time shipments	—	—	—	—	—
Downtime	—	—	—	—	—
Space for expansion	—	—	—	—	—
Plant location	—	—	—	—	—

(continued)

Source: Merritt L. Kastens, *Long-Range Planning for Your Business* (New York: AMACOM, 1976), pp. 52–53.

Figure 2-9. *Continued*

Category	I	II	III	IV	V
Organization and administration					
Ratio of administrative to production personnel	—	—	—	—	—
Communications	—	—	—	—	—
Clear-cut responsibilities	—	—	—	—	—
Management turnover	—	—	—	—	—
Management information	—	—	—	—	—
Speed of reaction	—	—	—	—	—
Marketing					
Share of market	—	—	—	—	—
Product reputation	—	—	—	—	—
Brand acceptance	—	—	—	—	—
Selling expense	—	—	—	—	—
Customer service	—	—	—	—	—
Distribution facilities	—	—	—	—	—
Sales organization	—	—	—	—	—
Prices	—	—	—	—	—
Number of customers	—	—	—	—	—
Distribution costs	—	—	—	—	—
Market information	—	—	—	—	—
Work force					
Hourly labor	—	—	—	—	—
Clerical labor	—	—	—	—	—
Salespeople	—	—	—	—	—
Scientists and engineers	—	—	—	—	—
Supervisors	—	—	—	—	—
Middle management	—	—	—	—	—
Top management	—	—	—	—	—
Training costs	—	—	—	—	—
Management depth	—	—	—	—	—
Turnover	—	—	—	—	—
Technology					
Product technology	—	—	—	—	—
New products	—	—	—	—	—
Patent position	—	—	—	—	—
R&D organization	—	—	—	—	—
Engineering design capability	—	—	—	—	—

- Companies that pursue a *differentiation strategy* relying on product-line depth, product quality, service, distribution, or brand identification to create a competitive advantage.
- A *low-cost strategy* based on economies of scale, the experience curve, manufacturing facilities and equipment, and access to raw materials.
- A *focus strategy* based on the boundaries of a competitor's product line and served markets.

Any effort to categorize groups of organizations into finite categories has to be tempered with judgment. The fact is that many organizations will merge one or more broad generic strategies in order to either maintain their presence in the marketplace or increase their share of market. For example, Deere & Company, the farm and industrial equipment manufacturer, has been moving on a solid course of survival and growth for a long period. It saw a treacherous agricultural market during the 1984–86 period, when recession caused 2,000 farmers per week to sell out. As one of Deere's executives pointed out, "We can't rely on wage rates going down, we can't rely on markets going up, we've got to drive costs down."

Deere's successful strategies can be grouped as follows:

1. Create a *low-cost* advantage. For example, costs of a small sprocket wheel were reduced by 50 percent. The cost of engines for construction machinery have been knocked down by $357 or 27 percent. And on a model-by-model basis, the industrial equipment division claimed its newest machinery was coming in at 30 to 35 percent lower costs than previous lines.
2. *Focus* on segments of opportunity. One of these segments was the lawn tractor business, which had been booming with $650 million in sales and is expected to reach $1 billion, even against aggressive Japanese competitors such as Honda.
3. *Differentiate* through market and product development: (a) manufacture engine blocks for General Motors; (b) make axles and chassis for recreational vehicle manufacturers, such as Winnebago, which means creating line extensions of existing designs for specialized use; and (c) develop relationships with General Motors to supply it with 40,000–50,000 diesel engines. The joint relationship permits Deere to experiment with materials such as ceramics that could give it a competitive edge.

Thus, the Deere example shows the use of several generic strategies working within one organization.

Operating Profile

A third framework for analyzing competitor strategies is the development of an operating profile to analyze the marketing strategies and tactics employed by competitors. Figure 2-10 presents a basic format for evaluating your key competitors. Using expanded forms, answer all questions that are applicable to your situation. When information is missing, yet desirable to have, more intensive competitor intelligence is called for. (Sources of competitor intelligence are discussed in Chapter 4.)

Figure 2-10. *Worksheet for profiling competitors' strategies.*

Where applicable, indicate the practices and characteristics of major competitors for each of the marketing strategies.				
	Competitor A	*Competitor B*	*Competitor C*	*Competitor D*
Market				
Market Dimension				
What size market does each competitor operate in? Be specific with respect to:				
Segments (geographic, demographic, psychographic)				
Single market				
Multimarket				
Total market				
Regional market				
National market				
International market				
Market Entry				
How do competitors usually enter a market? Is there a market leader among competitors? Who are the followers? Identify by:				
First-in strategy				
Follow-the-leader strategy				
Last-in strategy				
Market Commitment				
How much commitment do competitors give to a specific market in terms of priorities and resources?				
Major commitment				

	Competitor A	Competitor B	Competitor C	Competitor D
Average commitment				
Limited commitment				
Market Demand How flexible are competitors in changing strategies for different market situations?				
Prune markets when demand slackens				
Concentrate on key markets when demand increases				
Harvest profits when sales plateau				
Market Diversification How have competitors responded to diversification opportunities?				
Added new businesses or added another stage of production or distribution				
Diversified into unrelated businesses				
Product				
Positioning How efficient are competitors in monitoring customer perceptions and identifying customer niches as related to:				
Positioning a single brand				
Positioning a multiple brand				
Repositioning older products				
Product Life Cycle How efficient are competitors in extending the life cycle of their products as related to:				
Promoting more frequent usage				
Finding new users				
Finding more uses for product				
Finding new uses for product's basic materials				

(continued)

Figure 2-10. *Continued.*

	Competitor A	*Competitor B*	*Competitor C*	*Competitor D*
Product Competition				
To what extent do competitors attempt to gain a larger share of a market by introducing:				
Competing brand				
Private label				
Generic product				
Product Mix				
Where do competitors stand in relation to width and depth of product lines?				
Single product				
Multiple products				
Product systems				
Product Design				
How much manufacturing and design flexibility do competitors display as related to:				
Standard products				
Customized products				
Standard product, modified				
New Products				
What has been the pattern of competitors in relation to the following areas of new product development?				
Innovation				
Modification				
Line extension				
Diversification				
Remerchandizing existing products				
Extending market for existing products				
Product Audit				
How flexible have competitors been in monitoring their product lines as displayed by:				
Line reduction				
Line elimination				

	Competitor A	*Competitor B*	*Competitor C*	*Competitor D*
Price				
New Products				
What has been the pattern of competitors in pricing new products? Do they tend to use:				
Skim (high) pricing				
Penetration (low) pricing				
Psychological (odd/even) pricing				
Follow-the-leader pricing				
Cost-plus pricing				
Established Products				
What has been the pattern of competitors in pricing established products? Do they tend to use:				
Slide-down (gradual reduction) pricing				
Segment pricing				
Flexible pricing				
Preemptive (reacting to competitors') pricing				
Loss-leader pricing				
Promotion				
Advertising				
To what extent do competitors use advertising to do the following:				
Support personal selling				
Inform target audience about availability of product				
Persuade prospects to buy directly from advertising				
Sales Force				
What is the profile of competitors' sales forces with respect to:				
Sales force size				
Sales force territorial design				
Compensation systems				

(continued)

Figure 2-10. *Continued.*

	Competitor A	*Competitor B*	*Competitor C*	*Competitor D*
Training				
Technical or service backup				
Sales Promotion How well do competitors integrate sales promotion with their advertising and sales force strategies? Is sales promotion used to:				
Encourage more product usage				
Induce dealer involvement				
Stimulate greater sales-force efforts				
Distribution				
Channel Structure What has been the distribution strategy of competitors in reaching customer markets?				
Direct distribution to end user				
Indirect distribution through intermediaries (distributors, dealers)				
Channel Dimension Are competitors displaying any strategies that could alter their distribution methods? Are they looking at:				
Exclusive (restricted) distribution				
Intensive (widespread) distribution				
Selective (high sales potential) distribution				
Multiple Channel Are competitors adding channels that complement or compete against existing ones to reach new markets?				
Complementary channels				
Competitive channels				
Channel Control Are any competitors attempting to control distribution channels through the following approaches?				

	Competitor A	Competitor B	Competitor C	Competitor D
Adding a wholesaling function				
Adding a retailing function				
Controlling more of the manufacturing process				
Adding franchises				
Combining with other organizations to achieve purchasing economies				

Summary of Competitor Analysis Conduct a competitor analysis by examining customer selection (which competitors customers choose), competitor segments (how competitors divide up the market), behavioral purchase patterns (why customers buy from your competitors and not from you), and competitive strategies (your competitors' plans to gain market share against you).

Industry Analysis

The third part of the external analysis is industry analysis. An industry is the sum of many parts: sources of supply, existing competitors, emerging competitors, alternative product and service offerings, and various levels of customers from intermediate types such as original equipment manufacturers (OEM) to end users. Within these powerful factors are a range of influences that also affect an industry.

Case Example

Cincinnati Milacron Inc. Cincinnati Milacron Inc. (known as "the MILL") has made a strategic change from being a leader in the machine tools industry to becoming a leader in advanced manufacturing systems. The MILL saw its dominance in machine tools deteriorate during the early 1980's through the inroads of imports. In fact, in 1985 the company reported its first losing year since the Depression.

The transition was painful for Milacron. Management observed the operating statistics of declining market share and lowering earnings, and saw the urgency for corrective action.

Placing emphasis on conducting an industry analysis, management saw a brighter future in producing automated manufacturing systems for companies that were developing products primarily made of plastics and light space-age materials.

An industry analysis revealed tremendous growth in parts for cars and airplanes using new materials such as composites made of epoxies and graphite fibers. For example, industry analysis indicated that more than half the aircraft in the 1990's would be made of composite materials. Milacron geared its flexible manufacturing systems to helping customers create shapes out of those new materials. Further analysis in specific industries prompted the MILL to make laser equipment that welded hypodermic needles without affecting their hollow insides.

Fortunately, Milacron's forward-looking mentality, along with the appropriate industry analysis, helped the company achieve a position as the leading U.S. plastics machinery producer. The industry analysis created a framework that permitted management to examine the various interacting and, sometimes, conflicting forces and to form a usable strategy. As a result, by 1986 Milacron was in an excellent position to blunt the efforts of plastics machinery imports with a new line of machines that molded plastics.

Conducting an Industry Analysis Figure 2-11 illustrates the interacting forces that make up an industry analysis. It proceeds from the broad analysis of suppliers, existing competitors, emerging competitors, alternative product offerings, and customers (Level 1) to a finite listing that can be used as a checklist (Level 2).

Level 1 Analysis

Suppliers

If industries are dominated by a few suppliers that maintain control of the flow of materials that usually results in control of prices, then a powerful influence is exerted on all the other forces within the industry. A review of supplier practices at key stages of the industry's evolution will provide you with a clue to future patterns of supplier behavior, which in turn will result in alternative strategies. Such analysis has had the effect of driving user organizations to other countries for sources of supply, to joint ventures, or to new technologies. On the other hand, when suppliers see the threat of losing their dominance

Figure 2-11. *Industry analysis.*

Level 1—Profile:

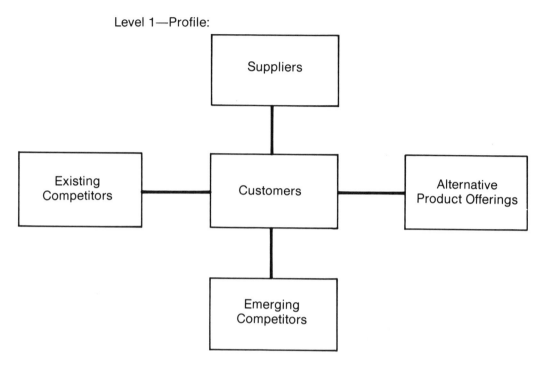

Level 2—Identify:

- Current demand for product
- Future potential for product
- Industry life cycle
- Emerging technology
- Changing customer profiles
- Frequency of new product introductions
- Level of government regulation
- Distribution networks
- Entry and exit barriers
- Marketing innovation
- Cost structures

in an industry, cooperative relationships can be formed (as shown by the case example of Cummins Engines working in unison with its suppliers).

While suppliers are normally thought of in terms of materials, labor is also a form of supply with the same factors influencing the analysis and subsequent strategy decisions.

Existing Competitors

How do you rate the intensity of competitive actions? Examine the pattern of price wars. Which competitors seem to retaliate first against movements in prices? Review the amount of advertising and identify the themes of the advertisements. Is there a tendency to "knock the competition" or is it a more professional approach? Is there a warlike environment that is changing the character of the industry?

You can also characterize existing competitors within an industry by answering the following questions:

- How would you rank the commitment of most competitors to the industry? Is there a major, average, or minor commitment?
- How diverse are the competitors in their objectives and strategies? Are there some entrepreneurial firms using innovations to increase market share? Are there more established firms that are ready to hold their markets "at all costs"?
- What is the nature of the products in the industry? Have they reached a commodity status or is there a tendency toward product differentiation?
- Is the industry plagued with overcapacity or undercapacity? What effect would each condition have on the strategies of competitors?

Emerging Competitors

The entry of new competitors over the last 25 years in many U.S. industries—such as steel, cars, consumer appliances, textiles, footwear, and, now, high technology—has had a devastating effect on the established companies. In conducting an industry analysis there is a tendency to focus only on existing players. The wrenching lesson from this experience is that you must identify and analyze emerging competitors with the same intensity of detail as you apply to existing ones. The job is more difficult when applied to emerging competitors because patterns of behavior are not always visible. However, there is sufficient evidence since the early 1960's, particularly from foreign competitors, to make reasonable assumptions. For example, most foreign competitors, especially from Asian countries, will enter an industry with low prices to increase market share as rapidly as possible regardless of profitability. If good distribution is difficult to achieve, they will produce for the private label of established companies in the industry while at the same time introducing their own brand. The value of knowing your competitors is demonstrated by the ancient

Chinese commentator Sun Tzu over 2,000 years ago in his writings on warfare. (The term *enemy* is easily interchangeable with competitors to absorb the wisdom of his concepts.)

> "Know the enemy and know yourself; in a hundred battles you will never be in peril."
>
> "When you are ignorant of the enemy but know yourself, your chances of winning or losing are equal."
>
> "If ignorant both of your enemy and of yourself, you are certain in every battle to be in peril."

Alternative Product Offerings

Using the lessons from analyzing emerging competitors, you should give similar emphasis to alternative products or services. It is appropriate in this type of analysis to employ the skills and knowledge of R&D and manufacturing and product designers in your organization, who are more likely to be aware of substitute products. Outside industry specialists from academia, research organizations, and other industry consultants are also useful sources of information. The auto industry provides a familiar example of how aluminum is replacing steel and how plastics are increasingly providing an alternative to aluminum.

Customers

Customers are classified at all stages of the buying cycle: from end-use consumer to industrial and commercial buyers as well as intermediaries such as distributors, wholesalers, and retailers. Each stage represents a force within an industry that warrants investigation. Answering the following questions will provide you with insights about the influences or power of customers:

- Do customers tend to dictate buying terms because of large-volume or concentrated purchases?
- Are customers knowledgeable about costs of raw materials and manufacturing and do they use such information as bargaining power?
- Is there a threat of key customers using backward integration to take over the suppliers' functions?
- Is there sufficient product differentiation or can customers simply switch from one supplier (domestic or foreign) to another?

Level 2 Analysis: Checklist

Industry analysis continues with Level 2, a more detailed analysis that should be used as a checklist:

Current demand for product: Indicate, in quantitative terms, the demand or usage of your product in sales, dollars, units, pounds, number of users, share of market, or whatever measurement provides a reliable indication of demand.

Future potential for product: Use a time frame of three to five years to forecast the potential for your product and try to use the same unit of measurement as that for determining current demand.

Industry life cycle: Identify, even in broad terms, the stage the industry is in in its life cycle—for example, introduction, growth, maturity, or decline (product life cycle is discussed in Chapter 9).

Emerging technology: Identify specific technology that is currently available or may be in use even on an experimental basis with competitors; determine where the technology is coming from and who holds patents or copyrights.

Changing customer profiles: Use segmentation techniques (identified earlier in this chapter) to track any emerging changes in demographics, geographics, or psychographics.

Frequency of new product introductions: Monitor the introduction of new products to establish if there is an industry pattern that can serve as a standard for your own level of product development.

Level of government regulation: Determine if government regulation is increasing or declining and assess the impact on your industry.

Distribution networks: Indicate if there are any innovations in the use of distributor channels—for example, emphasis on pushing the product through distributors or pulling the product through the channel by influencing the end user or eliminating distributors entirely. Also determine if there is evidence of forward integration in which producers are acquiring distributors.

Exit and entry barriers: Assess the ease or difficulty of entering and exiting an industry. The entry barriers include amount of capital investment needed, extent of economies of scale, access to distribution channels, and opportunities for product differentiation. Exit barriers include types and value of fixed assets; length of presence needed in market through labor contracts; leases; providing services and parts to customers; government regulations; social responsibilities to communities and workers; level of emotional attachment to the business or industry; and special relationships with other divisions in the organization or with outside attachments to warehousing, transportation, or financial institutions.

Marketing innovation: Determine if there are innovations involving areas such as just-in-time delivery, telemarketing, demonstrations, seminars, new promotional incentives, advertising, and sales-force utilization.

Cost structures: Evaluate the impact of economies of scale on costs and profits as they relate to manufacturing, purchasing, R&D, marketing, and distribution. Determine specifically the impact on costs of the current movement to automation and its potential impact on your industry.

Summary of Industry Analysis

Industry analysis helps you define many factors in your industry: customer profiles, existing and emerging competitors, products, and technology. By giving you a picture of the overall industry from all these aspects, industry analysis lets you see industry trends into the future so you can stake out opportunity areas for growth.

Remember that industry analysis consists of two levels. First, it requires a *broad analysis* of suppliers, existing competitors, emerging competitors, and alternative product offerings to give you a wide picture of the entire industry. Second, it entails a much more *detailed analysis* of conditions related to product, customers, technology, cost, distribution, and other factors. In your own analysis, use the checklist provided for Level 2 analysis to consider each of these factors in your own business situation.

Environmental Analysis

The fourth, and final, part of the external analysis is environmental analysis. Consider the following case of Humana Inc. and its problems in introducing a new product in 1986. It will provide you with a perspective on environmental considerations and how they can affect your business.

Case Example

Humana Inc. Humana Inc., a large hospital chain, ventured into the health insurance business during the mid-1980's. The first product of this new venture was a group insurance plan, *Humana Care Plus.* The intent was to channel patients to its hospitals, reasoning that employers would choose its plan because of low premiums and that policy holders would be attracted to Humana hospitals because of lower deductibles.

The original product launch for *Humana Care Plus* did not do well. Even with $350 million in premiums it still wasn't making money. In fact, its losses contributed to the company's first quarterly earnings drop in 15 years.

What went wrong? Customer analysis revealed that only 46 percent of *Care Plus* members were actually using Humana facilities. However, premiums were calculated on a 70 percent user rate. Additional analysis revealed another aspect of market behavior: doctors (that is, the distribution network) failed to steer patients to Humana hospitals. Their behavior was influenced by a strong need to retain independence of action and they therefore specified hospitals other than Humana's. There was also a rebellion among the doctors, who feared that severe cost cutting at hospitals would lead to poor-quality treatment.

In response, Humana considered all the ramifications of the social and environmental issues and mounted an educational program to convince doctors of the quality care at Humana hospitals.

Humana's situation reveals a range of environmental factors at work; some are visible, others are submerged. The case shows how considerations such as sociocultural, demographic, and economic forces can have a bottom-line impact on the success or failure of a new product launch. Marketers tend to be too narrow in viewing their products and markets, yet the forces in the environment are too powerful to ignore.

Conducting an Environmental Analysis The question "What went wrong?" is raised in most unsuccessful product launches. Typically, the answers fall back to an inadequate analysis of customers' market behavior and of competition, and to the broader considerations of environmental factors. There are six key components of environmental analysis, as shown in Figure 2-12. Use the following scenarios as guidelines for evaluating your own market and product. To respond to some of the situations, hard facts are needed; for others, intuition can also be used to provide valid answers. Certainly, interacting with other individuals within your company or group can reveal additional insights. However, be sure that the gathering of "nice to know" information is not the intent; rather, the intent is the conscious effort to use environmental issues to develop your competitive strategies.

Demographics

What potential do the following circumstances hold for your product or service?

1. World population is expected to grow from 4.4 billion in 1980 to 6.2 billion by the year 2000. Although much of the popula-

Figure 2-12. *Environmental analysis.*

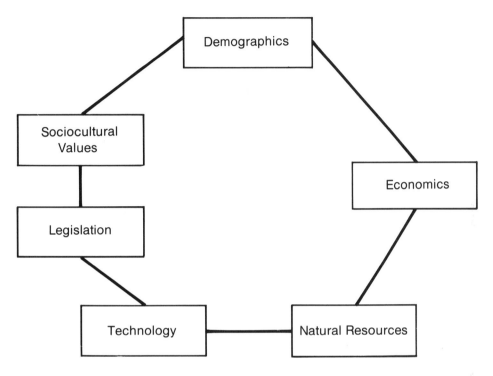

tion growth will occur within poor countries, there will be potential markets for foods, medicines, machines, clothing, agricultural products, and various low-technology products.

2. The 1980 census revealed that the U.S. population stood at 233 million, and the projection is for very slow growth to 264 million by the year 2000. Environmental issues contributing to the slowdown in the birth rate are the movement to smaller families, the increasing number of women working outside the home, and improved methods of birth control. Possible areas of growth include convenience items, new types of foods, quantity and styles of clothes, and number of automobiles per family.

3. The graying of America is a demographic fact. The U.S. median age is now 30 and is forecast to reach 35 by the year 2000, and the over-65 age group will show the second-largest increase in the coming decade, up by 20 percent. Other available facts indicate that (a) the 15–24 age group will decrease by 17 percent by the end of the decade, (b) the 25–34 age group will undergo a growth of 14 percent, (c) the 35–54 age group will have the greatest increase of all age groups, up 25 percent, and (d) the 55–64 age group will diminish by 2 percent in this de-

cade. Within each of these age populations, there are opportunities for products and services such as sports equipment, travel, clothes, recreation, medical services, insurance, financial services, and transportation.

4. The profile of the American family is changing. The changes can be summed up as later marriages, fewer children, more divorces, and more working wives. Each of these factors can form a market segment that could hold potential for new products and services ranging from advisory services to household appliances.

5. The 1970's and 1980's spawned a new type of household—namely, the nonfamily household—taking several forms:
   • Single-adult households consisting of individuals who are either single, separated, widowed, or divorced.
   • Two-person, cohabitant households consisting of unmarried individuals sharing the same living quarters.
   • Group households where three or more individuals of the same or opposite sex share living quarters as well as sharing all expenses.

   Again, these categories represent potential segments of opportunity for a variety of products and services ranging from travel to furniture, from financial to legal.

6. Within the United States, it is reported that 46 million Americans move each year. That figure represents approximately one out of five. Within this tremendous mobility, the geographical shifts are as follows: movement of people to the Sun Belt states, movement from rural to urban areas, and movement from the city to the suburbs. (However, there does appear to be a recent countermove back to the center city, especially in those areas where urban renewal has been successful.) This movement is characterized by young adults and some older adults whose children have grown up and have sufficient resources to be attracted by the cultural and recreational facilities available to them. This population shift has tremendous potential for such products as automobiles, air conditioning, styles of clothes, resorts, and other lifestyle services and products.

7. Currently, there is a better-educated white collar population in the United States than in previous generations. Sixty-six percent of Americans over age 25 have high school degrees and 16 percent have college degrees—and the percentages continue to rise. The U.S. Bureau of Labor Statistics predicts the most growth in the following occupational categories: engineering, science, medicine, computers, social science, retail buying, selling, sec-

retarial, construction, refrigeration, health service, personal service, and protection. These categories will increase the demand for a variety of financial services, real estate, quality products, and books and other publications.

8. There has been a large increase in the United States of an Asian population with the Chinese constituting the largest group, followed by the Japanese, Filipinos, Koreans, and Vietnamese. Over the last few years a number of organizations have been isolating these ethnic and racial groups and serving them specific foods, clothing, furniture, and other products.

Economics

What potential do the following circumstances hold for your product or service?

1. The real income growth in the United States has stagnated. Statistics show that the per capita income is at $8,728 and the median household income is at $19,684. In addition, the economic figures show a reduction in disposable personal income (the amount people have left after taxes). There has also been a reduction in discretionary income, the amount left after paying for food, clothing, shelter, insurance, and other necessities. The implications are that a large portion of the population will negatively affect the sales of automobiles, large appliances, and vacations. However, there has been a significant rise in two-income families, which has increased average family income. Therefore, income distribution in the United States is a factor that should be examined for its potential in determining how and which groups purchase products and services.

2. With the intensity of competition, particularly from Japan and other Asian countries, there· is a tremendous pressure on U.S. firms to become more competitive. Robotics and other forms of automated manufacturing—or, in many cases, firms giving up manufacturing in the United States and buying finished products abroad—have resulted in the downsizing of U.S. organizations. This movement is reflected in the new lean organizations, such as Uniroyal, du Pont, Dow Chemical, United Technologies, Xerox, Chrysler, General Motors, and AT&T, where layoffs of managers number into the thousands. The skilled professional manager has now been temporarily or permanently displaced. You need to determine the impact of this new phenomenon on the economy and on the purchasing power of groups in specific geographic segments.

3. The effect of low savings and high debt can have an impact on bank accounts, bonds and stocks, real estate, insurance, and all forms of products and other services. The culprit behind much of the high debt is the credit card. While the use of credit cards is a visible factor, a good portion of bad debt is blamed on the recessions plaguing the industrial, farm, and oil segments of the economy, as well as on lenient bankruptcy laws.

4. The various economic cycles have an impact on consumer spending patterns. During downturns in the economy the basics of food, housing, and clothing require a good part of household income. During rising economic periods, such products as transportation, medical care, and recreation take on an increasing proportion of expenditures. It is especially important to utilize economic forecasting if your business is income-sensitive. With sufficient forewarning, you can take the steps necessary to exploit the economic cycle or to guard against its negative effect on your operation.

Natural Resources

What potential do the following circumstances hold for your product or service?

1. U.S. government reports indicate that diminishing supplies of oil, coal, and various minerals could pose a serious problem; that the quantities of platinum, gold, zinc, and lead are not sufficient to meet demands. In addition, silver, tin, and uranium may be in short supply and at even higher prices by the turn of the century. And by the year 2050, several more minerals may be exhausted if the current rate of consumption continues. Diminishing supplies of other resources, such as wood and water, are continuing to pose problems in many areas of the world. While firms that use these resources face cost increases and potential shortages, for other firms there is the exciting prospect of discovering new sources of materials or alternative synthetic products for natural resources.

2. The availability and cost of energy continue to be major factors for the future economic growth of the United States and other countries around the world. Specifically, oil prices fluctuated from $2.23 a barrel in 1970, to $34.00 a barrel in 1982, and to $18.00 in 1986. In the meantime, there has been an intensive search for alternative forms of energy, with investigations taking place to harness solar, nuclear, wind, and other forms of

energy. Some firms are searching for ways to make practical products using alternative forms of energy, such as the joint venture between automobile companies and electric utilities to come up with a reliable electric automobile.

Technology

What potential do the following circumstances hold for your product or service?

1. The often quoted statistic that 90 percent of all the scientists who ever lived are alive today sums up the accelerating pace of technological change. Only in the past few years has technology resulted in a tremendous number of new products such as word-processing typewriters, telecopiers, personal computers, and audio and video links from workplace to home to other distant locations. New technological advances are changing the way workers are handling their jobs. For example, farmers can use a product that looks like a ray gun to help detect if crops need watering.

   Scientists at AT&T Bell Laboratories are developing a new generation of computers that use light instead of electrical signals. Instead of chips made from silicon, researchers are working on optical transistors or switches made from new polymers. These new chips are capable of processing laser-beam signals with incredible speed, more than a thousand times faster than silicon transistors can process electrical signals.

2. The United States still leads the world in research and development expenditures, with Japan a close second. In 1986, the federal government alone handed out more than $60 billion in research and development funds. The United States is reported to have 12,000 academic, government, and industrial laboratories. Research continues in such areas as cancer cures, chemical control of mental illness, household robots, new types of nutritional foods, clones, and other types of spectacular products. While such leaders in R&D as Merck & Co., Inc., AT&T, Dow Chemical, Kodak, IBM, and Eli Lilly and Company all spend above average in their research, other organizations are forming joint ventures with either U.S. or foreign organizations to bolster their research and development capability.

   Within this R&D thrust, the managements of the various organizations are concerned that the basic research results in marketable products. Thus, the emerging trend is to add marketing people to the R&D research teams in an effort to achieve a stronger marketing orientation.

Legislation

What potential do the following circumstances hold for your product or service?

1. Businesses are in various stages of regulation and deregulation. Some of the businesses that have entered into the deregulation phase are airlines, banks, and insurance companies. Yet these, too, are constantly being watched for possible infractions of the law. In general, legislation has a number of purposes: first, to protect companies from one another with respect to competition; second, to protect consumers from unfair business practices; and third, to protect the larger interest of society against unscrupulous business behavior. You should have a good working knowledge of the major laws protecting competition, consumers, and the larger interest of society. It also becomes increasingly important to be aware of how the competition is behaving within the context of federal, state, and local legislation for opportunities that may affect you.

2. Within the political and legal environment, the number of public interest groups is increasing. These groups lobby government officials and put pressure on managers to pay more attention to minority rights, senior citizen rights, women's rights, and consumer rights in general. They also deal with such areas as cleaning up the environment and protecting natural resources.

Sociocultural Values

What potential do the following circumstances hold for your product or service?

1. Society holds a variety of values; some are classified as primary beliefs and values and tend to be long-lasting. These values relate to work, marriage, charity, and honesty. They are usually passed on from parents to children and are reinforced within the institutions of schools, churches, businesses, and government. There are also a range of secondary beliefs that are subject to change and are within the marketer's ability to influence. Such beliefs can range from when individuals get married and how

much debt should be carried, through educational advertising and the provision of products and services.
2. Subcultures rise and fall, from the flower children of the 1960's, to the yuppies of the 1980's, to the variety of religious cults, all with different beliefs, preferences, and behaviors. Each has a major impact on hairstyles, clothing, sexual norms, and the types of products and services purchased.
3. Cultural values also come and go and can be categorized as follows:
   - How people relate to themselves.
   - How people relate to others.
   - How people relate to institutions.
   - How people relate to society.

Summary of Environmental Analysis The case example demonstrated how one company, Humana, suffered a failed marketing strategy because it ignored powerful environmental forces operating at the time. Had Humana been aware of doctors' concerns and of the demographic and economic forces influencing its success in the market, it could have shaped a strategy that responded to environmental factors.

In conducting your environmental analysis, focus on six categories of environmental factors: demographics, economics, natural resources, technology, legislation, and sociocultural values. The scenarios provided should help you focus on the major environmental events that might affect your marketing strategy. In your own business, you will have to go beyond the specific trends noted in this chapter and consider new and changing environmental factors as they appear. Sources of information include demographic and economic reports, congressional accounts of new and pending legislation, periodicals citing breakthroughs in technology, and sociocultural trends reported in newsweeklies and evident in daily life. Further, you may need to focus on the differences in environment in different areas of the country or world. For instance, in the United States, state laws often vary considerably. Whatever your approach, environmental analysis requires a broad outlook and flexibility beyond the immediate scope of your market.

Summary of External Analysis

This chapter was intended to give you a broad overview of how to analyze external market conditions in order to fashion competitive strategy. In it, we examined four key components: (1) customer analysis, (2) competitor analysis, (3) industry analysis, and (4) environmental analysis.

Customer Analysis The function of marketing is to plan, price, promote, and distribute want-satisfying products and services to customers at a profit. In order to fulfill that function, a company must know what customers want and how to deliver it to them. *Customer analysis* tells you exactly that.

Market and Product Segments

Segmentation means splitting the overall market into smaller segments with similar characteristics so you can *concentrate* on particular needs of groups that are underserved, and therefore gain entry or expansion in the market. Your ability to correctly identify an emerging, neglected, or poorly served segment—also referred to as niche or target marketing—is crucial to developing successful competitive strategy. Some common ways to segment a market include grouping by demographic, geographic, psychographic, and product attribute factors.

Patterns of Customer Behavior

By knowing how customers think, behave, and make decisions regarding products and services, you can direct your marketing strategy toward their behavior. The "behavioral cycle" is a complex interaction of six factors: stimulus, sensation, predisposition, perception, motives, and customer behavior.

Unfilled Wants and Needs

Marketing demands that businesses display a customer-driven orientation; that they determine the unfilled wants and needs of customers, and then satisfy them. Managers must understand not only *what* these needs are, but how to *communicate* breakthroughs to customers. Four types of communication sources include (1) advocate impersonal, (2) advocate personal, (3) independent impersonal, and (4) independent personal. By evaluating the impact of each of these sources, and by understanding the role of *opinion leaders,* you can determine the best forms of publicity for your product in particular market segments.

A manager also must know how customers *adopt* new products and services. On an individual level, a customer adopting an innovation passes through five distinct phases: awareness, interest, evaluation, trial, and adoption. On a group level, customers adopt a product at different times after its appearance. The key to using this information in meeting unfilled wants and needs is to combine communication with adoption factors in order to reach customers and cause successful long term use.

Competitor Analysis As an actor in the marketplace, your company is constantly at odds with other firms that are trying to increase their own market share, perhaps through some of the same customer analysis as you have done. Thus you need a sharp picture of your competitors' relative positions in the marketplace in order to implement effective moves and to uproot their inroads. *Competitor analysis* examines competitors from four angles: (1) how customers select products and services from competitors, (2) how competitors segment the market, (3) how customers display their purchase patterns as they relate to competitors, and (4) how competitors develop their strategies. You can compare competitors by factors in the marketing mix and you can identify the major characteristics of competitors' strategies to form a reliable profile that can be used to project their future actions.

Analyzing competitors' strategies is one of the most important parts of competitive analysis, because from your knowledge of competitors' strategies you can correctly devise your own strategies to select a target market and position your product against the competition. Such analysis also helps you shape pricing, promotion, and distribution strategies.

Industry Analysis By considering many interrelated factors, industry analysis gives you an integrated picture of how customers, competitors, and environment interact within your industry. The analysis operates at two levels. At the first level, it provides a broad inquiry into suppliers, existing competitors, emerging competitors, and alternative product offerings. At the second, more detailed level, it examines specific market features that could affect your marketing effort. These features include current product demand, future product potential, industry life cycle, emerging technology, changing customer profiles, frequency of new product introductions, level of government regulations, distribution networks, entry and exit barriers, marketing innovation, and cost structures.

This analysis forces you to look beyond the narrow dimensions of products and customers to view the variety of forces that make up an industry.

Environmental Analysis Powerful forces of demographics, economics, natural resources, technology, legislation, and sociocultural values can "make or break" marketing efforts for your business. Through *environmental analysis,* you can judge the dimensions and impacts of events in each of these categories and design your strategy decisions to take them into account.

By presenting a set of environmental scenarios now operating in the world, this section permits you to consciously interact with and react to the variety of statements and ask yourself the overriding question for each, "What potential does this factor hold for my product or service?" The statements also serve as models for trends that may emerge in the coming years and may affect your strategies.

3

Internal Analysis

Objectives
To enable you to

1. Conduct an *internal analysis* along seven dimensions: performance, strategy, strategic priorities, cost, portfolio, financial resources, and strengths/weaknesses

2. Compare four basic *organizational alternatives:* functional, geographic, product management, and market

3. Determine whether your organization uses a *customer-oriented or product-oriented focus* in setting strategic priorities

4. Analyze the impact of *cost behavior* on the selection of competitive strategies

5. Conduct a *strengths/weaknesses analysis* to find the distinctive competencies in your firm

Figure 3-1 illustrates the two major components of competitive analysis: external analysis (see Chapter 2) and internal analysis. Internal analysis enables you to "look in the window" to examine the capabilities of your own organization or business unit in defending or attacking markets. Analyzing your strengths and weaknesses in an organized manner will help you match your strong points against competitors' weak spots when executing a competitive attack.

Case Example

PPG Industries, Inc. PPG Industries, Inc. is the world's largest supplier of flat glass and coatings for the housing and automobile industries. The strategic challenge facing the Pittsburgh-based company was to shift its business from the mature U.S. housing and automobile markets to the fast-growing high-technology business. The toughest job for management was ridding the company of its

Figure 3-1. *A framework for competitive analysis.*

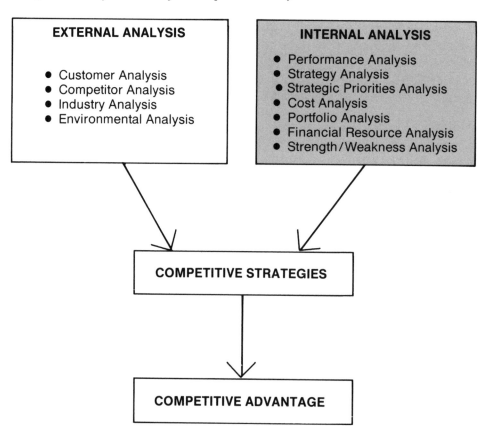

overcautious character that had led to a lack of implementation. As an internal analysis disclosed, PPG traditionally preferred to study moves rather than to make them, and to penalize risk takers rather than reward them.

During 1986, the environment of the company changed when the company transferred to a more aggressive leader. As the new CEO, Vincent Sarni said, "For those who don't perform, we will either change their job or get rid of them." The urgency to change attitudes was also expressed by another executive in PPG who said, "We have to create a survival attitude." Such urgency was also evident in the goals of doubling chemical sales and boosting average returns on investment from 10 percent to 14 percent; in the reduction of emphasis on depressed commodity chemicals; and in the expansion into higher-margin growth businesses. Those growth areas included acrylic coatings that make aluminum siding for houses far stronger; auto primers that protect metal from rust years longer; auto topcoats that go over metal and rubber in one application; and coatings for steel beams that keep them from buckling in a fire. All of these new products and markets represented a daring strategy for Sarni,

who invested only in those products that could leapfrog over
his competitors' technology. Said Sarni, "The top-performing
company is one that anticipates change and deals with it.
You've got to spend on research and you've got to have the patience to let it pay off."

The PPG case exposes many issues related to the internal capabilities of a company or division: attitudes, strategic priorities, and organization among them. It is exactly the function of internal analysis
to enable you to determine what condition or state of readiness your
operation is in to win against competition. To get a complete picture
of your organization, you need to evaluate it along the following
lines:

- *Performance analysis, by organization or business unit,* relates
  to structure, people, culture, tasks, systems, resource utilization,
  innovation, and productivity.
- *Strategy analysis* examines the ability to react to aggressive competition, to defend existing markets, and to attack new markets.
- *Strategic priorities analysis* concerns the long-term effects on
  strategic direction, commitment to quality, customer orientation,
  and human resource development.
- *Cost analysis* relates to achieving competitive advantage.
- *Portfolio analysis* reviews markets and the strengths of business
  units in each market.
- *Financial resource analysis* studies the availability of cash within
  different competitive scenarios.
- *Strengths/weaknesses analysis* surveys areas of distinctive competencies and types of unique assets.

Performance Analysis

Internal analysis begins with an examination of the organizational
structure of a company, division, business unit, or department. It is
within the structure that business life exists: the interrelationships with
those of the same level, with superiors, or subordinates. It is within
the organizational unit that marketing plans or product, promotion,
pricing, and distribution strategies emerge. It is where leadership is
exercised, which, in turn, influences the attitudes and morale of individuals within the organizational unit. Various schools of thought
exist on the merits of a highly structured or loosely run operation. In
any event, a structure does exist. You need to determine what kind

of structure exists within your own company or unit and to evaluate its effectiveness in supporting your goals and strategies.

Organizing for Marketing Consider for a moment the possibility that no one is officially in charge of your firm's marketing effort. Either of two equally disastrous results would then be likely: (1) there might be no marketing effort at all, since no one would be responsible for it; or (2) each manager might embark on his or her own marketing effort. Either way, chaos would reign in the absence of organization.

Organization is a human endeavor. It involves the structuring of various elements to achieve a smooth interplay among them and to generate a synergism that makes the whole more than the sum of its parts. The relationships between people (positions) and the work they perform (activities) are two basic elements that can be structured within a company. Organization by positions may be called *structural organization* (or chain of command), while organization by activities is usually labeled *process organization* (Table 3-1). Structural organization identifies the authority and responsibilities associated with each job. Since this job-related package normally changes very little over time, it can be considered static. When converted into a diagram, it takes the form of an organization chart. In contrast, the main objectives of process organization are to streamline the accomplishment of specific tasks and to facilitate control over the progress of a project. Thus, it should be clear that the nature of process organization is dynamic—that is, task-related—and therefore subject to review and possible change. The result of process organization is represented graphically in the form of a flow chart.

Structural organization is a necessity; in any company there has to be at least one person who is officially assigned ultimate responsibil-

Table 3-1. *Comparison of the Key Characteristics of Structural and Process Organizations.*

Type of Element	*Type of Organization*	*Main Purpose*	*Nature*	*Graphic Representation*
Positions	Structural	Identify authority responsibilities.	Static	Organization chart
Activities	Process	Streamline task accomplishment and facilitate progress control.	Dynamic	Flow chart

Figure 3-2. *The role of organization in the marketing management cycle.*

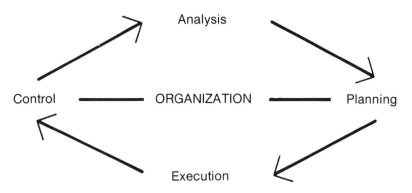

ity for the conduct of the firm's marketing effort. The role of structural organization within your firm's marketing effort is to provide the framework within which the core elements of the marketing management cycle—*analysis, planning, execution,* and *control*—can function (Figure 3-2). Structural organization must offer stability, support, and a frame of reference for these revolving functions.

Basic Organizational Alternatives Your current organization may have been appropriate when it was instituted, but could conceivably have outlived its usefulness. The product–market mix of your firm, as well as the competitive situation in the marketplace, may have changed dramatically over the years. Whatever the present structure, it should probably be reviewed for its adequacy and possible improvement. Only an organization that is fully in tune with the market will realize its potential. In trying to evolve the optimum organizational setup to achieve competitive advantages, you should examine the four major alternatives open to most firms: *functional organization; geographic organization; product organization;* and *market organization.*

Functional Organization

Functional organization of the marketing area works best for small to medium-size companies. It assigns responsibilities and creates positions in accordance with the various functions to be performed, resulting in a horizontal division of labor, which in turn results in specialization. The basic strength of this approach lies in the fact that the ultimate responsibility for a given marketing function rests with a

Figure 3-3. *Functional organization with line and staff subgroupings.*

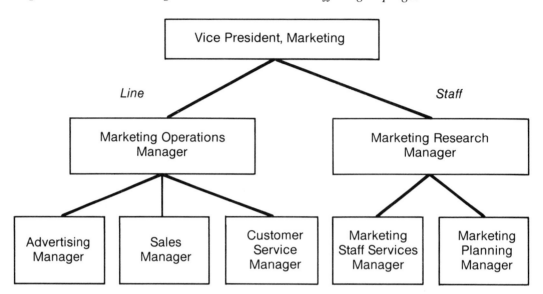

single individual. Functional organization is the only setup in which there is no duplication or paralleling of functions. Within a functional framework, the responsibility of each manager thus extends to the entire product and market mix.

As the number of functions for separate managers increases, the marketing vice-president's span of control may become too broad for a direct reporting relationship. In such a case, subgrouping of the existing functions into operations and staff will prove helpful (Figure 3-3). This distinction is basic to organizational thinking.

Operations, or line, personnel are responsible for conducting a firm's business, with the results of their efforts reflected in profit and loss statements. Staff people, on the other hand, make up a company's think tank, a group of internal consultants or advisers. They research, analyze, and recommend; but they do not make the decisions. Properly handled, the interplay of line and staff can be quite productive: Line people can concentrate on getting the job done without having to do their own research; and staff personnel can focus on thorough investigation and analysis, as well as on the development of sound proposals, without the distractions arising from day-to-day demands.

But as a firm grows, this kind of functional setup can become rather unwieldy and cumbersome, unable either to respond quickly or to pay proper attention to specific products or markets. Concentration of functional responsibility in one person, initially a virtue, now becomes a drawback. To avoid dilution of effort, further specialization and more individualized attention to products and markets are needed.

If you want to continue to achieve optimum results, duplication of functions—that is, having the same functions performed in different sections of the marketing area—is the price that inevitably has to be paid for growth.

Geographic Organization

Some firms choose to organize their marketing effort along geographic lines. (United Air Lines, for example, has created separate marketing structures for the eastern, central, and western parts of the United States.) A geographic subdivision can be accomplished easily because territorial borderlines can be drawn along geopolitical boundaries. Also, the sales effort is readily integrated into the marketing effort, since the former is usually organized along geographic lines already. Furthermore, geographic organization makes sense because consumers in different parts of the country behave differently.

Product Management Organization

An alternative approach that a sizable number of firms have been following since the early 1930's is the product management system. Created in the late 1920's by Procter & Gamble, this arrangement employs both functional managers, who act as resource managers, and product managers, who serve as program managers. This form is called a matrix organization, because each resource manager interacts with each program manager. Entered graphically in a matrix, the functions represent rows, while the products appear in columns. (See Figure 3-4.)

Product management becomes necessary when the complexity of the product mix threatens to overtax the functional system, resulting in a dilution of effort that leaves many products virtually unattended. The advent of product management brings order and focus to this disarray by clearly lodging responsibility for the fate of a specific product or product line with a single individual, ensuring it the attention it requires. This approach fosters individualized marketing programs for each product or product line and aggressive internal competition for funds and sales force time.

The responsibilities of a product manager are many. He or she must:

- Provide for the assigned product line a continuing series of programs and projects designed to improve market position and profitability.

Figure 3-4. *Product management organization.*

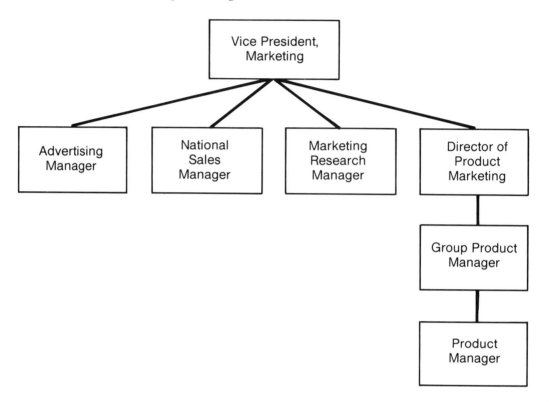

- Mold the marketing effort according to changing consumer demands.
- Coordinate the activities of the firm's functional units with a view toward achieving short- and long-range product objectives.
- Act as an intelligence center for all relevant information concerning the product line.
- Analyze market potential and develop marketing strategies.
- Generate advertising campaigns.
- Stimulate interest in and support of the product line among the sales force and distributor network.

A product manager has to be an initiator, communicator, coordinator, and evaluator. He or she must interact continually with other members of the organization: division management, advertising agency, advertising manager, marketing research manager, packaging director, national sales manager, production manager, research and development manager, and credit and accounting manager.

The main advantage of the product management system is that every product or product line has its own advocate whose personal career is directly dependent on the success or failure of the line administered. (And the sky is the limit: Lee Iacocca, the CEO of Chrysler, is the former product manager of Ford's Mustang. Conversely, if a product line goes under, so does the product manager.)

The primary drawback of product management is that the product manager's authority is usually not commensurate with the area of responsibility. In contrast to a basic organizational principle indicating that responsibility and authority should coincide, product managers are held responsible for bottom-line performance without being in a position to make the crucial decisions. They can recommend, suggest, even urge, but they cannot decide.

Thus, the mark of a superior product manager is vision coupled with persuasiveness—the ability to identify significant trends, correctly assess their relevance, and persuade others to act. In a sense, a product manager has to be an internal salesperson, continually selling to others to gain acceptance and support for his ideas. In addition, it is sensitivity to market changes and sheer hard work that make for a successful product manager. Understandably, these positions are occupied mainly by energetic young people on their way up who are looking for a chance to prove themselves and to acquire the skills and expertise that will serve them well in positions of authority.

Market Organization

Focusing too strongly on an individual product or line may well detract from the main mission of your firm—namely, to serve the needs of its chosen customers rather than those of its existing products. Thus, many firms are revamping their organizations to become customer-oriented instead of product-oriented. Figure 3-5 illustrates the differences between the two approaches, using a simplified example of three product lines being marketed to three markets.

Whatever is lost in product expertise in such a reshuffling effort is gained in market expertise. Each market manager becomes a specialist in the particular needs and problems of a specific group of customers. In many other respects, market organization is comparable to product organization: Marketing managers also have to develop annual and long-term sales and profit plans and do not have their own support systems, either. Therefore, they must rely on much the same set of tools as their product manager counterparts.

Figure 3-5. *Comparison of product and market organization.*

Product Organization

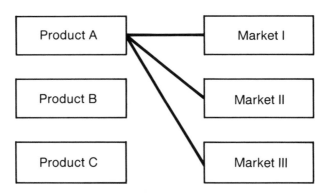

Market Organization

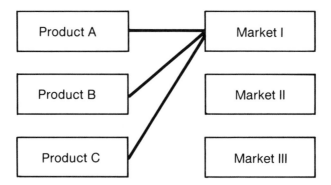

Choosing the Given such a range of choices, it is not easy to decide on the opti-
Right Setup mum solution for your firm. The following guidelines should prove
helpful.

- While a company with a small number of product lines can do
  well with a functional organization, a wide range of lines requires product management.
- If your product mix is fairly homogeneous, you can rely on a
  functional organization, whereas a heterogeneous collection of
  products warrants product management.
- Highly technical and complex products require product expertise,
  which is the cornerstone of the product management system.
- Mostly homogeneous markets can be served by a functional or
  product setup, while heterogeneous markets demand a market or-

ganization that responds to their unique needs and buying patterns. An example of the latter situation is the common division of the food-marketing business into grocery and institutional marketing.

- The size of your firm is another factor. If it is of small or medium size, a functional organization is likely to work well for you. The geographic dispersion of your markets should also be considered. If they are regional, or otherwise fairly concentrated, a product or market setup is a good choice. But if they are dispersed over a large area, you should look into the advantages of a geographic setup.

Answering some questions will also assist you in determining the adequacy of your marketing organization. Is it efficient: That is, does work get done with a minimum of waste, and does your setup respond swiftly to changes in the marketplace? Are all jobs clearly delineated as precise responsibilities and areas of authority? Is your structure internally consistent or the result of historic accidents? Is it up to date and consonant with the company's current and expected future situation? Is it streamlined, with no unnecessary management layers or make-work jobs? Finally, does it represent the optimum use of the firm's talent pool? Negative responses will pinpoint the need for a change.

Formal and Informal Organization At this point, a word seems in order about the distinction between formal and informal organization. Your firm's formal organization is represented by its official reporting relationships and authority structure as reflected in its organization chart. In a sense, it is the "on paper" organization as laid out in the latest reorganization plan. In contrast, informal organization is based on actual friendships and antipathies. In spite of its invisible, behind-the-scenes character, informal organization is very real and powerful, and often conflicts with your official organization chart.

Your firm is a living organism; it is people, and people cannot be boxed in and be expected to behave like robots. Therefore, you should examine carefully the "real" power structure in your firm before you make any changes. A reorganization or streamlining that collides with the informal organization might well prove counterproductive, no matter how well thought out it is otherwise.

You should try to identify the true leaders as well as the friendship and influence patterns in your organization. The head of a department may be powerless against a subordinate who deals directly with a higher-up. On the basis of a bowling friendship, an individual in one department may achieve swift cooperation in another department, circumventing official channels. It is largely an exercise in futility to try to change personal relationships and patterns of influence in the informal organization. Rather, it is better to make them work for you or, if they are negative, to neutralize them.

Your formal organization creates the framework for the functioning and interplay of the people within it. Although it is modified by informal relationships, an efficient and up-to-date setup is, nevertheless, an indispensable prerequisite for a goal-directed and successful marketing effort.

Strategy Analysis

The ability to react to aggressive competition, to defend existing markets, and to utilize the resources of the organization is the mark of an effective operation. The 3M case exemplifies such an operation and how it responded to opportunity.

Case Example

Minnesota Mining & Mfg. Co. In 1986, 3M organized a new group to aggressively move into the consumer market. Up to that point, the $7-billion company had only marginal results in its ability to reach end-user markets, which generated about $500 million in sales in 1985. Within the new autonomous group, the company is aiming to rapidly reach a $1-billion sales mark.

The new group relies on small entrepreneurial teams to develop new products that are spun off into separate businesses as they grow. Initially the group got 5,000 products, all of which came from other sectors of 3M. According to the group's strategy, it has no intention of taking 3M into a frontal attack on consumer markets already crowded with well-entrenched marketing giants. The plan is to squeeze sales increases out of 3M's older products, such as Scotch® tape and sandpaper, and to find markets for some of the newer ones, which include scouring pads, surgical tapes, and do-it-yourself home energy products such as caulks and weather stripping, auto supplies, and Scotchgard® fabric protectors. The opportunity is great because of the range of product technologies within 3M that have not yet been adapted for consumer markets. As Ernest Moffet, Jr., who initially headed the group, said, "To make that pay off all we've got to do is apply a consumer marketing mentality."

Moffet is putting high hopes on his ability to take a product that has been successful in the industrial sector and apply it to the consumer end of the business. For example, Magic Plus®, a new version of Scotch® tape, was introduced as an office product and then introduced into consumer markets. The mainstay of 3M's strategy is to enter with strength into the consumer market with new and existing products.

Obviously, a successful strategy is greatly influenced by some basic values and beliefs:[1]

1. A belief in being the best. David Ogilvy wants those in his advertising agency to believe they are working in the best agency in the world.
2. A belief in the innovation of the details of execution, the nuts and bolts of doing the job well. Pepsico and Frito-Lay, Inc., both stress strategy execution.
3. A belief in the importance of people as individuals. Tandem Computers Inc., for example, makes employee freedom a central value. There is no formal organizational chart and few formal rules.
4. A belief in superior quality and service. Procter & Gamble is one of the firms that focuses on product quality.
5. A belief that most members of the organization should be innovators coupled with a corresponding willingness to support failure. One Hewlett-Packard theme is that innovative people should be placed throughout the organization.
6. A belief in the importance of informality to enhance communication. Tandem Computers has regular Friday beer parties at all its offices throughout the world, stresses an open door policy with everyone communicating on the same level, and sponsors a retreat involving its best people selected across the organization and across levels.
7. Explicit belief in the importance of economic growth and profits.

In many situations, those basic values and beliefs that were finely honed in organizations over many years are now being put to the test as mergers, acquisitions, downsizing, or simply the breaking up of organizations becoming more rampant. There are also new strategic alliances or consortiums that go so far as to blend international cultures. For example, in 1986 a new consortium let France's Groupe

[1]The list is adapted from T. J. Peters and R. H. Waterman, Jr., *In Search of Excellence: Lessons from America's Best-Run Companies* (New York: Harper & Row, 1982), p. 285.

Bull and Japan's NEC Corporation share in the computer operations of Honeywell Inc. The blend consisted of an American boss, a French-run board, and a healthy dose of Japanese technology. Three diverse cultures had to meld in an attempt to develop a strategy that would work in computer markets against such heavyweights as IBM and Digital Equipment, as well as in the controls business that is basic to Honeywell.

Strategic Priorities Analysis

Your internal analysis continues with an examination of how your organization, and particularly how your group, looks at its long-term strategic priorities. The focal point from which strategic priorities emerge is determined by the level of market orientation within your organization. Does a customer-driven mentality exist in your organization or is it just given lip service? The amount of commitment to product quality and market development is reflected in the mentality of those determining strategic priorities.

Case Example

CertainTeed Corporation CertainTeed Corporation, the fiberglass and buildings materials manufacturer, has had a remarkable turnaround. In one year (1985), its earnings of $57 million on $1.1 billion in sales was a 30 percent increase over the previous year's $43 million, and a gigantic $68-million turnaround since the company posted loses of $11 million in 1981.

CertainTeed's success came with an innovation in fiberglass that helped it jump ahead of its major competitor, the Manville Corporation, to gain 25 percent of the insulation market. Credit must also be given to its new president, Michel Besson, who took over the mismanaged company. In addition to better people management, Besson immediately pushed for product expansion. He set up an intensive research and development capability that resulted in a new, lighter-density fiberglass insulation that launched the company into the growing market for fiberglass-reinforced products. Today, CertainTeed's fiberglass–plastic compounds end up in everything from ship moldings to bathtubs to side panels of the Pontiac Fiero. The result? CertainTeed's fiberglass division contributed 76 percent of the company's earnings on 43 percent of its sales during the mid-1980's.

CertainTeed faced the strategic priorities question by taking a long view of its market and by launching a major effort in product innovation. However, mere wishful thinking did not make this type of R&D activity work. Here are the actions taken:

1. Management created an internal environment where functional managers worked in harmony within a *market-oriented* organization.
2. Managers at middle and upper levels participated in identifying the *strategic direction* of the organization.
3. Managers developed a customer-oriented mentality and learned how to *recognize new growth markets* and launch appropriate products.
4. Managers participated in a *planning system* that pulled together all the innovations into a coordinated strategic thrust.

The CertainTeed case illustrates the transition from a product orientation to a customer orientation and how that change affected its long-term strategic priorities.

Consumer-Oriented vs. Product-Oriented Concepts

The consumer-oriented concept of marketing is a far cry from the old product-oriented philosophy, whereby the producer developed a product without input from the ultimate buyer and then used promotional pressure to persuade the consumer to buy it. In contrast to this one-way approach, the consumer-oriented concept is cyclical in nature, putting the consumer at the beginning and the end of the marketing process. Figure 3-6 illustrates the metamorphosis of the consumer from the role of recipient of a given product to shaper of that product.

The product-oriented concept is myopic and usually distorts efforts to develop strategic priorities. It focuses on the needs of the seller and thus leaves a company vulnerable to the inroads of competitors who may be more sensitive to consumer needs and desires. Table 3-2 offers more details on the differences between the two perspectives.

As both Figure 3-6 and Table 3-2 point out, marketing research is a key element of consumer-oriented marketing. It enables a company to specify what features a forthcoming product should have, because consumer preferences and problems have been investigated. *Instead of trying to create markets for products, you are now attempting to provide products for markets.* The entire thrust of your firm is now aimed at discovering and exploiting market opportunities. This re-orientation is accompanied by another remarkable change: Companies are no longer married to technologies and existing products but rather to consumers and their evolving wants and problems.

Figure 3-6. *The concepts of marketing.*

Product-Oriented Marketing

Consumer-Oriented Marketing

Case Example

Reynolds Reynolds Metals Co., long a leader in aluminum foil products,
Metals Co. learned that housewives were unhappy about the long roasting
time and the lack of visibility associated with the use of their
foil. Instead of disregarding this information because of limitations inherent in this metal, Reynolds took up the challenge
and developed a new product, the Brown-In-Bag, which with-
stands high temperatures, retains natural meat juices, and re-

Table 3-2. *Characteristics of the Two Concepts of Marketing.*

Product-Oriented	*Consumer-Oriented*
Focus on product	Focus on consumer
Emphasis on volume	Emphasis on profit
Insignificant marketing research	Thorough marketing research
Engineering self-guided	Engineering guided by marketing
Primarily interested in production economies	Primarily interested in providing need satisfaction
Aiming for short-term gains	Aiming for long-term relationships
Management engineering-oriented	Management marketing-oriented

duces cooking time. The product was a tremendous success upon introduction and the firm found it difficult to keep up with demand.

Consumer Orientation and Its Impact on Strategic Priorities Henry Ford came close to destroying his company by insisting on producing only one model in one color. The Johnson Products Company, Inc. had been doing a sizable business selling hair straighteners to blacks who wanted to imitate white hairstyles. But the company experienced considerable difficulty when it failed to react swiftly to a change in the attitudes of its black consumers. After restructuring its marketing philosophy, Johnson rebounded and in the United States is the largest seller of cosmetics specially formulated for the black consumer.

These examples show that it is imprudent, if not outright dangerous, to disregard the consumer. Simply stated, your marketing effort should be directed toward satisfying consumer wants at a profit. This philosophy, known as a marketing concept, should permeate your entire organization. It represents your best corporate insurance for survival and growth in a competitive marketplace.

Pushing products that have been developed in isolation from the consumer will not be successful for long. Only consumer satisfaction breeds the loyalty that results in repeat business. The ability to create satisfaction is based on understanding the needs and wants of your consumers. Marketing research is the most effective tool for accomplishing this end. A well-conceived marketing operation must employ a consumer-oriented concept.

Characteristics and Benefits of Consumer-Oriented Marketing

Following this examination of the philosophical aspects of the consumer-oriented concept of marketing, it is appropriate to take a closer look at its operational characteristics and impact. Table 3-3 highlights ways in which the concept penetrates every facet of your marketing effort, and lists the benefits to be derived from its application. You may want to convert the specific action suggestions into a personal checklist. By using such a systematic approach, you can pinpoint and improve areas of weakness.

Implementation of Consumer-Oriented Marketing

How can you implement a new marketing concept if your firm is still using the old product-oriented approach? Table 3-4 presents a sample

(text continues on p. 126)

Table 3-3. *The Consumer-Oriented Marketing Concept and Marketing Behavior.*

Area	Action	Benefit
Organization	Set up a separate marketing function under a vice-president who reports directly to the company president.	Stresses importance of marketing and puts it on equal footing with other functional areas, such as engineering and production.
Planning	Base corporate planning on marketing research, sales forecasts, and marketing plans.	Keeps corporate effort truly attuned with market.
	Try to project technological and market trends sufficiently far into the future.	Provides adequate lead time for developing programs, products, and facilities for future markets.
	Set objectives and communicate basic assumptions and objectives.	Creates a common framework for planning that becomes clearly goal-oriented.
Control	Institute tight feedback system to check results of marketing activities.	Keeps your "ear to the ground" and enables timely corrective action.
Research on consumer behavior	Investigate consumer wants, needs, desires, problems, habits, views, satisfactions, and dissatisfactions.	Establishes necessary communications link to consumer to fine-tune marketing effort.
Legal aspects	Examine legal ramifications of planned marketing activities.	Determines legal requirements and framework for your marketing effort.
International marketing	Adjust marketing effort to specific environment.	Makes marketing more suited to particular circumstances and likely to be more successful.
Marketing strategy	Identify target markets and cultivate them carefully.	Pinpoints specific needs and wants in order to serve them better, which, in turn, breeds loyalty.

Area	Action	Benefit
Product	Base product specifications on marketing research.	Keeps product design in line with consumer wants and problems.
	Make package appealing and distinctive.	Makes "silent salesperson" on the shelf easily recognized and persuasive.
	Select memorable, meaningful brand name.	Suggests important quality of product and is remembered.
Pricing	Set prices in line with product's market value, as perceived by consumers.	Ensures optimum salability because product is neither underpriced nor overpriced in consumers' eyes.
Promotion	Stress benefits that consumer will derive from product instead of glorifying its features.	Gives consumers good, convincing reasons to buy your product over others.
	Position product properly with respect to competition.	Gives product clear-cut profile in consumers' minds.
	Aid your dealers through displays, point-of-purchase materials, and generous advertising.	Generates consumer business and dealer loyalty.
Selling	Advise your customers on how they can derive the most profit from your product instead of overloading them with stock.	Makes your salespeople welcome because they bring profits.
	Train your dealers in product knowledge and sales techniques.	Makes knowledgeable dealers do better long-term business.
Distribution	Be selective in choosing distributors, have them fit distribution policy objectives.	Associates your product with the right kind of outlet.
	Give your dealers adequate support in terms of product availability and service.	Gives dealers good reasons to buy from your company.

Table 3-4. *An Action Program for Implementing the Consumer-Oriented Marketing Concept.*

Step	Result
1. Find out what your ultimate buyers like/dislike about your product and the way in which it is marketed	Provides invaluable assessment of what you are doing right/wrong
2. Determine which changes and/ or new products they would like to see	Shows how you can protect your business and make more money
3. Examine the differences that consumers perceive between your product and its better selling competitors, if any	Enables you to evaluate and, possibly, correct your competitive positioning
4. Draw up a plan aimed at improving consumer satisfaction and profits	Setting objectives and aiming to achieve them is the only way to grow systematically
5. Ensure top-level and full organizational support	New marketing programs can only be successful if they enjoy the full support of the entire organization
6. Initiate appropriate modifications and/or development projects	A steady flow of tailor-made new products emerges from your laboratories
7. Test consumer reaction to new product(s)	You "feel out" probable large-scale reception of your new product and can make final adjustments
8. Launch new product(s) in market	Full-scale presentation and availability of your innovation to your target market
9. Follow up with consumer research to find out whether the changes you instituted paid off	Feedback permits you to modify current situation and steamline future activities
10. Keep attuned to evolving trends in the marketplace	Helps you to foresee changes and deal with them early

action program that includes an assessment of your firm's internal situation and culminates in a continuous monitoring of developments in the marketing environment. The result column gives information on the benefits of each step in the program. You can use the table as a checklist for actions performed and benefits to be derived. (You might also find it helpful to use the left-hand margin for designating a time frame for the individual steps with respect to a specific product or product line, and for indicating the initials of those persons responsible for each area.)

The summarizing format of this program provides an overview and permits further detail in line with your firm's strategic priorities. Without a vigorous enactment program, the "good idea" of the consumer-oriented marketing concept, initially greeted with great enthusiasm, becomes too easily diluted, neglected, and ultimately abused. It is easy to bask in the self-congratulatory, ivory-tower atmosphere of new product ingenuity and, in the process, forget the most important element—the consumer. The consumer-oriented marketing concept brings you back to the basics of sensitivity to consumer needs. Periodic reapplication of this action program can provide your company with invaluable "life" insurance. You must continue to be aware of the dynamics of the marketplace because needs and problems change, as do attitudes and habits. Catering to these changes differentiates your product in a consumer's mind from those of your competitors, thus creating a firm niche for it in the marketplace. Failure to recognize or regard these changes could spell disaster for your product and your company.

Cost Analysis

Case Example

Russell Corporation Russell Corporation, one of the country's largest producers of athletic uniforms, has 35 to 40 percent of the market. The uniqueness of Russell is that this Alabama-based sportswear maker can survive against its Asian competitors and still command a leading market share in the late 1980's. The sales and earnings are also impressive: In 1972, the company was earning about 3 percent on sales of $75 million, while in 1986, it earned 8 percent on sales of $355 million—almost double the industry average.

The company's success resulted from achieving a competitive cost advantage and developing a capability to respond quickly to customer needs. Its president, Eugene Gwaltney, summed up his strategy: "It's pretty hard to make a football uniform on Monday in Japan or Korea and get it over here by Friday." Russell outfits the National Basketball Association and every National Football League team except the New York Giants.

But uniforms account for only 35 percent of Russell's sales. Half its billings come from simpler items: tee shirts, fleeced sweatshirts, and warm-up suits sold through department stores and chains such as Sears and Wal-Mart—as well as from private label arrangements with Nike and Levi-Strauss. The company strategy also employed a *cost improvement* approach. Currently Russell's production lines are the quietest, cleanest, and most automated in the industry.

The Russell case illustrates the wide impact of costs as they relate to distribution, product mix, manufacturing cost efficiencies, and all other areas of the marketing mix.

Costs have broad implications for your selection of competitive strategies. Do you use a low-cost strategy? Do you pursue a differentiation or innovation strategy? Do you employ a concentration strategy? To decide on a strategy, you will need to understand cost from the standpoints of the *experience curve* and *sales forecasting*.

Experience Curve

The value of understanding the experience curve is in being able to examine costs as they relate to strategy options for your own company as well as for your competitors.

Much of the work on the experience curve began in the mid-1960's when the Boston Consulting Group (BCG) and others conducted thousands of cost studies that showed each time the cumulative volume of a product doubled, the total value-added costs—including administration, sales, marketing, and distribution, in addition to manufacturing—fell by a constant and predictable percentage. Further, the cost of purchased items usually fell as suppliers reduced prices as their costs fell, also due to the experience effect. This relationship between costs and experience is called the experience curve.

Figure 3-7 shows a variety of examples from BCG studies. Look at the electronic component situation as an example. You see that the slope of the line is 70 percent. This slope indicates that the unit cost will be reduced 30 percent each time the cumulative production doubles.

Key Factors Causing the Experience Curve

Knowing that costs will be reduced by a fixed percentage each time production doubles is only part of the equation. The other parts are in knowing which factors are contributing to the experience curve and then consciously incorporating those factors in planning your strategy. Some of the key factors are labor productivity, work methods, production efficiency, and product design and materials.

Labor Productivity

Labor productivity goes beyond the factory floor to the white collar jobs of middle management. During the 1980's, there was a trend to

Figure 3-7. *Some examples of experience curves from BCG studies.*

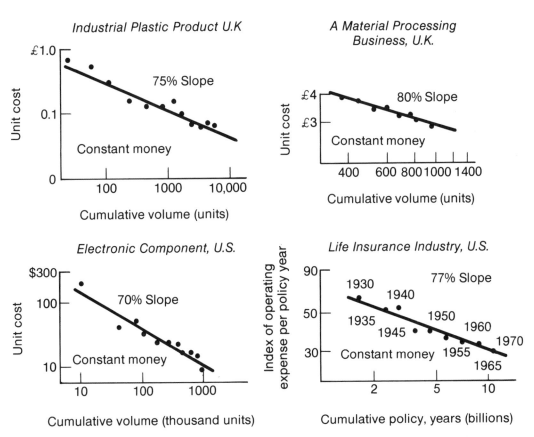

Source: Barry Hedley, "A Fundamental Approach to Strategy Development," *Long Range Planning* (December 1976), p. 4.

simply wipe out layers of management and reduce the organization
into a "lean and mean" operation. In place of permanent workers,
there has been growth in the use of contingency or temporary workers
who are used on an as-needed basis, which further reduces labor costs
in such areas as employee benefits. Concurrent with the downsizing
of organizations, continued productivity can be encouraged by permitting middle managers to become more innovative and entrepreneurial in planning and strategy development.

Work Methods

Paralleling labor productivity are the methods workers use to complete a task. Outside consultants used to be hired to examine and
make recommendations about such methods. A newer approach focuses the problem solving with the worker on the job using tech-

niques such as quality work circles, which often result in the redesign of work operations and the simplification of the methods.

Production Efficiency

Tremendous progress has been made in factory automation with the use of robots, computer-aided design (CAD), and computer-aided manufacturing (CAM). While some companies faltered initially and did not experience cost reductions, the evidence is clear that such factory automation can significantly reduce costs to the point that unit costs of manufacturing can be less than those of the most inexpensive Asian labor. During 1986, one of IBM's fully automated manufacturing plants in Kentucky produced computer printers at a lower cost and at a higher quality than those it previously purchased from its Far East sources.

Case Example

International Rectifier Corporation International Rectifier Corporation provides a dramatic example of a bold movement into making the experience curve contribute to its marketing strategy. During 1986, this Los Angeles firm was about to open its new automated semiconductor manufacturing facility after pouring into it a hefty $82 million. The plant was expected to be the most automated semiconductor facility in the United States up to that time. It would certainly be the only commercial plant where the entire manufacturing process, from printing integrated circuits on silicon wafers to putting finished chips in protective housings, is accomplished in one continuous process. As one of its executives indicated, "We're betting we can produce a high-volume item in the United States better than anywhere in the world." If the facility lives up to expectations, it will cut production costs in half, slash wafer-to-package time to just one week instead of eight, and boost the yield of all work shifts. Output per worker will be a phenomenal $350,000 a year—more than double the industry average.

Product Design and Materials

Greater efficiency through experience is gained when product design and manufacturing work together. Also contributing to efficiency is the use of new space-age materials, such as ceramics, and new lightweight metals and epoxies. However, for an increasing number of U.S. companies, the efficiencies may not be realized completely if the trend continues toward separating product design from manufacturing through the shifting of production to overseas locations.

Strategy Implications

The implication of the experience curve is that it is prudent to accumulate experience faster than competitors do. One approach to accumulating experience suggests pursuing a first-into-the-market strategy and going for a large share of the market. Another is to be a follow-the-leader into a market, assess the mistakes of the leader, and move rapidly to dominate an emerging, neglected, or poorly served market segment. If you can accumulate experience faster than competitors, with the corresponding reductions in costs, then you have the advantage of price flexibility to use as a weapon to attack a competitor's position.

The negative side of this scenario shows the possibility of becoming a slave to the experience curve by adopting a production-driven mentality rather than a market-driven orientation. For example, if the production-driven approach prevents responding to changing consumer patterns; to customer demands for just-in-time delivery; to accepting orders for short-run customized parts; or to reacting to competitors' innovations, then the cost efficiencies will have a negative effect in a changing marketplace. Ford's Model T automobile is a classic example of just such a situation. The Model T eventually suffered a severe decline that almost resulted in the bankruptcy of the company. Even though consumer demands shifted to heavier, closed-body cars offered by General Motors, Henry Ford was inflexible in moving away from the highly efficient, cost-effective production techniques that he so methodically developed but that disregarded changing consumer patterns.

A more modern example of a balanced approach to the application of the experience curve is illustrated by Japan's Toyota Motor Corp. Because of the contributions to the experience curve over years of aggressive automation, attention to labor productivity through work circles, and problem solving by employees at the assembly line, as well as the other factors already discussed, Toyota, in 1986, turned out more than 3.67 million vehicles with roughly the same number of production workers (23,000) that it had in the late 1960's when it was building only a million cars a year. In contrast, at Ford Motor Company it took 37,000 workers to produce 3.2 million vehicles. With Toyota's production efficiencies continuing to improve to a next-generation "flexible body line" already in operation in its U.S. plants, there is an aggressive push for greater market share. Obviously, the experience curve works.

In summary, the marketing strategy implications of the experience curve are:

1. A competitive advantage can be achieved if you *accumulate greater experience than your competitors.* The resulting cost advantage (assuming selling prices are constant) can be used to plow back investment to achieve additional manufacturing efficiencies, as in the example of Toyota; to improve products; to shore up the marketing effort; or to build market share through lower prices, which also serves to unbalance competitors' expansion moves. If it is your strategy to use low price to buy market share rapidly, it is essential that a plan be implemented to gain experience as rapidly as possible, certainly faster than your competitors. Further, the push for market share should be done early in the product's life cycle.

2. Within the context of competitor analysis, it is important to *examine your competitors experience curves.* It is not a simple task and certainly needs the cooperation of your production managers, purchasing agents, and financial staff to create examples of different experience curves under a variety of pricing scenarios.

3. Experience curves can be used to *forecast costs,* which in turn can be used to set potential prices. However, costs and prices are usually calculated on the basis of a reasonably accurate sales forecast. The major quantitative contribution marketing people can make to these calculations is to provide a reliable sales forecast.

Sales Forecasting

Role and Impact

Attempts to foretell the future are as old as mankind. In business, however, such attempts are particularly significant because they can influence those cost and price decisions resulting from the experience curve. Figure 3-8 shows the role of sales forecasting in the corporate planning process. The position of sales forecasting on the diagram shows the need for good, solid, thorough marketing research in order to elevate sales forecasting from the level of sheer soothsaying to that of a serious and significant managerial effort. But the diagram also

Figure 3-8. *The role of sales forecasting in corporate planning.*

clearly points out the far-reaching impact that sales forecasting can have on the entire experience curve.

In order to pinpoint the exact nature of a sales forecast, it should be distinguished clearly from a number of related terms. *Market potential* is the grand total of possible sales available to all sellers of a product in a given market. *Company sales potential* is the maximum portion of the market potential that a company can reasonably hope to capture by efficient use of its resources. *Sales forecast* is that fraction of the company sales potential that your division will attempt to achieve. Finally, *actual industry and company sales* are self-explanatory terms, representing the realized levels of sales.

Company sales are the result of the interaction of your company's marketing effort with marketing opportunities within the constraints imposed by the competition and the general economic climate. Taking these contributing factors into account, it is the task of forecasting to furnish decision makers with a set of alternative sales potentials derived from projections of possible market situations and of the probability of occurrence of each one.

As a manager, you will use these sales potentials as a frame of reference in assessing your marketing opportunities. By evaluating the payoffs of marketing strategies applied to the potentials, you can employ company resources so as to take full advantage of the opportunities open to you. The outcome of this process is your sales forecast.

Sales forecasting is an organized effort to predict the future level of sales, given a certain marketing strategy and specified assumptions about prevailing conditions. It proceeds by examining past events and developments as well as present knowledge and experience to project future sales tendencies. But merely projecting past figures into the future as if they were isolated from events is not sales forecasting. You need to combine objective, factual inputs with subjective judgment.

Judgment is essential for meaningful sales forecasts. In fact, forecasts are typically generated in cycles; that is, they are made, refined, and then revised. These cycles are repeatedly run through until, in the opinion of the forecaster, the optimum combination of marketing strategy and sales results occurs. Decisions about marketing strategies and assumptions about variables in the marketplace create alternative "what if" scenarios that have to be altered until a given input produces a desirable projected outcome. At this point, the sales forecast becomes binding, and its individual product and/or territorial elements are converted into sales quotas that serve as a basis for evaluating actual peformance of individuals and the firm as a whole.

A well-managed forecasting program will make prognoses in time to allow corrective measures, not when developments are unalterably in progress. Such a program will also provide for frequent comparisons of actual-to-forecast figures in order to enable revision and strategic action during the forecast period. No forecast should ever be allowed to go unmonitored or become outdated. Instead, it should be used as a powerful tool to govern your firm's course and fix responsibilities.

The job of sales forecasting should not be treated as an academic exercise. It is the purpose of sales forecasting not only to help anticipate future events, thus preparing your firm to cope with them, but also to result in the development of strategic means for controlling them. Only in this way will your firm become the master, rather than the victim, of its fate. It is this strategic element of forecasting that is frequently overlooked.

Techniques

Although various computer models are available to do sales forecasts, time and budget restrictions often bar their use. Rather, marketing executives usually have to rely on a set of relatively simple, quick, do-it-yourself techniques that substantially reduce the time and money required in forecasting. There are a number of such forecasting techniques that, along with subjective judgment, add precision to sales estimates.

Fortunately, sales forecasting methods are not mutually exclusive. Rather, it is advisable to use multiple approaches for arriving at estimated sales. If they all yield similar results, you can place great confidence in your figures. If, however, they diverge widely, you should find out why and reconcile them before a commitment is made. A multiple-method procedure acts as a system of checks and balances, assuring you of meaningful composite predictions.

Nonmathematical forecasting techniques can be roughly subdivided into (1) judgmental methods, involving the opinions of various kinds of experts such as executives, salespeople, and informed outsiders, and (2) buyer surveys and market tests.

Judgment from the Extremes. Judgment from the extremes involves asking for an expert's opinion as to whether or not future sales are likely to be at an extremely high or extremely low level. If the expert's reaction is that neither seems probable, the range between the extremes is successively reduced until an approximate level of expected sales is reached. Resulting in a range rather than a single-figure estimate, this approach is appropriate in situations where experts feel incapable of giving one-level forecasts.

PERT-Derived Method. The approach taken by PERT (Program Evaluation and Review Technique) is to make three estimates: an optimistic estimate *(O)*, a most likely estimate *(M),* and a pessimistic estimate *(P).* Instead of asking for accompanying estimates of the likelihood of occurrence of each one, a standard equation is applied in order to arrive at the expected value *(EV)* or forecast:

$$EV = \frac{Q + 4M + P}{6}$$

With this method, a measure of real values against expected ones, the standard deviation can be developed. Taking, for instance, an optimistic sales estimate of 250 (figures in thousands), a most likely estimate of 240, and a pessimistic estimate of 200 (dollars or units), the expected value can be computed as follows:

$$EV = \frac{250 + 4(240) + 200}{6}$$
$$= 235$$

The standard deviation is then derived by means of the following formula:

$$SD = \frac{Q - P}{6}$$
$$= \frac{250 - 200}{6}$$
$$= 8.33$$

According to probability theory, the true value lies within two standard deviations plus or minus from the expected value, with about 95 percent probability. The true value of sales, therefore, can be expected to lie in a range from $235 \pm 2(8.33)$, or between 218.34 and 251.66.

Group Discussion Method.   The accuracy of a PERT-derived forecast hinges heavily on the ability of the expert(s) to produce realistic estimates. As a quick check on figures arrived at by other methods, the PERT approach can be very useful. But the analyst frequently feels that a number of specialists should be invited to participate in forecasting. Most often, the team meets as a committee and comes up with a group estimate through consensus. This group discussion method has the advantage of merging divergent viewpoints and moderating individual biases. You should, however, guard against the potential disadvantage of domination of the discussion by one or more individuals, or superficial response because of a lack of individual responsibility.

Pooled Individual Estimates Method.   While the pooled individual estimates method avoids the potential pitfalls of group discussions, it also lacks the benefits of group dynamics. A project leader simply merges separately supplied estimates into a single estimate, without any interplay with or between the participants.

Delphi Technique.   An increasingly popular method for forecasting is the Delphi technique, which overcomes the drawbacks of both group discussion and pooled individual estimates methods. In this approach, group members are asked to submit individual estimates and assumptions. These are reviewed by the project leader, revised, and fed back to the participants for a second round. Participants are also informed of the median forecast level that emerged from the previous round. Domination, undue conservatism, and argument are eliminated because of the written, rather than oral, procedure, and the group members benefit from one another's input. After successive rounds of estimating and feedback, the process ends when a consensus emerges.

Jury of Executive Opinion. As mentioned, the experts consulted in one or more of these methods are typically recruited from one of three pools: executives, salespeople, and informed outsiders. A jury of executive opinion is often composed of top-level personnel from various key functions such as sales, production, and finance. The major advantage of this type of source is that forecasts can be arrived at quickly. This advantage is, however, easily outweighed by the disadvantage inherent in involving people in the estimating process who, in spite of their high rank, are relatively unfamiliar with the forces that shape marketing success.

Composite of Sales Force Opinion. The composite of sales force opinion approach collects product, customer, and/or territorial estimates from individual salespeople in the field. Since they are in constant contact with customers, salespeople should be in a position to predict buying plans and needs. They may even be able to take into account probable competitive activity. Salespeople who call on relatively few industrial accounts and work very closely with them are likely to produce the best forecasts. Conversely, salespeople who call on many accounts in visits that are widely spaced will be of relatively little help in predicting sales.

Few companies simply add up their sales force's estimates to compute the sales forecast. Since sales quotas are frequently based on these estimates, a salesperson will tend to be conservative or pessimistic in estimating sales. This tendency can be partially corrected by rewarding accuracy and distributing records showing the accuracy of past forecasts, or by allocating promotional support to a territory in line with the sales estimate (in which case it may, of course, become a self-fulfilling prophecy).

To counter the additional problem that many salespeople are unfamiliar with broad economic trends, many firms supply their salespeople with basic assumptions to guide their estimates. In spite of its drawbacks, the effort may well be worth it. For one thing, morale is likely to be higher if salespeople have had a hand in their own forecasts and quotas.

Outside Experts. When it comes to outside experts, any knowledgeable source could be consulted—for example, trade associations or economists. Marketing researchers are another valuable resource, together with dealers and distributors. However, it is generally difficult to assess the degree of familiarity with industry conditions and trends of such outsiders. Thus, they should be used with caution and only in a supplementary capacity.

Consumer Surveys. The judgmental methods just described involve estimates by people who are not themselves the ultimate buyers. Some observers consider this fact a weakness and suggest getting the word directly from "the horse's mouth." Surveys of consumer buying intentions are particularly appropriate when past trends (such as energy consumption) are unlikely to continue or historical data (as for a new product or market) do not exist. This technique works best for major consumer durables and industrial capital expenditures, since these types of buying decisions require a considerable amount of planning and lead time, and the respondents are able to predict their own behavior with reasonable accuracy. However, other kinds of consumer purchases are not planned sufficiently in advance and can thus only be guessed at. A substantial bias may be involved because the interviewee might want to please the interviewer, or might give an arbitrary answer because he cannot predict his own behavior in an unfamiliar situation. In addition to the possible drawback that prospective purchasers might be unwilling to disclose their intentions, it should be remembered that answers given refer to future, and thus hypothetical, behavior rather than actual behavior.

Test Marketing. The problem of accuracy can be remedied by using the test-marketing approach whereby a new product, or a variation in the marketing mix for an established one, is introduced in a limited number of test cities. The entire marketing program that is scheduled on a national basis is put into effect, scaled down to the local level, but otherwise identical in every detail, including advertising, pricing, packaging, and so forth. The new marketing effort now has to compete in a real sales environment. Purchases, if any, are actual, not hypothetical. If carefully chosen and monitored, test markets can provide a significant minipicture of the full-scale reaction to the planned change. On the basis of actual sales results in the test markets, sales forecasts are simply scaled up by appropriate factors.

Table 3-5 summarizes the methods discussed.

Portfolio Analysis

Portfolio analysis consists of formal models that provide a systematic approach to assessing competitive position and to determining investment levels. In practice, portfolio analysis is used for self-contained organizational units—divisions, strategic business units

Table 3-5. *Comparison of Nonmathematical Forecasting Methods.*

Method	*Nature*	*Benefits*	*Drawbacks*
Judgmental			
Judgment from the extremes	Successive narrowing of high–low range	Range instead of single figure	Depends on individual estimating
PERT-derived	Weighing of three alternative estimates	Possibility of determining confidence range	Depends on individual estimating
Group discussion	Group consensus estimate	Merges divergent views, moderate biases	Domination by one individual, superficiality
Pooled and individual estimates	Averaging of individual estimates	Avoids group discussion pitfalls	Lacks group dynamics
Delphi technique	Successive written rounds of estimating with feedback from other participants	Eliminates domination, conservatism, superficial response	Lacks group dynamics
Jury of executive opinion	Top-level committee	Quick	Unfamiliar with market conditions
Composite of sales force opinion	Adjusted estimates from individual salespeople	Front-line expertise, motivational tool	Bias due to impact on compensation, unfamiliar with economic trends
Outside experts	Merging of outside opinions	No bias due to personal interests	Difficult to assess degree of expertise
Market			
Consumer surveys	Consumer interviews about buying intentions	Directly from "the horse's mouth"	Hypothetical behavior
Test marketing	Sale in limited number of cities	Actual sales results	Costly, time-consuming

(SBU), departments, and product lines—in which investment decisions have to be made on a market-by-market or product-by-product basis. Your job is to seek out the information needed for these portfolio approaches and to determine which approach suits your particular business. The results can be of immeasurable help in systematically analyzing your situation and in developing competitive strategies.

Case Example

Hewlett-Packard Co. Hewlett-Packard Co., the highly successful computer and instrument manufacturer, was reorganizing for continued growth against competitors during the mid-1980's. It was being attacked from all sides: IBM and AT&T at the top; Digital Equipment Corp. and Data General Corp. head to head; Nixdorf Computer, and Hitachi from abroad. And that formidable lineup didn't account for the hard-driving smaller firms—such as Apollo Computer Inc., Sun Microsystems Inc., Daisy Systems Corp., and Tektronic—or other competitors creating market niche challenges for many of Hewlett-Packard's 9,000 products.

Organizationally, Hewlett-Packard has been a loosely knit collection of 50 autonomous divisions, each responsible for its own production and marketing. It is best described as an engineering-oriented company, run by engineers for engineers. In the past, the organizational format has worked well, reaching revenues of $6.6 billion.

But changing patterns in market behavior began to emerge. For example, large customers insisted that whatever equipment they bought must fit together into a unified system. Further, the buying influence was no longer left solely with the engineer. Consequently, the loosely run engineering-oriented organization resulted in inefficient selling practices (several salespeople from various divisions calling on one prospect) and delays in developing new product systems (engineering workstations and high-powered desktop computers). Opportunities in these growth segments fell to the smaller, faster-reacting competitors.

While organizational changes were needed to change the company into a market-driven company, there was an urgent need for analyzing products and markets using the formal techniques of portfolio analysis. Hewlett-Packard undertook portfolio analysis for its 50 autonomous divisions and then for its major product lines.

Models

BCG Growth–Share Matrix

With a technique developed by the Boston Consulting Group, the portfolio of businesses or products can be tracked. BCG Growth–Share Matrix (Figure 3-9) graphically shows that some products may be in a strong position relative to those of competitors, while other products may be in a weaker position. Each product has its own total strategy depending on its position in the matrix. Each product is represented by a circle in the matrix and from the positioning of these circles management can determine the following information:

Figure 3-9. *A BCG Growth–Share Matrix.*

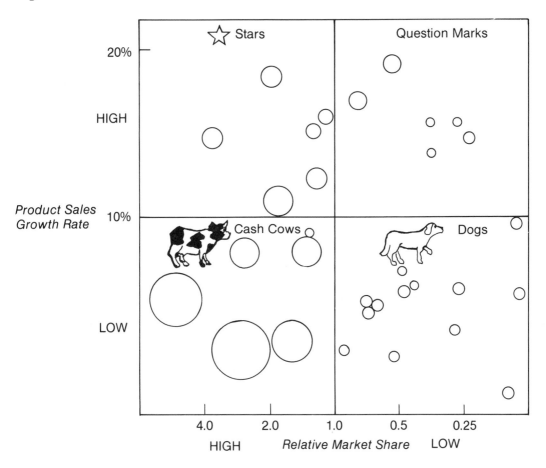

- Dollar sales, represented by the area of the circle.
- Market share, relative to the firm's largest competitor, as shown by horizontal position.
- Growth rate, relative to the market in which the product competes, as shown by vertical position.

In addition, the quadrants of the matrix categorize products into four groups:

1. *Stars:* products that have high market growth and high market share. These products need constant attention to maintain or increase share through active promotion, product improvement, and careful pricing strategies.

2. *Cash cows:* products with low market growth and high market share, market dominance, and strong cash flow. The object for this group of products is to maintain market dominance without

the benefit of large expenditures for promotion and with minimal outlay for R&D. The central idea behind the cash cow is that businesses with a large share of market are more profitable than their smaller-share competitors.

3. *Question marks* (also known as problem children or wildcats): products with potential for high growth in a fast-moving market but with low market share. They absorb large amounts of cash (usually from the cash cows) and are expected to reach the status of a star.

4. *Dogs:* products with low market growth and low market share, reflecting the worst of all situations. A number of alternatives are possible: maintain the product in the line to support the image of being a full-line supplier, eliminate the product from the line, or harvest the product through a slow phasing out.

As you review the growth–share matrix, note on the vertical axis that product sales are separated into high and low quadrants. The 10 percent growth line is simply an arbitrary rate of growth and represents a middle level. For your particular industry the number could be 5 percent, 12 percent, or 15 percent. Similarly, on the horizontal axis there is a dividing line of relative market share of 1.0 so that positioning your product in the lower left-hand quadrant would indicate high market leadership, and in the lower right-hand quadrant, low market leadership. The important interpretations to make from the matrix are as follows:

- The amount of cash generated increases with relative market share. (This point was borne out in the section covering the experience curve.)

- The amount of sales growth requires proportional cash input to finance the added capacity and market development. If market share is maintained, then cash requirements increase only relative to market growth rate.

- From a marketing manager's point of view, cash input is required to keep up with market growth. Increasing market share usually requires cash to support advertising and sales promotion expenditures, lower prices, and other share-building tactics. On the other hand, a decrease in market share may provide cash for utilization in other product areas.

- In situations where a product moves towards maturity, it is possible to use enough funds to maintain market position and use surplus funds to reinvest in other products that are still growing.

In summary, the BCG Growth–Share Matrix permits you to evaluate where your products and markets are relative to competitors and what investments are needed relative to such basic strategies as building share for your product, holding share, harvesting, and withdrawing from the market.

General Electric Business Screen

The BCG Growth–Share Matrix focuses on cash flow and uses only two variables: growth and share. The General Electric Business Screen (Figure 3-10), on the other hand, is a more comprehensive, multifactor analysis that provides a graphic display of where an existing product fits competitively in relation to a variety of criteria. It also aids in projecting the chances for a new product's success.

The key points in using the GE Business Screen are:

Figure 3-10. *General Electric Business Screen.*

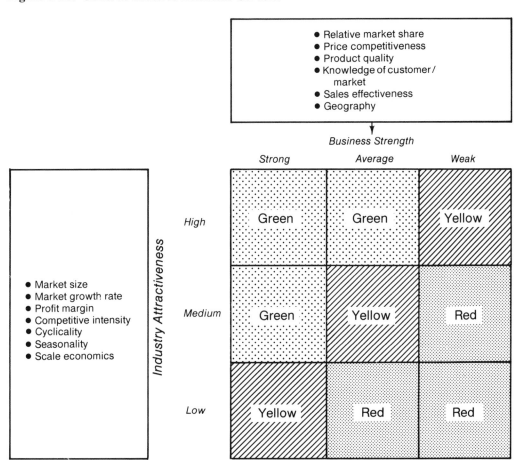

1. *Industry attractiveness* is shown on the vertical axis of the matrix. It is based on rating such factors as market size, market growth rate, profit margin, competitive intensity, cyclicity, seasonality, and scale of economies. Each factor is given a weight classifying an industry, market segment, or product as high, medium, or low in overall attractiveness.

2. *Business strength* is shown on the horizontal axis. A weighted rating is made for such factors as relative market share, price competitiveness, product quality, knowledge of customer and market, sales effectiveness, and geography. The results of the analysis show the ability to compete that, in turn, provides insight into developing strategies in relation to competitors.

3. The matrix is divided into three color sectors: green, yellow, and red. The green sector has three cells at the upper left and indicates those markets that are favorable in industry attractiveness and business strength. These markets have a "green light" to move in aggressively. The yellow sector includes the diagonal cells stretching from the lower left to upper right. This sector indicates a medium level in overall attractiveness. The red sector covers the three cells in the lower right. This sector indicates those markets that are low in overall attractiveness.

A more comprehensive view of the factors contributing to industry attractiveness and business strength is given in Table 3-6, developed by Derek Abell and John Hammond. The variety of factors is not meant to overwhelm you but to provide for the practical application of any factors that could possibly contribute to a more meaningful analysis. To show the practical application of the GE Business Screen, Figure 3-11 illustrates the strategy options for each of the nine cells of the matrix.

Arthur D. Little Matrix

Another practical portfolio analysis approach is associated with the consulting organization Arthur D. Little Inc. In this author's experience it has been used by Becton, Dickinson & Co., a major manufacturer in the health care industry, for analyzing its market share for its various products. In Figure 3-12, some of Becton Dickinson's products are used to demonstrate the application of this matrix. First, note the similarities of this matrix to the other portfolio analysis approaches already discussed. The competitive positions of various products are plotted on the vertical axis according to such factors as leading, strong, favorable, tenable, weak, and nonviable. On the hor-

Table 3-6. *Factors Contributing to Market Attractiveness and Business Position.*

Attractiveness of Your Market	Status/Position of Your Business
Market Factors	
Size (dollars, units, or both)	Your share (in equivalent terms)
Size of key segments	Your share of key segments
Growth rate per year:	Your annual growth rate:
Total	Total
Segments	Segments
Diversity of market	Diversity of your participation
Sensitivity to price, service features, and external factors	Your influence on the market
Cyclicity	Lags or leads in your sales
Seasonality	
Bargaining power of upstream suppliers	Bargaining power of your suppliers
Bargaining power of downstream suppliers	Bargaining power of your customers
Competition	
Types of competitors	Where you fit, how you compare in terms of products, marketing capability, service, production strength, financial strength, management
Degree of concentration	
Changes in type and mix	
Entries and exits	Segments you have entered or left
Changes in share	Your relative share change
Substitution by new technology	Your vulnerability to new technology
Degrees and types of integration	Your own level of integration
Financial and Economic Factors	
Contribution margins	Your margins
Leveraging factors, such as economies of scale and experience	Your scale and experience
Barriers to entry or exit (both financial and nonfinancial)	Barriers to your entry or exit (both financial and nonfinancial)
Capacity utilization	Your capacity utilization
Technological Factors	
Maturity and volatility	Your ability to cope with change
Complexity	Depths of your skills
Differentiation	Types of your technological skills
Patents and copyrights	Your patent protection

(continued)

Source: Derek Abell and John Hammond, *Strategic Market Planning* (Englewood Cliffs, N.J.: Prentice-Hall, 1979).

Table 3-6. *Continued.*

Attractiveness of Your Market	Status/Position of Your Business
Technological Factors	
Manufacturing process technology required	Your manufacturing technology
Sociopolitical Factors in Your Environment	
Social attitudes and trends	Your company's responsiveness and flexibility
Laws and government agency regulations	Your company's ability to cope
Influence with pressure groups and government representatives	Your company's aggressiveness
Human factors, such as unionization and community acceptance	Your company's relationships

izontal axis, the maturity levels for the products are designated embryonic, growth, mature, and aging.

The key interpretations for this matrix are:

1. **Nonviable:** lowest possible level of competitive position.
2. **Weak:** characterized by unsatisfactory financial performance but with some opportunity for improvement.
3. **Tenable:** a competitive product position where financial performance is barely satisfactory. These products have a less than average opportunity to improve competitive position.
4. **Favorable:** a competitive position that is better than the survival rate. These products also have a limited range of opportunities for improvement.
5. **Strong:** characterized by an ability to defend market share against competing moves without the sacrifice of acceptable financial performance.
6. **Leading:** has the widest range of strategic options because of the "competitive distance" between the given products and the competitors' products.

An examination of the four Becton Dickinson products shows how this matrix worked during a particular period in those products' life cycle.

Automated radioimmunoassay (a sophisticated diagnostic product used in laboratories) is considered to be in its embryonic stage and to have a favorable competitive position. This favorable position of-

Figure 3-11. *Strategy options based on the GE Business Screen.*

Business Strength

Industry Attractiveness	Strong	Average	Weak
High	Premium—Invest for Growth: • Provide maximum investment • Diversify worldwide • Consolidate position • Accept moderate near-term profits • Seek to dominate	Selective—Invest for Growth: • Invest heavily in selected segments • Share ceiling • Seek attractive new segments to apply strengths	Protect/Refocus—Selectively Invest for Earnings: • Defend strengths • Refocus to attractive segments • Evaluate industry revitalization • Monitor for harvest or divestment timing • Consider acquisitions
Medium	Challenge—Invest for Growth: • Build selectively on strengths • Define implications of leadership challenge • Avoid vulnerability—fill weaknesses	Prime—Selectively Invest for Earnings: • Segment market • Make contingency plans for vulnerability	Restructure—Harvest or Divest: • Provide no unessential commitment • Position for divestment *or* • Shift to more attractive segment
Low	Opportunistic—Selectively Invest for Earnings: • Ride market and maintain overall position • Seek niches, specialization • Seek opportunity to increase strength (for example through acquisition) • Invest at maintenance levels	Opportunistic—Preserve for Harvest: • Act to preserve or boost cash flow • Seek opportunistic sale *or* • Seek opportunistic rationalization to increase strengths • Prune product lines • Minimize investment	Harvest or Divest: • Exit from market or prune product line • Determine timing so as to maximize present value • Concentrate on competitor's cash generators

Source: Bernard A. Rausch, *Strategic Marketing Planning* (New York: AMA Extension Institute, 1982), p. 88.

fers the manager a range of strategy options as long as the decisions relate to the overall corporate strategy.

Single-use hypodermic needles and syringes have a strong competitive position in a growth industry. Here, too, strategy options are fairly flexible and depend on competitive moves as well as on how quickly increases in market share are desired.

Blood collection systems (Vacutainers) have a leading competitive position in a mature industry in the United States. The Becton Dick-

Figure 3-12. *Arthur D. Little matrix applied to Becton Dickinson products.*

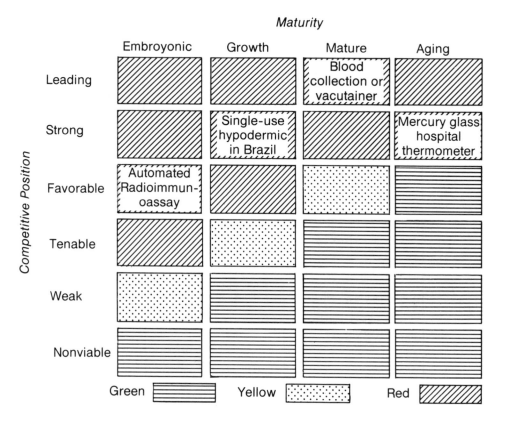

inson strategy is to hold existing market share by means of product differentiation.

Mercury glass hospital thermometers in the United States have a strong competitive position in an aging industry. This product has less price flexibility. However, by using service, repackaging, and distribution innovations, Becton Dickinson attempts to maintain its strong position before giving in to price reductions.

As in the GE Business Screen, a green-yellow-red system is used to indicate strategic options: green indicates a wide range of options; yellow indicates caution for a limited range of options for selected development; and red is a warning of peril with options narrowed to those of withdrawal, divestiture, and liquidation.

A Practical The example detailed in Figures 3-13, 3-14, and 3-15 represents an
Application actual analysis used by an electric utility company to examine and

Figure 3-13. *Market attractiveness analysis.*

	Rating	Weighting Factor
1. Market Size—Total		
Very small (less than $1 million/yr.)	1	
Small ($1–$10 million/yr.)	2	
Medium ($10–$25 million/yr.)	3	(.05)
Large ($25–$100 million/yr.)	4	
Very large ($100+ million/yr.)	5	
2. Market Size—Reasonable Potential		
(Added Gross Revenue/Yr.)		
Very small (less than $500,000/yr.)	1	
Small ($500,000–$1 million/yr.)	2	
Medium ($1–$5 million/yr.)	3	(.15)
Large ($5–$10 million/yr.)	4	
Very large ($10+ million/yr.)	5	
3. Market Growth Rate—Total Market		
Declining	1	
Stable	2	
Slow growth (0%–3%)	3	(.10)
Medium growth (4%–9%)	4	
Fast growth (10+%)	5	
4. Competitive Intensity		
Superior competition	1	
Strong/active competition	2	
Moderate competition	3	(.10)
Slight/some competition	4	
No competition	5	
5. Required Investment		
Very high ($10+ million)	1	
High ($1–$10 million)	2	
Moderate ($100,000–$1 million)	3	(.05)
Low (Under $100,000)	4	
None (0)	5	
6. Payback—Total Investment ÷ net		
annual sixth-year revenue		
1 year or less	5	
2 years or less	4	
3 years or less	3	(.15)
4 years or less	2	
Over 4 years	1	

(*continued*)

Figure 3-13. *Continued.*

	Rating	Weighting Factor
7. Type of Load—Time		
On-peak only	1	
Mostly on-peak	2	
Peak and off-peak	3	(.10)
Mostly off-peak	4	
Off-peak only/interruptible	5	
8. Type of Load—Hours Used		
Less than 1 hour/day	1	
1–3 hours	2	
4–6 hours	3	(.10)
7–9 hours	4	
10 or more hours	5	
9. Seasonality		
Summer load	1	
Year-round, peaks in summer	2	
Year-round, even all year	3	(.10)
Year-round, peaks in fall, winter, spring	4	
Winter, fall, spring load (low/none in summer)	5	
10. Cyclicality		
Cyclical—in phase with auto industry	1	
	2	
Somewhat cyclical	3	(.10)
	4	
Not cyclical at all	5	

prioritize its portfolio of end-use applications for electric energy, as expressed in kilowatt hours (kwh). The output of such an analysis is then used in a strategic marketing plan, an example of which is given for this utility company in Chapter 6.

The analysis occurs in two stages. First, an analysis is done of end-use applications against ten factors in each of two categories: *market attractiveness* (Figure 3-13) and *business strengths* (Figure 3-14). Each of the ten factors is specified by a range of criteria with an assigned rating number of 1 to 5. Then, a weighting factor indicating the relative importance of each factor is also assigned in order to come up with a rating score. While the scoring can be done by an individual, for best results it is recommended that a team approach be used to gain qualified input from individuals representing different functional areas of the company. In this sample analysis, the group consisted of nine individuals who formed a strategy team.

Figure 3-14. *Business strengths analysis.*

	Rating	Weighting Factor
1. Relative Market Share		
Under 10%	1	
10–25%	2	
26–50%	3	(.05)
51–75%	4	
Over 75%	5	
2. Share Growth		
Declining	1	
	2	
Stable	3	(.15)
	4	
Growing (or already > 90%)	5	
3. Price Competitiveness—Operating Cost		
Electric cost more than 100% higher	1	
Electric cost up to 100% higher	2	
Electric cost up to 25% higher	3	
Electric competitive	4	(.15)
Electric less expensive/no viable competition	5	
4. Product Quality/Performance		
Not as good	1	
	2	
Same as competition	3	(.10)
	4	
Better than competition	5	
5. Knowledge of Customers/Markets		
Not knowledgeable/much less than competition	1	
Not very	2	
Somewhat/same as competition	3	(.10)
Knowledgeable	4	
Very knowledgeable/much better than competition	5	
6. Brand Recognition		
(Recognition of/Preference for Electric)		
Electric (virtually) unknown/competition preferred	1	
Electric not as well known as competition	2	
Electric as well known as competition	3	(.10)
Electric better known than competition	4	
Electric preferred/competition (virtually) unknown	5	

(*continued*)

Figure 3-14. *Continued.*

	Rating	*Weighting Factor*
7. Distribution Network		
No distribution network exists	1	
Distribution exists, but favors competition	2	
Distribution exists and is neutral	3	(.10)
Distribution exists and favors electric	4	
Superior distribution exists and favors electric	5	
8. Sales Effectiveness		
(Ability to Gain Share)		
Not at all	1	
Not very effective	2	
Somewhat effective	3	(.10)
Effective	4	
Very effective	5	
9. Fit with Current Business		
None	1	
Poor	2	
Fair	3	(.10)
Good	4	
Very good	5	
10. Unique Marketing Advantages		
No, strong disadvantage	1	
No, minor disadvantage	2	
No, about same	3	(.10)
Yes, minor advantage	4	
Yes, strong advantage	5	

In the second stage, the scores of end-use applications are compiled in rank order to identify those markets having high potential, medium potential, and low potential. This ranking is particularly valuable for product and service development, budget allocations, deploying the sales force, selecting advertising media, developing other promotional support, and devising overall competitive strategies. In this electric utility example, the competitor is natural gas.

The results of the preliminary screening of 21 different end-use applications for electric energy are shown in Figure 3-15. Among the end-use applications identified as having high potential are lighting

Figure 3-15. *Preliminary evaluation of marketing opportunities based on analyses shown in Figures 3-13 and 3-14.*

End-Use Application	Market Attractiveness Rating	Business Strengths Rating	Combined Rating
Nonresidential interior lighting	3.40	4.70	8.10
Residential security lighting	3.95	3.85	7.80
Street lighting	3.65	4.05	7.70
Arc melting	3.60	3.80	7.40
Commercial lighting	3.45	3.50	6.95
Induction melting	3.10	3.40	6.50
Induction heating	3.20	3.25	6.45
Dual fuel	3.50	2.75	6.25
Commercial OPL	3.25	2.85	6.10
Residential resistance heat	3.30	2.74	6.05
Electric ranges	2.55	3.45	6.00
Residential heat pump	3.10	2.85	5.95
Commercial resistance heat	3.40	2.45	5.85
Electric dryers	2.60	3.15	5.75
Commercial cooking	3.05	2.55	5.60
Residential OPL	3.15	2.45	5.60
Residential water heating	3.20	2.10	5.30
Cool storage (ice storage)	2.85	2.25	5.10
Air-to-air heat pump	2.50	2.25	4.75
Water source heat pump	2.35	2.35	4.70
Heat storage	2.75	1.90	4.65
Average	3.14	2.98	6.12

and melting. The fact that a particular end-use application did not rank relatively high does not mean the application doesn't or should not fit in the strategic marketing plan. It simply means that it might be of interest for the intermediate or long term, or fits in a particular geographic market, such as areas where there is no natural gas service or where the competition is oil or propane. Further refinement of the screening process occurs in the objective setting and action-step phases of the strategic marketing plan, where the example's team came to grips with achievable sales objectives for a particular end-use application; the resources required for each objective; and the balancing of available resources against priority targets.

You can use this extremely valuable technique to evaluate your own product and market opportunities.

154   The Framework for Competitive Analysis

Financial Resource Analysis

Case Example

Campbell Soup Company Campbell introduced a radical change to its corporate strategy during the mid-1980's: It shifted from mass marketing to regionalization. For example, in Texas and parts of California where consumers like food with a more zesty taste, Campbell made its nacho cheese soup spicier. At a major sports event, a local Campbell sales manager used part of her ad budget to sponsor a related radio promotion. Another local manager arranged hot samples of Campbell soups at a ski resort.

To move toward regionalization, Campbell shifted its focus to marketing by pushing decision making down to levels that were closer to the consumer. That move required more market-by-market planning, as the company tailored its products, advertising, promotion, and sales efforts to fit different regions of the country, and even individual neighborhoods within a city.

In turn, more skilled managers were needed who could develop comprehensive marketing plans, determine competitive strategies and tactics on the basis of the planning objectives, and then be able to identify the *financial implications* of those strategies. Such calculations as return on investment, return on sales, market share, breakeven, and marketing expense-to-sales ratios took on even greater meaning with regionalization as compared with the traditional centralized Campbell organization that developed a single set of products and marketing programs for a mass market that was viewed with little or no differentiation.

Further, not only were the middle managers required to act as business managers, but local sales staffs were converted into autonomous marketers as the company moved forward in dividing the United States into 22 regions. No longer were they extensions of the corporate office; every regional staff studied its own marketing strategies and implemented them.

Financial analysis is an essential part of an internal analysis. It provides you with the means to quantify your strategy decisions. This section concentrates on those areas of financial analysis that a general manager or marketing manager needs to understand to conduct an internal analysis. The following financial measures are key parts of a financial analysis.

Return on Investment There are several approaches to calculating return on investment (ROI) depending on how "investment' is defined. The most often used is:

$$ROI = \frac{\text{Net Income}}{\text{Investment}} \times 100\%$$

Return on Sales

$$ROS = \frac{\text{Net Income}}{\text{Total Sales}} \times 100\%$$

Cash Flow CF = (Net Income + Depreciation) − (change in plant and equipment) − (change in working capital)

In some organizations, the term *cash flow* is used to identify cash flow from operations only and does not include cash flow arising from balance sheet changes, as noted in the equation.

Market-Share Analysis While not used in traditional financial analysis, market share is useful because of its financial implications to ROI.

Before a calculation can be made, you need to determine which of the four measures of market share will be used:[2]

1. **Overall market share:** The company's overall market share is its sales (in units or dollars) expressed as a percentage of total industry sales. Industry practice or historical company reporting patterns will usually dictate the form of measurement. You will also have to consider how you want to define the market as it relates to the product lines offered by your company. Consistency and accuracy of what is being measured are the criteria.

2. **Served market share:** The company's served market is its sales expressed as a percentage of the total sales to its served market. The served market is that segment that can be reached and served by the company's marketing effort. It could be a geographic region or a particular product line of expensive (or inexpensive) products. If you use this category of market share, don't be lulled into a false sense of security. You could have an 85 percent share of a regional market with a limited product line, yet have only 15 percent of the total industry. Again, good judgment and consistency should prevail. Served market is particularly useful if it is your strategy to expand on a segment-by-

[2]The list is adapted from P. Kotler, *Marketing Management: Analysis, Planning, and Control,* 5th edition (Englewood Cliffs, N.J.: Prentice-Hall, 1984), p. 747.

segment rollout to other geographic regions or customer categories.

3. **Market share relative to top three competitors:** This market share shows the company's sales expressed as a percentage of the combined sales of the three largest competitors. This measure is especially valid when three or four companies command the major share of the market (fuel oil and cold cereals, for example). If your company has 30 percent of the market and its three largest competitors have 20 percent, 10 percent, and 10 percent, then your company's relative market share is 75 percent (30% of 40%). On the other hand, if each of the four companies had 25 percent of the market, then any company's relative market share would be 33 percent (25% of 75%).

4. **Market share relative to a leading competitor:** In some cases a company may simply track its sales as a percentage of the leading competitor's sales. This measure is effective when the industry is fragmented with very small competitors and your growth is measured against the dominant competitor.

According to Kotler, a useful way of analyzing market share movements is in terms of the following four components:[3]

$$\begin{array}{l} \text{Overall} \\ \text{market} \\ \text{share} \end{array} = \begin{array}{l} \text{Customer penetration} \times \text{customer loyalty} \times \text{customer selectivity} \\ \times \text{ price selectivity} \end{array}$$

where

Customer penetration is the percentage of all customers who buy from this company.

Customer loyalty is the purchases from this company by its customers expressed as a percentage of their total purchases from all suppliers of the same products.

Customer selectivity is the size of the average customer purchase from the company expressed as a percentage of the size of the average customer purchase from an average company.

Price selectivity is the average price charged by this company expressed as a percentage of the average price charged by all companies.

Marketing Expense-to-Sales Analysis One of the key financial ratios to watch is marketing expense-to-sales. When you are monitoring different strategies in situations such as either defending market share or aggressively pursuing market share,

---

[3] Kotler, *Marketing Management*, p. 748.

it becomes a platform for projecting the financial impact of future strategy approaches. The components of this ratio comprise sales force-to-sales, advertising-to-sales, sales promotion-to-sales, marketing research-to-sales, and sales administration-to-sales. The ratios can be monitored either through a chart, which graphically shows deviation from budget, or from the more typical periodic budget variance reports.

Break-even Another key financial consideration is the minimum sales revenue
Analysis necessary to cover costs. This revenue is the product of two factors: *quantity* and *price*. The quantity factor is crucial here because it represents the number of units that must be sold just to recover costs. This quantity is called the *break-even* quantity.[4]

How Break-even Analysis Works

To get the most out of break-even analysis, your cost accounting system must be able to separate each relevant cost category into its fixed and variable components. On a total cost level, the terms *fixed* and *variable* refer to whether or not the amount varies with the output. A cost item is considered fixed if its total amount is unaffected by the number of units produced—for example, advertising expenditures. Variable cost, on the other hand, refers to items that are dependent on output. The most obvious examples are direct material and direct labor. These costs can be determined on a per-unit basis. Unlike fixed costs, they are not incurred when there is no production. In marketing, sales-force commissions are an example of a variable cost.

The distinction between fixed and variable cost is basic to break-even analysis. When variable unit cost is deducted from the price of the item, the resulting figure is called *unit contribution*. The thinking behind this terminology is that it makes no sense to produce (and sell) any product whose direct manufacturing cost cannot be recovered in the selling price. After all, you can avoid these costs by not producing the unit. On the other hand, fixed costs are incurred in any case; there is virtually nothing that you can do about them. So, any excess of price over unit variable costs will go first toward covering fixed costs. Whatever money is left over—that is, if you sell more units than are necessary to cover costs—is a profit.

[4]The material on break-even analysis is adapted from Norton Paley, *Pricing Strategies and Practices* (New York: AMACOM, 1983), pp. 42–47.

The break-even point can be identified with the help of a basic formula:

$$QB = \frac{F}{P - V}$$

where:

    QB = break-even quantity: the minimum sales quantity necessary at a given price to cover your product's total costs
    F = total fixed costs attributable to your product
    P = alternative price levels for your product
    V = unit variable cost of your product

The equation makes it evident that altering any of its elements will affect the result significantly; increasing or lowering your fixed costs, your price, and/or your unit variable cost will immediately be reflected in the quantity needed to break even. What you are doing, in essence, is dividing your fixed costs by your unit contributions in order to determine how many units you need to sell to recover your fixed costs.

An Illustration

To illustrate how break-even analysis works, let us presume that your firm has developed a new product whose production will require an additional investment of $60,000. At an estimated economic life span of five years, this original amount results in fixed annual depreciation costs of $12,000. Assume further that corporate management has assigned your innovation a share of general overhead amounting to $26,000 per year, and that the variable unit cost is $10. You can then modify the break-even formula to read:

$$QB = \frac{I + O + A + D}{P - V}$$

where:

    QB = break-even quantity
    I = depreciation of additional investment necessary for the production of your innovation
    O = your new product's share of corporate overhead
    A = alternative advertising budgets
    D = alternative levels of distribution expenditures
    P = alternative price levels for your product
    V = unit variable cost of your product

This example is deliberately simplified, but it does show a number of elements of your fixed costs related to your decision: depreciation of incremental productive investment; compensation for use of corporate services and facilities; advertising expenditures; and distribution cost allowances. These cost factors, while they do not vary with the output level, are, nevertheless, flexible in the sense that they can be adjusted upward or downward by managerial decisions. Thus, break-even management becomes both a task and an opportunity for goal-directed executive decision making.

Inserting into the formula those figures that will remain unchanged throughout all our calculations, we arrive at the following outcome:

$$QB = \frac{12,000 + 26,000 + A + D}{P - 10}$$

$$= \frac{38,000 + A + D}{P - 10}$$

Since your depreciation, share of overhead, and variable unit cost are given figures, the minimum quantity necessary to cover your costs is solely a function of your marketing mix, represented in this case by varying advertising and distribution budgets, as well as by the price of the proposed innovation. Seven combinations of the elements of your marketing mix are shown in Table 3-7.

For each of the three variable elements (price, advertising, and distribution), two alternative price levels are being considered, producing a total of eight combinations or mixes. Combined marketing expenditures range from a low of $20,000 to a high of $100,000. Which of these mixes—and, thus, expenditure levels—is preferable and should be implemented is, however, impossible to determine with the amount of information before you at this point. The additional data you need to arrive at a meaningful choice are presented in Table 3-8.

Table 3-7. *Alternative Marketing Mixes.*

Mix No.	Price (P)	Advertising Budget (A)	Distribution Budget (D)
1	$16	$10,000	$10,000
2	16	10,000	50,000
3	16	50,000	10,000
4	16	50,000	50,000
5	24	10,000	10,000
6	24	10,000	50,000
7	24	50,000	50,000

Table 3-8. *Break-Even Analysis.*

Mix No.	Fixed Costs (F)	Break-Even Volume (QB)	Expected Volume (QE)	Total Costs (C)	Revenues (R)	Profits/ Losses (Z)
1	$ 58,000	9,667	12,400	$182,000	$198,400	$16,400
2	98,000	16,333	18,500	283,000	296,000	13,000
3	98,000	16,333	15,100	249,000	241,600	−7,400
4	138,000	23,000	22,600	364,000	361,600	−2,400
5	58,000	4,143	5,500	113,000	132,000	19,000
6	98,000	7,000	8,200	180,000	196,800	16,800
7	98,000	7,000	6,700	165,000	160,800	−4,200
8	138,000	9,857	10,000	238,000	240,000	2,000

In each instance, the total fixed costs were arrived at by adding their four ingredients: $F = I + O + A + D = 38,000 + A + D$. In line with our equation, the break-even volumes (QB) for the different mixes were computed by dividing the two unit contributions for $P - 10$ ($16 - 10 = \$6$ and $\$24 - 10 = \$14$, respectively, from Table 3-7) into the appropriate fixed-cost amounts. The expected volume (QE) column contains reasonable demand estimates, that is, executive predictions of actual demand levels in units, given the applicable marketing mix. The last three columns of Table 3-8 $(C, R, \text{and } Z)$ proceed under the assumption that the expected volume materializes; in other words, they use the QE figure as their basis of computation.

What Is the Best Mix?

With all the figures in, which is the best mix? It is impossible to give an absolute answer to this question, because the answer depends on your goals.

If you are aiming for the highest possible profit, you will have to choose Mix 5. But this choice, as straightforward as it seems, is not without danger. For example, the higher price providing substantially higher unit contribution may very well attract competitors. Another advantage to your competitors is that the expected volume constituting less than one-fourth of the demand level leaves much of the market unattended and gives them ample room for market penetration. Although the total costs of Mix 5 are the lowest, it is a high-risk choice that will, at best, give you a limited market share and leave you vulnerable to competitive inroads.

A more conservative approach on your part would be to choose between Mixes 1 and 6, both of which will cost and yield you nearly the same. Of the two, the greatest quantity above the break-even volume results from the application of Mix 1. At the same time, the demand level estimated for this mix is one and one-half times as high as that for Mix 6, which would likely result in a larger market share.

The illustration has been analyzed at length to demonstrate the kind of analytical thinking that goes into break-even analysis. But there is also room for creative thinking and dynamic management concerning the break-even volume. This fact becomes evident from Figure 3-16, which illustrates part of the material presented in Tables 3-7 and 3-8.

Four of the mixes in the illustration have been selected for a comparison of the highest profits and losses. Since the price is the same, the revenue curves are identical for Mixes 1 and 3, on the one hand, and Mixes 5 and 7, on the other. Also, the same total-cost curves apply to Mixes 1 and 5 as well as to Mixes 3 and 7, respectively. As can be seen, the higher price of $24 reduces the break-even volume to less than one-half of the original quantity and produces the highest profit at the expected level of demand, if the austerity budget proposal is employed. Also, total costs reflecting $50,000 for advertising and $10,000 for distribution result in losses at the two demand levels generated by the pricing alternatives under consideration.

Several insights emerge. One is that raising your price—everything else remaining the same—lowers the break-even point, provided the market behaves as expected. If such a favorable market response is likely at the higher price, you can reduce your risk substantially, because you need far fewer units than before to cover your costs and start making a profit. Another fact to consider is that the higher the level of total costs you begin with, the greater the quantity you have to sell to cover them.

Summary of Break-even Analysis

It becomes evident that break-even figures are not simply fixed and unalterable. Rather, they are the result of your decisions and subject to active management. Toward this end, it is well to remember that your break-even point is determined by three factors: *your fixed costs,* *your unit variable cost,* and *your price.* (A fourth element, demand level, is not under your direct control and so is omitted here.)

Figure 3-16. *Break-even chart.*

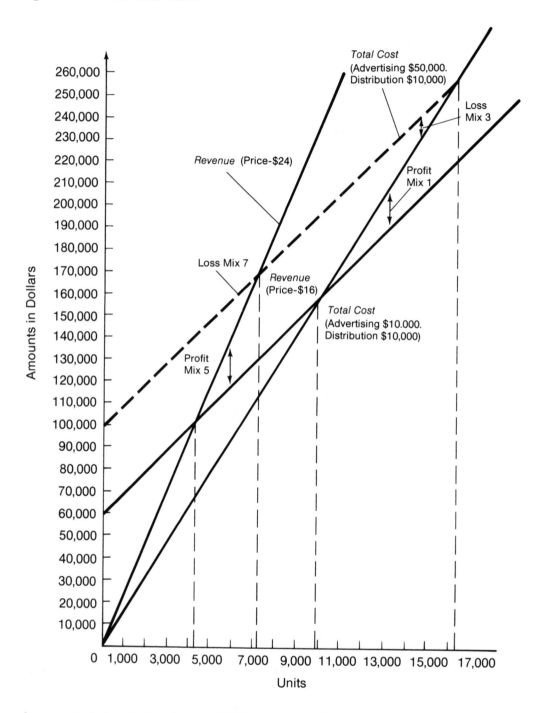

Source: Marketing Update, Issue 9 (1977), p. 4. Published by Alexander-
    Norton Publishers, Inc.

Implications of The greater value of financial analysis lies not in your ability to do
Financial the calculations, but in your understanding the implications of those
Resource ratios. Some useful conclusions come from a project first begun by
Analysis General Electric in the 1960's: PIMS (Profit Impact of Marketing
Strategy). It was later turned over to the Strategic Planning Institute,
a nonprofit corporation governed by approximately 200 member companies, representing almost 2,000 businesses. The data contributed
by those businesses form an empirical base that provides useful strategic planning information. Much of PIMS data and conclusions are
based on many of the financial analysis measurements just discussed,
such as ROI, market share, cash flow, and expense-to-sales ratios.
The major findings of the PIMS analysis are summarized in the following brief statements.[5]

1. **The Impact of Investment Intensity**
   As investment intensity rises, ROI declines.
   Large investment plus high marketing intensity equals poor
   ROI.
   Capacity utilization is vital when fixed capital intensity is
   high.
   High capital intensity plus small market share equals disaster.

2. **The Impact of Market Share**
   ROI is closely related to relative market share.
   Market share is most profitable in vertically integrated indus-
   tries.
   High R&D spending depresses ROI when market share is
   weak.
   Capacity utilization is most important for low-share busi-
   nesses.
   Heavy marketing depresses ROI for low-share businesses.
   Market share and quantity are partial substitutes for each other.

3. **The Impact of Market Growth Rate**
   A rapid rate of new product introduction in a fast growing
   market depresses ROI.
   R&D is most profitable in mature, slow-growth markets.

4. **The Impact of Life Cycle Stage**
   A narrow product line in the early or middle stage of the life
   cycle is less profitable than at the later stage.

---

[5]For a quantitative and detailed discussion of each item, see D. Abell and J. Hammond, *Strategic Market Planning* (Englewood Cliffs, N.J.: Prentice-Hall, 1979).

5. **The Impact of Marketing Expense-to-Sales Ratio**

    High R&D plus high marketing depresses ROI.

    High marketing expenditure depresses ROI, especially when quality is low.

6. **The Impact of Relative Market Share on Cash Flow**

    High relative share improves cash flow, while high growth decreases it.

    High share and low investment intensity produces cash, while low share and high investment intensity results in a cash drain.

    High relative share produces cash, especially when marketing intensity is low.

7. **The Impact of Investment Intensity on Cash Flow**

    Low or medium growth coupled with low investment intensity produces cash, while high growth coupled with high investment intensity is a cash drain.

    Harvesting share when investment intensity is low produces cash, while building share when investment intensity is high is a cash drain.

    Investment plus marketing intensity results in cash drains.

    Few new product introductions coupled with low investment intensity produces cash.

Strengths/Weaknesses Analysis

This last component of internal analysis, strengths/weaknesses analysis, is actually an integration of both internal and external analysis. It thus provides an excellent summary and how-to exercise for the complete concept of competitive analysis by examining the strengths and weaknesses of your own firm in the context of the strengths and weaknesses of your competitors.

Case Example

Syntex Corporation   Syntex Corporation, the eleventh largest drug company in the United States, utilized the excellent techniques of historical perspective and strengths/weaknesses analysis as a means of determining a strategy for the future. In the 1960's, Syntex was America's success company; it learned how to synthesize steroids that eventually were used in making birth control pills.

However, about 1970, U.S. Senate hearings raised questions of possible hazards of the pill. Sales dropped, earnings plunged 50 percent, and the stock toppled from $80 to $20. Syntex eventually recovered from its reliance on birth control pills and moved into other areas of drugs. Its next rise to power was again dependent on a single product, with the development of Naprosyn, an anti-inflammatory product used for treating arthritis. That product and others within the line grew 14 percent worldwide during 1986, but still accounted for 43 percent of Syntex's $949-million sales for 1985.

While concentrating efforts to dominate the field, management wisely undertook a strengths/weaknesses analysis and saw the vulnerability of maintaining a one-product-only strategy. Using its market dominance in birth control pills and anti-inflammatory products, management began using the profits and redeploying Syntex's strengths into the bigger and riskier drug market growth areas, such as the cardiovascular, immunological, and gastrointestinal markets. In just a 12-month period, 26 drugs were put under development.

Syntex's management understood the marketing battlefield. They battled such companies as SmithKline Beckman Corp. and its top-selling line of pharmaceuticals. They also fought a sales environment, trying to convince doctors that Syntex's products were better than current therapies. To win those battles, Syntex doubled its sales force of 750 over a five-year period; it also spent heavily to develop new products, allocating about 14.5 percent of its total sales to research, one of the industry's highest rates.

The case illustrates the practical value of a strengths/weaknesses analysis: how it affected Syntex's product development, its competitive strategy against such companies as SmithKline Beckman, and its selling tactics employed to reach doctors. The analysis resulted in management's moving Syntex from concentrating on a few well-chosen market niches to becoming a full-line pharmaceuticals producer.

The strengths/weaknesses analysis questionnaire presented as Figure 3-17 consists of 100 questions that serve as a marketing audit. They contribute to the total competitive analysis in two ways:

1. They analyze marketing operations and key environmental factors affecting your company (external analysis).
2. They assess your company's strategic marketing capabilities and determine what strategies can be used to increase competitive advantage (internal analysis).

The analysis itself consists of three parts. First, it analyzes the *overall marketing environment* in which your firm operates. By looking at such things as consumers (ultimate buyers), customers (intermediate buyers), competitors, and environment (political and legal factors,

Figure 3-17. *Strengths/weaknesses analysis questionnaire.*

Part I: Reviewing the Firm's Marketing Environment

Consumers

1. Who are our ultimate buyers?
2. Who or what influences them in their buying decisions?
3. What are our consumers' demographic and psychographic profiles?
4. When, where, and how do they shop for and consume our product?
5. What need(s) does our product satisfy?
6. How well does it satisfy?
7. How can we segment our target market?
8. How do prospective buyers perceive our product in their minds?
9. What are the economic conditions and expectations of our target market?
10. Are our consumers' attitudes, values, or habits changing?

Customers

11. Who are our customers—that is, intermediate buyers (wholesalers and/or retailers)?
12. Who or what influences them in their buying decisions?
13. Where are our customers located?
14. What other products do they carry?
15. What is their size, and what percentage of our total revenue does each group represent?
16. How well do they serve our target market?
17. How well do we serve their needs?
18. How much support do they give our product?
19. What made us select them and them select us?
20. How can we motivate them to work harder for us?
21. Do we need them?
22. Do they need us?
23. Do we use multiple channels?
24. Would we be better off setting up our own distribution system?
25. Should we go direct?

Competitors

26. Who are our competitors?
27. Where are they located?
28. How big are they overall and, specifically, in this product area?
29. What is their product mix?
30. Is their participation in this field growing or declining?
31. Which competitors may be leaving the field?
32. What new domestic competitors may be on the horizon?
33. What new international competitors may be on the horizon?
34. Which competitive strategies and tactics appear particularly successful or unsuccessful?
35. What new directions is the competition pursuing?

Other Relevant Environmental Components

36. What are the legal constraints affecting our marketing effort?
37. To what extent does government regulation restrict our flexibility in making marketing decisions?
38. What requirements do we have to meet?
39. What political or legal developments are looming that will improve or worsen our situation?
40. What threats or opportunities does technological progress hold in store for us?
41. How well do we keep up with technology in the lab and in the plant?
42. What broad cultural shifts are occurring that may affect our business?
43. What consequences will demographic and geographic shifts have for our business?
44. Are any changes in resource availability foreseeable?
45. How do we propose to cope with ecological constraints?

Part II: Reviewing Marketing Management Procedures and Policies

Analysis

46. Do we have an established marketing research function?
47. Do we conduct regular, systematic market analyses?
48. Do we subscribe to any regular market data service?
49. Do we test and retest carefully before we introduce a new product?
50. Are all our major marketing decisions based on solidly researched facts?

Planning

51. How carefully do we examine and how aggressively do we cope with problems, difficulties, challenges, and threats to our business?
52. How do we identify and capitalize on opportunities in our market-place?
53. What care is given to the determination of gaps in needs?
54. Do we develop clearly stated and prioritized short-term and long-term marketing objectives?
55. What are our marketing objectives?
56. Are our marketing objectives achievable and measurable?
57. Do we have a formalized annual marketing planning procedure?
58. Do we use management by objectives (MBO)?
59. What is our core strategy for achieving our marketing objectives?
60. Are we employing a push–pull strategy in dealing with our customers and consumers?
61. How aggressively are we considering or employing diversification?
62. How effectively are we segmenting our target market?
63. Are we allocating sufficient or excessive marketing resources to accomplish our marketing tasks?
64. Are our marketing resources optimally allocated to the major elements of our marketing mix?

(continued)

Figure 3-17. *Continued.*

Planning

65. How well do we tie in our marketing plan with the other functional plans of our organization?

Implementation and Control

66. Is our marketing plan truly followed or just filed away?
67. Do we continuously monitor our environment to determine the adequacy of our plan?
68. Do we use control mechanisms to ensure achievement of our objectives?
69. Do we compare planned and actual figures periodically and take appropriate measures if they differ significantly?
70. Do we systematically study the contribution and effectiveness of various marketing activities?

Organization

71. Does our firm have a high-level marketing office to analyze, plan, and oversee the implementation of our marketing effort?
72. How capable and dedicated are our marketing personnel?
73. Is there a need for more training, incentives, supervision, or evaluation?
74. Are our marketing responsibilities structured to best serve the needs of different marketing activities, products, target markets, and sales territories?
75. Does our entire organization embrace and practice the marketing concept?

Part III: Reviewing Strategy Aspects of the Marketing Mix

Product Policy

76. What is the makeup of our product mix and how well are its components selling?
77. Does it have optimal breadth and depth?
78. Should any of our products be phased out?
79. Do we carefully evaluate any negative ripple effects on the remaining product mix before we make a decision to phase out a product?
80. Have we considered modification, repositioning, and/or extension of sagging products?
81. What additions, if any, should be made to our product mix?
82. Which products are we best equipped to make ourselves and which items should we buy and resell under our own name?
83. Do we routinely check product safety and product liability?
84. Do we have a formalized and tested product recall procedure?
85. Is any recall imminent?

Pricing
86. To what degree are our prices based on cost, demand, and/or competitive considerations? 87. How would our customers react to higher or lower prices? 88. Do we use temporary price promotions and, if so, how effective are they? 89. Do we suggest resale prices? 90. How do our wholesale or retail margins and discounts compare with those of the competition?

Promotion
91. Do we state our advertising objectives clearly? 92. Do we spend enough, too much, or too little on advertising? 93. Are our ad themes and copy effective? 94. Is our media mix optimal? 95. Do we make aggressive use of sales promotion techniques?

Personal Selling and Distribution
96. Is our sales force large enough to accomplish our marketing objectives? 97. Is it optimally organized according to geographic, market, or product criteria? 98. Is it adequately trained and motivated, and characterized by high morale, ability, and effectiveness? 99. Have we optimized our distribution setup, or are there opportunities for further streamlining? 100. Is our customer service up to par?

technology), you can create a picture of external forces shaping your business situation. Second, it reviews *marketing management procedures and policies* in areas such as analysis, planning, implementation and control, and organization. This review provides a look at the internal workings of your organization as they relate to competitive fitness for strategy. Third, it examines strategy aspects of the *marketing mix* by considering policy around product, pricing, promotion, and distribution. This third part is a good integration of the way your organization is responding to external forces, providing a test of internal responsiveness to the environment and market orientation.

For best results, form a task force to provide objective answers to the questions. Some organizations obtain excellent results by calling in a knowledgeable consultant to work with the task force. If you can keep in mind that the purpose of this time-consuming analysis is to develop competitive strategies and thereby create competitive advantage, perhaps the laborious task can be justified. By using this questionnaire, you should be able to identify what makes your company or division or product outstanding; compare your overall distinctive competencies and specific strengths with those of your competitors; and, similarly, identify the weaknesses you have that can prevent you from achieving a competitive advantage. (Chapter 7 provides specific ways of incorporating these findings into competitive strategy.)

Summary of Internal Analysis

There are seven basic components of internal analysis that together will give you a picture of your organization.

1. Through **performance analysis,** you can evaluate the organization of your company or business unit. Whether you organize by function, geography, product, or market will depend on the size of your firm, your product mix, and the character of the market.

2. **Strategy analysis** is a way to examine the attitudes and directions your organization or business unit has chosen. It can answer questions such as: Is it best to use available resources? How can the business readjust product lines and marketing efforts to meet market needs?

3. **Strategic priorities analysis** gives you a more focused look at how well you are pursuing a *customer-oriented* strategy that puts the needs and wants of customers first. Learn to provide products for markets, rather than creating markets for products, in order to exploit new and profitable market opportunities.

4. **Cost analysis** has two components. First, the experience curve shows you that as cumulative production (or experience with a product) increases, costs decrease. You can assess your experience by looking at labor productivity, work methods, production efficiency, and product design and materials. Second, you should engage in *sales forecasting* in order to predict and, therefore, control future levels of sales. Both of these factors give you a way to evaluate and manage costs.

5. **Portfolio analysis** takes place in a smaller organizational unit, such as a division or strategic business unit (SBU). It helps you assess your competitive position systematically in order to determine investment levels. The three portfolio models include the BCG Growth–Share Matrix, the General Electric Business Screen, and the Arthur D. Little Matrix.

6. **Financial resource analysis** offers a range of quantitative techniques for identifying the financial implications of strategies.

The major techniques include return on investment, return on sales, cash flow, market-share analysis, marketing expense-to-sales ratio, and break-even analysis.

7. Finally, your **strengths/weaknesses analysis** summarizes both the internal and external aspects of competitive analysis. It examines your strong and weak points in comparison with those of your competitors so that you can concentrate in areas of the highest potential for market expansion.

THREE

Marketing Research and Planning

Part Three first presents a framework for a total marketing and competitor intelligence system (Chapter 4), including guidelines and how-to techniques on data collection methods (Chapter 5). The intent is not to turn you into a marketing researcher or a specialist in constructing marketing intelligence systems, but, rather, to show you the systems and inputs that you can organize within your business to assist in developing competitive strategy.

This part, then, answers the question: What do you do with all the competitive analysis and other marketing data? Chapters 6 and 7 describe a structure for the organized sorting of the information to permit systematic viewing of the material in order to develop a competitive strategy. That structure is the *strategic marketing plan*.

4

Developing a Marketing
Intelligence System

Objectives:
To enable you to

1. List the applications of *marketing intelligence systems* as they relate to developing competitive strategies
2. *Input* and *process information* within the framework of a total marketing intelligence system
3. Understand the differences between *marketing research* and a marketing intelligence system
4. Develop a *competitor intelligence system*

You cannot expect to optimize your company's marketing effort without an adequately functioning marketing intelligence system. Action without information leaves results to chance, as opposed to planning your course and controlling the outcome. Strategic marketing planning and the development of tactics require an effective and efficient information system.

Scores of U.S. companies are discovering that marketing intelligence systems can be used as potent strategic weapons. By using information in a variety of new ways, organizations find they can better support their basic products, offer new services that extend their markets, and create new products and businesses that distinguish them from their competitors.

Case Examples

Dana Dana Corporation made a tremendous rebound in its core busi-
Corporation nesses of original-equipment auto and truck parts, replacement

parts, and industrial machine components. After struggling for several years (1982 earnings plummeted 46 percent below 1980), Dana's reported 1985 earnings rose 119 percent to $112 million on sales of $2.8 billion.

Part of Dana's recovery strategy involved shifting its product mix from the highly cyclical original-equipment parts business to the stable replacement market for auto and truck parts. Further, Dana concentrated on the aftermarket by increasing its already extensive network of independent parts dealers by 50 percent, to 900. Supported by sharp pricing and a marketing strategy that focused on packaging components into coordinated repair kits, the Toledo-based company showed a rapid sales gain, and over a period of just three years tripled its market growth rate. In another display of aggressive marketing action, it also manufactured gears identical to those designed by its competitor, Clark Equipment Co., as a means of rapidly grabbing market share.

The type of aggressive strategy demonstrated by Dana relied on market surveillance to monitor changing customer needs and to react quickly to competitive moves. To achieve such quick response, Dana used a marketing intelligence system that functioned as an early warning system for decision making and action.

Owens-Corning Fiberglass Corporation In another example, Owens-Corning Fiberglass, the home insulation company, turned the information developed by in-house R&D into what has proved to be a lucrative new marketing tool. For example, when it was conducting research to develop new insulation materials several years ago, the company generated extensive data on the energy efficiency of a wide variety of house designs. It applied that information to boost sales of its home insulation products. Owens-Corning developed a computer program that uses these data to come up with energy efficiency ratings for new designs. It started to offer builders free evaluations of their building designs if they agreed to buy all of their insulation from the manufacturer and meet a minimum standard of energy efficiency.

Information, Intelligence, and Decision Making

Today's marketplace does not allow for a great deal of management by instinct and intuition. Still, many managers feel compelled to utilize that approach because they find management science techniques overwhelming and intimidating. As is often the case, a compromise between the two extremes seems to be the answer. In highly volatile environments, instinct and intelligence—in this context a management tool, not a personal trait—must be combined for effective marketing management. While it is not easy to work through the quantitative language often accompanying sensitive intelligence, the alternative of "flying by the seat of your pants" is hardly promising.

In a competitive world, scientifically based information is undoubtedly needed to support and streamline your decision making. To adequately satisfy this need, information sources and flows must be managed. This management can be accomplished by clearly defining your information requirements, which will, in turn, govern the acquisition and processing of information.

The process of building a complex marketing information system may start with this simple thought: "If I knew exactly what happened in the past, I would have a better feel for the future." This statement reveals the marketer's desire to develop a mechanism to supply meaningful and up-to-date intelligence that can improve decision making. You should be able to refer questions to a current and consolidated reservoir of information responsive to the "If I knew . . ." wishes. Such a reservoir is often referred to as a data base, and the method and process of inquiry are typical of information systems.[1]

Contrary to a common misconception, intelligence systems are not developed with the intention of replacing people with machines. Their purpose is to improve, not to replace, decision making. For example, the intelligence delivered by an information system will guide you in allocating scarce resources in a manner that will optimize profits. For obvious reasons, the cost of intelligence is justifiable only as long as it continues to improve decision making.

Such a system can accomplish the following:

- Monitor competitors' actions to develop counterstrategies.
- Identify neglected or emerging market segments.
- Identify optimum marketing mixes.
- Assist in decisions to add a product, drop a product, or modify a product.
- Develop more accurate strategic marketing plans.

Considering the wealth of material available on systems planning and development, this section can only highlight key developmental issues. It is intended mainly to give you an appreciation of what is involved in setting up and operating a marketing intelligence system.

[1] Note the distinction between information and intelligence: Information is simply an accumulation of random data, while intelligence is refined and systematized information.

Environmental Requirements for Systems Development

Get a Mandate The prime prerequisite for the development of a useful marketing intelligence system, one that cannot be bypassed, is an unequivocal *mandate* from top management. Amassing intelligence from multiple sources and forms is an intricate and continuing task that can be handled adequately only through formal efforts supported by top management. The mandate must be supported by a solid commitment of resources—people and dollars. Without such a commitment, an enormously challenging task will be turned into an exercise in frustration and will be impossible to accomplish. Systems development should not be made more expensive than it already is by illusory money-saving shortcuts and cheap substitute solutions. While not all members of your company's middle management may be in favor of an automated system, they must be made aware of top management's commitment to and support of the system.

Assemble a Team To undertake the designing and implementing of a marketing intelligence system, a fully budgeted, full-time *expert team* must be assembled. This team will expand and contract in size during the various phases of the system's development effort. The actual number of team members will also vary with the magnitude and complexity of the project. Sizable marketing intelligence systems have been set up by single individuals with the aid of data base management systems (DBMS) and consultants. Often, a small initial nucleus will have to take on the sizable burden of a cost/benefit analysis to evolve the first phase of a project before a skeptical management will lend additional support.

The high-powered members of your team should possess a multitude of talents: intimate knowledge of your business; extensive systems know-how; in-depth familiarity with computer hardware technology; considerable programming and software abilities (usually the most costly component of a system); strong analytical skills; and excellent managerial planning capabilities.

The most important members of the team are likely to be high-level representatives of the user community, those managers within your organization who will be using system outputs in their decision making. In all probability, you will want to represent this user community in person in order to make sure that all relevant information is generated by the system and that all information generated is relevant. This role, in effect, makes you the team's manager, since you will be specifying system parameters and ensuring that management gets what it needs to improve performance.

Use a DBMS In developing applications and programs for your company's marketing intelligence system, you will find that certain instructions are issued constantly. For example, some elements in your data base have to be updated regularly. Another common instruction is the development of files "keyed" on an important element such as customer name or customer type.

A *data base management system* (DBMS) incorporates these generic operations without requiring you to write a complex code into each of your applications every time a specific operation has to be executed. With the use of a DBMS, a considerable amount of programming cost can be saved and efficiencies gained in developing applications.

Prepare for But the very fact that you can gain efficiencies in program develop-
Programming ment by utilizing a DBMS can easily trap you into allocating too few other programming resources to your project. Despite all the advantages of a DBMS, you cannot expect it to be self-programming. Neither can you expect that a systems project such as your marketing intelligence system will work well if only one or two individuals are assigned the task of programming it.

In allocating resources, you therefore have to use managerial judgment. For example, if only one person is working on the programs, what happens to the project if he or she quits? If only a limited number of individuals are involved and you cannot afford to lose them, you may be placing yourself in a disadvantageous negotiating position. Also, if you personally do not possess the appropriate technical know-how, you are at the programmers' mercy and will lose control of the project.

Allow Time Another prerequisite for successful systems development is adequate time, a difficult and taxing aspect because management demands endless progress reports and diagrams as tangible evidence of the team's productivity. (Of course, there are techniques for staving off management's anxious expectations; for example, dividing your project into phases or building blocks and delivering them individually rather than in one complete package.) You should, however, realize that line management may be impatient for results and expect miracles in minutes. So you and the system developers have to sell your emerging marketing intelligence system to your management and colleagues with great creativity and skill.

Implementing the System

Specifying System Parameters Once you have secured a mandate for a systems development effort and assembled the project team, the arduous task of *system specification* must begin. This process encompasses several stages and covers the entire scope of your project.

Stage One

Your team must first *determine what your prospective system is supposed to accomplish.* The answer is usually, and unfortunately, rather vague: to provide management with concise, timely, and sensitive marketing intelligence. While the process by which this question is translated into a meaningful information mechanism is quite time-consuming, it is, nonetheless, necessary.

Just as successful marketing efforts begin with the identification of customer wants, the primary guiding factor of your systems design must be what users want. Frequent meetings and discussions with a variety of users are highly recommended. This interaction lets you explore questions such as:

- What types of decisions do the users make?
- What are the quantifiable and nonquantifiable elements of these decisions?

You should then develop a data element dictionary that specifies each element's significance as well as its current source, and cross-reference it to other elements. It may well be worthwhile to put this dictionary on the computer for future sorting, listing, and updating.

It is a good idea to begin your investigation by identifying critical elements in each of the marketing variable areas. Figure 4–1 illustrates the interrelationships among these system inputs, their processing, and your system's outputs. Note in the figure that input comes from a number of primary sources: product information, customer information, promotion plans, accounting data, competitor analysis, and environment and industry factors. Combined, these sources provide the unified data base of the marketing intelligence system. Later,

Figure 4-1. *Marketing intelligence systems flow.*

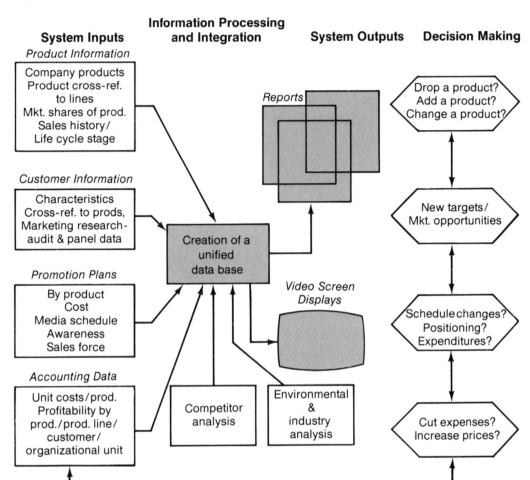

you will be able to process this information and sort out the data into an efficient external analysis delineating customer, competitor, industry, and environmental factors. It also shows how questions posed in the different decision-making areas can be addressed with the help of system outputs.

The capture of marketing information has to be orderly and systematic, so you must make a thorough review of your system's inputs:

- Are your sales order forms standardized?
- Can their content be readily transferred to the computer?
- Are they filled out properly?
- Do they include all relevant information?

- Can the results of market studies be easily transferred to this new data base?
- How are the inputs updated in a regular and consistent fashion?

A second group of questions should be asked:

- What constitutes concise, timely, and sensitive marketing intelligence?
- Do we have any today?
- Where?
- How long have we had it?
- Why isn't it enough?
- What is wrong with it?
- Is any part of it salvageable?
- If so, which part?
- Can it be adapted for our current and projected needs or do we have to start from scratch?
- Do our competitors have it?
- What is their source?
- What benefits do they derive from it?
- How much time did they spend in developing it?

Sifting through all of your company's information sources and attempting integration may prove to be a task that is not worth the effort. Rather, your project team would be well advised to concentrate just on major sources of information: current accounting systems that provide sales by territory, product, or customer type, as well as unit costs; and marketing research studies that contain product, promotion, distribution, pricing, and customer information.

It is the primary job of your team to consider how these sources can be integrated and enhanced. Top management has authorized your marketing intelligence system project because it cannot assimilate the varied and scattered bits of information available within your firm, and looks for intelligence instead of information.

Stage Two

Although defining the structure of your data base is a technical undertaking, it must be guided by sound business sense. Toward this end, you must *have a basic and general understanding of how marketing decisions should ideally be made in your industry:* Which factors should be taken into account, who should be responsible for data

generation and updating, and what stages are involved? Different industries require different strategy parameters and access to different
categories of information.

Stage Three

Specific organizational considerations will also influence your data
base structure. How is your firm organized: along product lines, by
customer type, or geographically? Is it structured along several lines
that foster intracompany competition? What information is to be restricted to use by single organizational units, and how will the security of the information be ensured?

Becoming The importance of any marketing intelligence system does not lie in
Operational the elegance of its logic or the harmony of the hardware in the computer center. Rather, its value is measured by its use by managers in
their decision-making activities. Therefore, high priority should be
given to getting your system into the mainstream of your company's
marketing management process.

If you were to market the system as a product, making it operational would be analogous to making a packaging decision. A poor
packaging strategy can damage the chances of a fine product. You
must package and deliver your system in such a manner that it will
be perceived as adding value and substance to the current marketing
decision-making process.

A marketing intelligence system is not supposed to inundate managers with reams of computer printouts but, rather, to synthesize variable activities to facilitate managerial decision making. Quite likely,
your firm will want to replace the flow of paper with *electronic information stations.* They are information sources—normally a video
screen hooked up to a remote computer with an input device—that
managers can use to obtain specific data. Hard-copy reports (computer printouts) are generally restricted to special requests.

The delivery mechanisms can be more or less costly and sophisticated, depending on your management's priorities.

- Will individual managers be allowed only to "read" available
  information, or will they be permitted to simulate alternative
  marketing scenarios?
- When will a manager be given access, and to what type of information?

• What types of hard-copy reports will be produced and where?

• Will managers be charged for their use of the system?

System Once your marketing intelligence system has been integrated into the
Maintenance mainstream of your marketing management process, requests for improvements in the level of data capture, data manipulation, and report
output are almost inevitable. Ideally, you will have anticipated these
requests—though not in precise detail—when you first designed your
system. If you decided on a high level of enhancements, you may
have selected, for example, a DBMS to accommodate different "cuts"
(presentation modes) of the data base or develop video screen reports
quickly.

In addition to enhancements, a development staff must be ready to
correct system "bugs." For instance, averages that have not been
computed accurately because the logic is incorrect in the software
may not be detected until the system is actually in use. Improvements
are very often required before a system can be considered operation-
ally useful. These improvements can bring in their wake considerable
modifications of your programming software and many require additional hardware as well. Systems building, like marketing itself, is a
discipline fraught with unknowns. To improve your odds, you should
follow the principles of *flexibility* and *contingency planning*. Flexibility is critical in software development and hardware design, since
few, if any, systems are complete on the first pass. When your system is operational, its developers must establish user liaisons, keep
alert for possible system "bugs" and problems, and provide remedies
as they occur. For preventing—or, at least, reducing—a variety of
operating problems, contingency planning cannot be stressed enough.

Your project team must consider many hundreds of "what if" situations in order to protect your system against potentially disastrous
consequences. Backups must be planned for, because Murphy's Law
("If anything can go wrong, it will") is a way of life in systems
development.

What You No marketing intelligence system can replace competent and effective
Can Expect line management, but it can help you run your business more effi-
From Your ciently and measure performance on a day-to-day basis. It should also
System be used to track progress toward long-term strategic goals and alert
you to significant structural and performance changes in your business as well as relevant environmental developments. Table 4-1 summarizes what your system can and cannot do for you.

Table 4-1. *Capabilities and Limitations of a Marketing Intelligence System.*

Can Do	Cannot Do
1. Track progress toward long-term strategic goals	1. Replace managerial judgment
2. Aid in day-to-day decision making	2. Provide all the information necessary to make an infallible decision
3. Establish a common language between marketing and "back office" operations	3. Work successfully without management support
4. Consider the impact of multiple environments on a strategy	4. Work successfully without confidence
5. Automate many labor-intensive processes, thus effecting huge cost savings	5. Work successfully without being adequately maintained and responsive to the user community
6. Serve as an early warning device for operations or businesses not on target	
7. Help determine how to allocate resources to achieve marketing goals	
8. Deliver information in a timely and useful manner	
9. Help service customers	
10. Enable you to improve overall performance through better planning and control	

A well-designed, customized marketing intelligence system will help you meet a number of objectives, such as:

1. Timely, accurate, and complete information for control over your marketing activities.
2. An early warning system indicating developing problems.
3. Adequate data on unusual problems to permit appropriate remedial action.
4. The necessary marketing and economic data to interpret financial results correctly.
5. Sufficient information to allow for the optimum allocation of human, financial, and material resources.

To satisfy these objectives and make your system operational and useful, you should develop it with a number of guidelines in mind, such as those presented in Table 4-2.

Table 4-2. *Guidelines for Systems Design.*

Do	Don't
1. Obtain top management support	1. Try to get grass-roots support for your system without top management support
2. Involve system users in the design of the system	2. Design and develop a system without strong user involvement
3. Identify information needs	3. Design your system without a clear picture of information requirements
4. Assemble a multitalented project team	4. Build a system with a limited resource base
5. Clarify the limits of the system	5. Try to develop a system that will facilitate every marketing decision your firm will ever make
6. Specify standard inputs and outputs of the system	6. Attempt to cope with a variety of nonstandard inputs and ad hoc output requests

Marketing Research Versus a Marketing Intelligence System

If you refer back to Figure 4-1, the diagram of a marketing intelligence system, you'll note that marketing research is listed within the system's input box identified as Customer Information. Marketing research is a vital form of input into a marketing intelligence system, but it is not a substitute for total marketing intelligence. At times there can be misunderstanding and legitimate confusion between the two systems. (Chapter 5 presents a detailed discussion of marketing research.) For your purposes and to clearly distinguish for senior management the differences between marketing research and a marketing intelligence system, see Table 4-3.

Developing a Competitor Intelligence System

Competitor Analysis The urgency for competitor intelligence and the magnitude of the activity earn it a distinct place in marketing intelligence. Perhaps this prominence is best described by the monitoring activities of four U.S. companies overseas. IBM, RCA, 3M, and Corning Glass have set up offices in Japan to monitor competitor activities and emerging tech-

Table 4-3. *Difference Between Marketing Research and a Marketing Intelligence System.*

Marketing Research	Marketing Intelligence System
1. Emphasizes handling external information	1. Handles both internal and external data
2. Is concerned with solving problems	2. Is concerned with preventing, as well as solving, problems
3. Operates in a fragmented, intermittent fashion on a project-to-project basis	3. Operates continuously and is a system
4. Tends to focus on past information	4. Tends to be future-oriented
5. Is not computer-based	5. Is a computer-based process
6. Is one source of information input for a marketing intelligence system	6. Includes other subsystems besides marketing research

nologies. According to Leonard Fuld, the head of Information Data Search Inc. (a fast-growing marketing intelligence firm), approximately 50,000 electronic bugging devices are now hidden in the offices and meeting rooms of U.S. corporations, with 10,000 more planted every year, usually by rival corporations. In addition, estimates show that corporate spending on electronic surveillance is already at $50 million a year and is growing by 30 percent annually.

This information provides just one example of how ferociously businesses are working to get information on competitors. But bugging competitors' meeting rooms is not the only method for obtaining such intelligence. The case example shows how one company, Texas Instruments, used competitor intelligence as part of an overall marketing intelligence system to gain competitive advantage.

Case Example

Texas Instruments, Incorporated Texas Instruments, Incorporated (T.I.), the large microchip manufacturer, made a phenomenal turnaround after a period of autocratic management and erratic finances. For example, in 1986 there was a $145-million loss in revenues of $4.6 billion, the result of a disastrous move into home computers. The lack of competitive analysis was reflected in a miscalculation of the market's need for a low-priced computer, inadequate knowledge of the competitors' strategies, and misjudgment of the effects of the downturn in the computer industry. Finally, under a new president, Jerry R. Junkins, the company began to plan for getting back on a growth track.

Under Junkins' leadership, T.I. began to apply greater sensitivity to external and internal analysis, with particular emphasis on competitor analysis. Attempting to attract customers to its custom-designed chips, T.I. decided to battle the Japanese head to head in high-volume, dynamic RAM markets when most other U.S. competitors were retreating. This competitive attitude infused the company with new vitality, reflected in the following aggressive strategies:

- T.I. *guaranteed* monthly shipping quotas to customers that wanted to institute just-in-time inventory programs. By 1987, it had already signed 50 such deals.
- It *innovated* by working on a system that would simulate a customer's proprietary chip design, test it, and deliver the results overnight.
- T.I. counted on a string of new product successes. Researchers developed a single-chip version of a powerful processor tailored for artificial intelligence (AI) applications. It also produced the first memory chip capable of storing 4 million bits of data—four times the capacity of the most advanced Japanese counterparts up to that point in time.
- Consistent with its aggressive, fighting-back attitude, T.I. filed suits charging Japan's eight leading producers with infringing on patents with computer memory chips. Next, it asked the U.S. International Trade Commission to ban imports of the offending chips, including those in finished goods.

We can review T.I.'s competitor analysis as a step-by-step process that led to its strategies:

1. **Competitors' size**—categorized by market share, growth rate, and profitability.
2. **Competitors' objectives**—both quantitative (sales, profits, ROI) and nonquantitative (technology innovation; market leadership; and international, national, and regional distribution).
3. **Competitors' strategies**—analyzed by internal strategies (speed of product innovation, manufacturing capabilities, delivery, marketing expertise) and external strategies (distribution network, technical field support, market coverage, and aggressiveness in defending or building market share).
4. **Competitors' organization**—examined by structure, culture, systems, and people.
5. **Competitors' cost structure**—examined by how efficiently they can compete, the ease or difficulty of exiting a market, and their attitudes toward short-term versus long-term profitability.

6. **Competitors' overall strengths and weaknesses**—identified by areas of vulnerability to attack as well as areas of strength that can be bypassed or neutralized.

Overall, T.I.'s ability to develop aggressive strategies was based on a comprehensive marketing intelligence system that served as a "window" through which to develop a clear image of the actions needed to sustain a competitive advantage.

Competitor Intelligence Model Figure 4-2 illustrates a model to show you how to organize the data coming into the system from diverse sources. Responsibility for the competitor intelligence model sits squarely on the shoulders of the marketing executive or any executive in charge of devising competitive strategies. In order to understand the flow of data, you need to examine each section of the model.

Collecting Field Data. At the top of the list is the *sales force,* which represents one of the most valuable sources of competitor intelligence. When salespeople are trained to observe key events and oriented to believe their input fits into the competitive strategy process, these men and women are first-line reporters of competitor actions. Communications with salespeople can be maintained by periodically traveling with them, by conducting formal debriefing sessions to gain detailed insights behind the competitor actions they observed, and by creating or expanding a section of the sales-force call reports to record key competitor information.

The other sources are more obvious areas of competitor information; but pay special attention to reverse engineering. This is a procedure whereby technical people and other product developers tear down a product and examine its components for methods of production, quality, and other details. In addition, a purchasing agent and financial analyst may cost out duplicating the product and determine financial considerations in order to provide insights into the competitors' operations.

Collecting Published Data. There are numerous sources of published information, from small-town newspapers, in which a competitor's presence makes front-page headlines, to large-city or national newspapers and magazines that provide financial and product information about competitors. Monitoring want ads provides clues to the types of personnel and skills being sought. Also, speeches by senior management of competing companies provide valuable insights into other firms' future plans, industry trends, and strategies under consideration. At times it is astonishing how much sensitive information is

Figure 4-2. *Functions of a competitor intelligence system.*

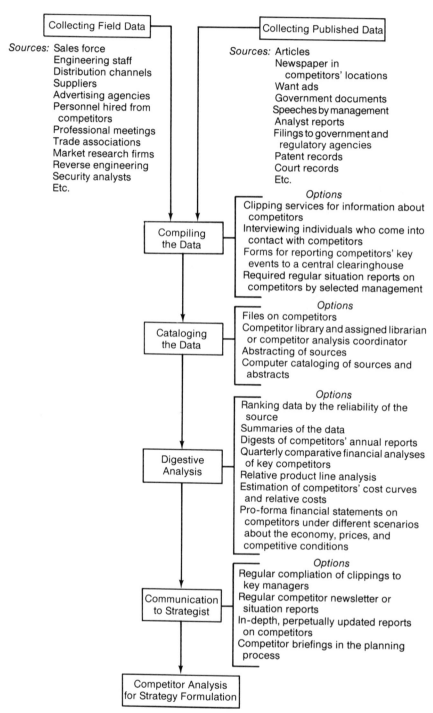

Source: Michael E. Porter, *Competitive Strategy* (New York: Free Press, 1980), p. 73.

provided in speeches that are given at a variety of trade shows and professional meetings and that subsequently get into print.

Compiling the Data.   Additional marketing intelligence sources are described in Figure 4-2, and the data from these should be noted on forms. For example, special forms should be developed for key events, such as trade shows, so that each individual attending the event can observe and report accurately on competitors' activities, pricing, new products, or special promotions.

Cataloging the Data.   The varied sources of data come together at this point in the system. Depending on the facilities available to you, the data should be organized and maintained by a secretary or, more appropriately, by a marketing analyst, manager of marketing intelligence, marketing research department, or librarian.

Digestive Analysis.   The first four procedures are mechanical ways of collecting, compiling, and cataloging data. The analytical and creative aspects now apply as you begin to synthesize the data to detect opportunities. It is appropriate to call in key functional managers from finance, manufacturing, and product development to assist in the analysis.

Communication to Strategist.   There are various approaches to communicate the synthesized information: oral reports at weekly staff meetings and the increasingly popular competitor newsletter.

Competitor Analysis for Strategy Formulation.   As has been mentioned elsewhere, the whole purpose of internal and external analysis and the entire competitor intelligence system is to develop competitive strategies.

Applications of the Competitor and Marketing Intelligence Systems

The broad purpose of competitor intelligence is to provide accurate information on your competitors' strengths and weaknesses so that you can attack those weaknesses. By focusing on the weaknesses of competitors' service, product, performance, price, promotion, distribution, or poorly served market segments, you dislocate and unbalance the competition. You thereby gain your objectives without costly market confrontations that may result in using your resources with little or no gain.

While it is in your best interest to be the driving force behind installing a marketing intelligence system and for gathering competitor intelligence, your most important role is to know where to apply the information.

Case Example

Honeywell Inc. Honeywell Inc., a Minneapolis-based company doing $6.6 billion in sales, undertook a strategic withdrawal from the computer business in 1986. The scorecard after 31 years showed that IBM had a 71 percent share of the large-frame market and Honeywell, just 3 percent; the balance was spread among the other manufacturers. Honeywell's managers decided to redirect its efforts toward areas of strength by concentrating its talents and capital in factory automation, where its 100-year-old expertise in controls gave it a solid chance for leadership.

Honeywell's strategic withdrawal was based on good judgment and industry trends. In factory automation, currently a business trend, it has a strong position. In 1985, Honeywell sold $1 billion worth of automated manufacturing systems, much of it to customers in the process industries such as oil refining, chemicals, pulp, and paper. Honeywell hopes to increase sales to $2 billion by 1990 by selling to automotive and electronics manufacturers that are beginning to automate. This segment of the business is projected at $10 billion a year and is growing by 15 percent annually.

Strategic withdrawal or expansion can be viewed through (1) market segmentation analysis, (2) product life cycle analysis, and (3) new product development, all of which have a foundation of solid marketing intelligence and competitor intelligence.

For *market segmentation analysis,* marketing intelligence system output can be used to

- Identify segments as demographic, geographic, and psychographic (behavior and life style), and by product attributes usage rates.
- Determine common buying factors within segments.
- Monitor segments by measurable characteristics—for example, customer size, growth rate, and location.
- Assess potential new segments by common sales and distribution channels.
- Evaluate segments to protect your position against competitor inroads.
- Determine the optimum marketing mix for protecting or attacking segments.

System output can be used in *product life cycle analysis* at the introduction stage to

- Determine if the product is reaching the intended audience segment and what the initial customer reactions to the offering are.

- Analyze the marketing mix and its various components for possible modifications—for example, product performance, backup service, and additional warranties.
- Monitor for initial product positioning to prospects—that is, to determine if customer perceptions match intended product performance.
- Identify possible points of entry by competitors in such areas as emerging or poorly served segments, product or packaging innovations, aggressive pricing, concentrated or innovative promotion, distribution incentives, and add-on services.
- Evaluate distribution channels for market coverage, shipping schedules, customer service, effective communications, and technical support.
- Compare initial financial results to budget.

Output can be used at the growth stage to

- Analyze product purchases by market segment.
- Identify emerging market segments and any new product applications.
- Conduct a competitor analysis and determine counterstrategies by type of competitor.
- Adjust the marketing mix for emphasis on specific components— for example, change in product positioning and shifting from a pull-through advertising strategy to a push advertising program through distributors.
- Decide on use of penetration pricing to protect specific market segments.
- Provide new incentives for the sales force.
- Monitor financial results against plan.
- Provide feedback on product usage and performance information to R&D, manufacturing, and technical service for use in developing product life cycle extension strategies.

At the maturity stage, system output can be used in product life cycle analysis to

- Evaluate differentiation possibilities to avoid facing a commodity type situation.
- Determine how, when, and where to execute product life cycle extension strategies—for example, finding new applications for the product to new market segments.
- Expand product usage among existing market segments or find new users for the product's basic materials.

- Determine potential for product line extensions.
- Continue to monitor on a competitor-by-competitor basis threats on market segments and threats to total market share and use competitor intelligence to develop strategies to protect market share.
- Evaluate financial performance, particularly profitability (if all went well you should be in a cash cow stage of the cycle).

And, finally, output can be used at the decline stage to

- Evaluate options such as focusing on a specific market niche, extending the market, forming joint venture with manufacturers or distributors, and locating export opportunities.
- Determine where to prune the product line to obtain the best profitability.
- Monitor financial performance as a means of fine tuning parts of the marketing mix.
- Identify additional spin-off opportunities through product applications, service, or distribution networks that could create a new product life cycle.

For *new product development,* marketing intelligence system output can be used as a preliminary screening device to

- Identify potential market segments as an idea generator for new product development.
- Determine the marketability of the product.
- Assess the extent of competitors' presence by specific market segments.
- Develop a product introduction strategy from test market to roll-out.
- Develop financial performance.

5

Marketing Research Techniques

Objectives:
To enable you to

1. Describe the characteristics and applications of the three basic methods of *primary data collection:* experimentation, observation, and interview
2. Compare the strengths and weaknesses of the three principal *interview research strategies:* in-person, telephone, and mail

3. List the potential applications of *focus group* interviews
4. Identify the *marketing mix factors* that affect a product's image and how an image can be researched
5. Identify the variety of sources for *secondary information*

Marketing research provides the necessary input and feedback to reduce the risks in decision making when marketing intelligence is used in planning competitive strategies. Such research is invaluable during every phase of the marketing process, from the inception of a new product or service idea through the stages of its evolution and market life, and, finally, to the decision to discontinue the product or service because it is no longer profitable.

As corporations grow more complex and marketing decision makers become further and further removed from the ultimate buyer, marketing research is the primary tool for bridging the communications gap and enabling managers to stay in touch with their markets. Better and more successful strategy decisions can be made when they are based on facts rather than hunch. These facts are the product of marketing research, which acts as a listening post between your company and the consumer. Marketing research can improve the effectiveness of your marketing decisions by providing accurate information about consumer needs or problems on which you can base your recommendations.

Marketing research is the systematic gathering, processing, and analyzing of relevant data to solve your firm's short- and long-term competitive problems, as well as to clarify its potential marketing opportunities. Ideally, your marketing research efforts should be *systematic, comprehensive,* and *objective.* They should be systematic because an unplanned undertaking cannot be interpreted quantitatively. They should be thorough and comprehensive because having only some of the truth can be misleading. And they should be objective—that is, reproducible and aimed at discovering the truth—because they are worthless if they set out to prove a preconceived idea.

However, the ideal is often not attained because of budget and time constraints. Some marketing research projects have to be completed rather quickly, and this haste severely limits their thoroughness. Similarly, insufficient funds allocated for marketing research limit the amount and quality of work that can be done.

Types of Data

You can get the data needed for marketing research either by turning to existing information *(secondary data)* or by generating your own *(primary data).* In general, a marketing researcher should try to avoid a primary study for reasons of time and cost. Instead, many marketing questions can be answered satisfactorily by utilizing secondary data. Only if this avenue proves to be inadequate should you consider primary research.

The distinction between the two types of data is a matter of purpose and control. Secondary data have been collected for another purpose; you have no control over their gathering, processing, and interpretation. Therefore, you have to check carefully to see how applicable they are in your case. The unit of investigation may have been different (for example, families instead of households); the sample size may have been insufficient; the wrong people may have been queried; the questions may have been leading; the data may now be obsolete. Even so, a thorough review of available secondary data is a must before you undertake a primary research project, because these data may provide all the answers you need. For instance, if you have to find out who the heavy users of powdered detergents are and where they are located, it would be unwise to go out and collect your own data at great expense. Data of this type are readily available from commercial suppliers. Even if you want to know who your own ultimate buyers are, you don't necessarily need to generate your own information; a professional data-collection organization may already have this information in its files.

Generating Primary Data

Of course, if you come up with "what if" questions, secondary data are no longer useful. They cannot address the issues of new product information, reactions to advertising, the impact of alternative pricing approaches, or the effect of a package change, among others. It then becomes unavoidable to generate your own data for the specific research purpose at hand. To help you do so, you have three major methods at your disposal that have been refined to a high degree of sophistication: experimentation, observation, and interviewing (Table 5-1).

Experimen- Experimental research aims to discover the impact of changes in an
tation independent variable on a dependent variable to help you optimize your marketing mix. It involves the creation of artificial situations in which all variables except the one to be tested are kept constant. This one experimental variable is deliberately manipulated to test its effect on the outcome, usually measured in terms of sales. An example of an experiment is a test-marketing setup in which different prices are charged for the same product in different cities to test the direct effect of price on sales.

To be meaningful, experimentation requires controlled situations, either in the field or in the laboratory. If influences from extraneous, uncontrollable variables (for example, dealer display) are found, the data will have to be adjusted accordingly. It is always advisable to employ *control groups,* in which no changes are introduced, to ensure the reliability of the experimental research. Each experiment must be designed and tailored to meet the specific needs of your project.

Observation Should you want to know the reactions of consumers to your product, packaging, advertising, or some other aspect of your marketing mix, observation can supply you with the input. Researcher and marketing manager could personally watch a test in order to get a firsthand look at the consumer's reaction to an intended change before implementing it on a large scale.

Observation involves recording the behavior of people or the re-

Table 5-1. *Highlights of the Three Basic Methods of Primary Data Collection.*

Why	How	Where	Data Collection Techniques	Examples	Checkpoints
Experimental Research					
To understand the association between two variables that may suggest a causal relationship	Manipulate the independent variable Measure the dependent variable Control certain extraneous variables and randomize as many others as possible	In a laboratory situation In field experiments	Personal interviews Telephone interviews Mail surveys Group discussions Depth interviews	Assess the effect of a promotional campaign Test the effect of product trial on future purchase behavior Determine the effectiveness of a TV commercial Select the most appropriate subscription plan for a magazine Study the effect of a consumer education program on product sales	Careful preplanning Rigorous problem definition Precise identification and definition of variables Use of control groups Adjustment for errors due to extraneous variables
Observation Research					
To observe and record consumer behavioral responses to marketing stimuli	Set up situation for consumer to take action Station observers or observational mechanisms to record consumer reactions	In the marketplace Under simulated field conditions in a laboratory-type situation	Watching and recording by trained interviewers or technicians Electromechanical equipment such as tachistoscopes (T scopes),	Conduct periodic store audits to track brand shares of a product Observe customer shopping patterns in a supermarket meat department	Careful preplanning Rigorous problem definition Simulation of test conditions as close as possible to actual market conditions

198

Interview Research

Purpose	Process	Setting	Techniques	Applications	Precautions
	Evaluate results		videotape recorders, audimeters, and psychogalvanometers (lie detectors)	Record pupil movements in a print copy test Evaluate prototype toys by observing children at play with them	Checking of customers to make sure they understand the tasks you want them to perform
To measure and understand consumer behavior, attitudes, or images related to a given marketing problem	Collect data from target consumers Compile data Analyze data Interpret results Conclude and recommend action plan	In marketplace with relevant consumers In the laboratory	Personal interviews Telephone interviews Mail surveys Group discussions Depth interviews	Collect demographic data on current customers Determine usage rates of company products Determine image of corporation among product nonusers Discuss merits and shortcomings of products available in a given market	Careful preplanning Rigorous problem definition Checking to make sure correct consumer group is surveyed Limitation of interviews to brief period Elimination of bias in key questions

sults of this behavior. It can sometimes be done without the knowledge or consent of the subjects, thus allowing them to behave uninhibitedly. The content of an observation can be recorded either by a person or by an electronic device. For example, you could personally observe the behavior displayed by consumers in selecting toys. In contrast, a surveillance camera or a psychogalvanometer (lie detector) are examples of electronic devices used to record consumer reactions.

Auditing and visual assessment, often referred to as ''looking'' research, is another kind of observation. By generating a count of the merchandise most recently moved through the nation's supermarkets, observation research gives you a capsule overview of the competitive framework for your product at a particular point in time.

As in experimentation—which borrows heavily from observation and interview—observation can be carried out either in the marketplace (traffic counts) or in a laboratory setting (pupillometric, or eye movement, studies). Whatever the circumstances, you use observation to find out what people do. Its big limitation is, of course, that it cannot tell you *why* they do what they do.

Interviewing   Interviewing is asking questions of selected respondents who are considered to possess necessary information and to be representative of the group under investigation. Such survey research can be conducted formally or informally, can be structured or unstructured, and can be disguised. If it is informal, the results cannot be extended to the underlying population. If it is structured, a formal list of questions (questionnaire) is used. And if it is disguised, the true purpose of the research is concealed from the interviewee. An example of an informal, unstructured, undisguised questioning technique is the focus group interview (see the later section in this chapter), while a mail questionnaire is a formal, structured, disguised technique.

These various characteristics explain why interviewing is by far the most widely and most frequently used approach in primary data generation. It is not as cumbersome and expensive as experimentation, and it digs beneath the observed behavioral surface in perception and motivation.

In order to get at the truth, however, a great deal of skill is required in executing a survey, because it is subject to even more human bias than either experimentation or observation. Bias on the part of both the interviewer and the respondent add to any inherent defects in the wording or sequence of questions.

Interview research can be conducted over a long period of time in order to monitor changes in your competitive environment, or it can be limited to a one-time snapshot of your market—highlighting, for instance, the impact of a particular advertising campaign. Like the other two methods, interviewing can be carried out either in the field (in supermarkets, shopping malls, or homes) or in the laboratory (inviting selected consumers into a research facility). A key rule in interviewing is to ask only necessary questions, because every additional question takes time, increasing the risk of consumer refusal. You should, therefore, refrain from asking questions that interest you personally but contribute little to the understanding of the subject at hand.

Three Approaches

Depending on the nature of your research task, the amount of money and time available, and the accessibility of the target group to be surveyed, conclusive interview research may take one of three forms:

1. **In-person interview:** Interviewer questions respondent face to face (a) in the privacy of the interviewee's home or office, or (b) in a central location by intercepting the consumer in a shopping mall or on the street.
2. **Telephone interview:** Interviewer conducts survey over telephone (a) in a local market, or (b) nationwide over WATS lines.
3. **Mail interview:** Survey questionnaire is mailed to selected respondents and returned by mail.

In choosing one approach over another, you have to look not only at your budget and time frame, but also at your likely rate of response and your response bias. The rate of response is the ratio of those who respond to the total number of people contacted. It is subject to a possible nonresponse bias resulting from the fact that the people who are not responding may differ substantially from those who do. If this discrepancy is significant, a question may arise as to whether the results are representative.

Response bias, on the other hand, is the distortion inherent in the answers given due to misinterpretation of the questions or deliberate misrepresentation. You will want to keep the rate of return as high, and the response bias as low, as the constraints of time and budget will allow.

Table 5-2 represents a comparison of the three interviewing techniques on the basis of a variety of criteria. It is designed to assist you in examining their relative merits and choosing the approach best suited to your particular research objectives.

Table 5-2. *Comparison of Relative Strengths and Weaknesses of the Three Principal Interviewing Techniques.*

	In Person	Telephone	Mail
Flexibility in data collection	Most flexible; can use visual aids, depth probes, various rating scales; can even alter direction of interview while still in progress	Fairly flexible, although visual aids and extensive rating scales cannot be used	Least flexible, but pictures and rating scales that do not require investigator assistance may be incorporated into a questionnaire; too many open-ended questions reduce response rate
Quantity of data obtainable	Fairly extensive data may be obtained, subject to respondent–investigator rapport	Generally limited by short duration of interview	Long questionnaires adversely affect response rate and are not recommended
Speed of data collection	Process of personally contacting respondents is time-consuming	Data available almost instantaneously; ideal for ad-recall and similar studies	Delays result from slow and scattered returns
Expense of data collection	Generally most expensive	Less expensive than in-person interview	Least expensive, depending on return rate
Investigator bias	Respondent–investigator interaction may significantly modify responses	Investigator bias, while present, is less serious than with in-person interview	No investigator bias
Lead time for respondents	Need to respond quickly to questions may result in incomplete or inaccurate data	Same problem as with in-person interviews	Respondents have time to think things over and do calculations to provide more detailed and accurate information
Sampling considerations	In-person interviews require detailed addresses of all respondents; problem may sometimes be overcome by using area and systematic sampling procedures	Problems resulting from imperfections in telephone directory may be controlled to some extent by using "random digit dialing" or "add 1" procedures	Mailing list is required; samples generated from unreliable lists introduce substantial selection bias

Nonresponse bias	Refusal rate is generally somewhat higher than with telephone interview	Callbacks can reduce nonresponse bias and are fairly inexpensive	Nonresponse bias could be very serious in cases where those who return the questionnaire differ substantially from those who do not
Sequence bias	No serious problem; investigator can record any changes respondents wish to make to answers to previous questions as interview progresses	Same problem as with in-person interviews	Respondents can see entire questionnaire and modify their responses to individual questions
Anonymity of responses	In-person, eye-to-eye contact may stifle frank interchange on sensitive issues	Obtaining frank responses is a problem, although less so than in in-person interview situations	Frank responses on sensitive issues can be obtained by guaranteeing anonymity
Identity of respondents	Easily available for future reference	Name and telephone number are available for future reference	May not be available in many cases; questionnaire may even have been filled out by someone other than intended respondent
Field control	Difficult and expensive	Centralized control is no problem; better-quality data result	Generally not a problem
Difficulty of reaching certain segments of population	The very rich are hard to reach, and investigators dodge very poor areas; most working men and women cannot be reached during normal working hours	Non-telephone-owning households cannot be reached; most working men and women are unavailable unless interviews are conducted in the evening and on weekends	Individuals with a low literacy level cannot be reached
Geographic coverage	Generally limited by cost considerations	WATS facilities permit wide coverage at reasonable cost	Geographic coverage is no problem
Investigator assistance	Easily available to explain instructions, provide help with unfamiliar terms and research procedures	Available, although not to the same extent as in in-person interviews	Not available; instructions may be misinterpreted; incomplete answers or blanks are fairly common

In-Person Interviewing: Flexibility with Depth

In-person interviewing produces not only a relatively high rate of response, but also an unusually high proportion of usable responses. It is the *most flexible* of the techniques, in that it can respond spontaneously to the unique conditions of each interview and also incorporate a variety of visual cues such as environmental situation, facial expressions, gestures, and body language. It allows for follow-up questions to clarify and specify answers given. Once a respondent has agreed to be interviewed in this mode, a considerable amount of time can be spent and extensive information can be obtained.

On the other hand, in-person interviews are the *most expensive* questioning technique and can be rather time-consuming to complete because they involve travel. Unless the interviews are conducted in the evening or on weekends, most respondents would necessarily be unemployed or retired persons. Geographic coverage is obviously limited by travel time and expense. Rising urban crime rates discourage many people from letting strangers into their homes.

The influence that the interviewer could potentially exert over the interviewee (intentionally or inadvertently) can be moderated by careful training and instructions. To prevent investigators from cheating or falsifying reports, supervisors can verify a certain percentage of questionnaires by contacting respondents.

All things considered, in-person interviewing is, in most instances, the best research method because it combines flexibility with depth and visual monitoring.

Telephone Queries: Growing in Popularity

If the nature of your study does not require consumer exposure to exhibits or product samples (for example, attitude surveys), you may be able to interview by phone. In contrast to in-person interviewing, in which control and supervision of the data-gathering process are difficult and expensive, calling interviewees from a central location provides a great deal of control.

Since about 95 percent of the households in the United States have telephones, lack of accessibility is not a serious problem. For various reasons, however, an increasing number of residential hookups are not listed. This difficulty can be dealt with through random dialing.

Phone interviewing is the *least time-consuming* of the three questioning techniques. It is generally less costly than face-to-face interviewing, even though it remains more expensive than mail (depending on the response rate). Outgoing WATS lines allow unlimited calls in a specified geographic area for a fixed fee. Interviewers can conduct the survey while sitting at a computer terminal, read the questions from the screen, and type in the responses directly. This direct input eliminates the time-consuming task of coding and keypunching questionnaire data.

Using the telephone, you can survey a relatively large number of people within a short period of time. This makes the telephone query particularly suitable for measuring customer reaction to your product and that of a competitor. With telephone interviewing, the response rate is good and callbacks are easy. Also, travel is eliminated and interviewer bias is reduced. However, you cannot ask intricate or intimate questions over the phone without the risk of people hanging up on you.

There is obviously a limit to the amount of information you can obtain in this way, since the maximum amount of time a person is willing to spend on the phone with an interviewer has been found to be 30 minutes; it may actually be considerably shorter, depending on the subject matter. Respondents may give incomplete or inaccurate information in an effort to get the interview over with.

Nevertheless, because of ease of administration, speed of response, flexibility, and wide coverage, phone interviews are rapidly gaining in popularity among marketers.

Mail Surveys: Large Scale, Low Cost

Although it is the slowest technique in the fieldwork stage, and the most susceptible to internal questionnaire bias, mail survey research can be the *most cost-effective* method available, potentially generating input from many people at relatively little cost. No interviewing staff is required, and no training or travel expenses are incurred. People in relatively inaccessible places can be contacted by mail: occupants of high-rise apartment buildings with doormen, owners of homes where servants handle callers, people living in remote rural areas, those in dangerous ghettos, or even hard-to-see executives.

The respondent can answer the questionnaire at his or her convenience and has time to look up any necessary information. There is no interviewer bias, and questions of a personal, embarrassing, or ego-involving nature (for example, on the use of hair dyes, contraceptives, or feminine hygiene products) are answered more readily through anonymous mail questionnaires.

Probably the most serious problem with mail surveys is motivating people to fill out the questionnaires. If the response rate is less than 20 percent, it will raise questions about how truly representative your

results are with respect to the underlying population. Since respondents tend to differ from nonrespondents, you cannot remedy the situation simply by increasing the size of your sample. Responses will
often come from people at the extreme end of the spectrum: those
who are very satisfied with your company or product and want to tell
the world about it, and those who are very dissatisfied and want to
make sure you know it. The large number of in-betweens frequently
cannot get very excited one way or another and thus feel no urge to
cooperate. To increase your response rate, you should follow up your
original sample by sending them another copy of your questionnaire
with a different cover letter. This action tends to increase returns
significantly.

In spite of these handicaps, mail surveys are widely used because
Another drawback to mail interviewing is that you never know for
sure whether the questionnaire is actually filled out by the intended
respondent. This task may be assigned to another family member or
a secretary who might misunderstand or misinterpret some questions.
Also, if the sequencing of questions is important, mail surveying may
be a poor technique because respondents can read the entire questionnaire before responding. And mail questionnaires cannot probe.

In spite of these handicaps, mail surveys are widely used because
they can reach thousands of participants at a reasonable cost, offer
wide geographic coverage, and can address issues that would otherwise be too sensitive.

Focus Group Interviews

Focus group interviews are a flexible, versatile, and powerful tool for
the decision maker. These interviews can furnish you with valuable
information on a variety of competitive and marketing problems in a
short span of time and at a nominal cost. But you have to keep in
mind their limitations. Focus groups are a *qualitative* research technique and should not be a device for headcounting. The results of
focus group interviews cannot be projected to your target market at
large. They may not even be representative and, certainly, cannot
replace the quantitative research that will supply you with the necessary numbers. But the interviews can improve the quality of your
quantitative research significantly. When there is no time for a well-
planned formal project, this technique can be called upon to supply
some factual and perceptual input for the managerial decision-making
process, which otherwise would have to rely exclusively on executive
suite conjecture.

Focus group interviewing involves the simultaneous interviewing
of a group of individuals—physicians, homemakers, police officers,
purchasing agents, or any other group of potential buyers or specifiers

representative of your market. A session is usually conducted as a casual roundtable discussion with six to ten participants. Fewer than six poses the danger of participants feeling inhibited. More than ten could result in some members not being heard. The idea, of course, is to get input from everybody. Although the length of a focus group interview varies, an average session lasts about two hours. Jetting around the country in a week, you can collect a good geographic cross-section of opinions. Thus, focus groups offer a quick and relatively inexpensive research technique.

Use focus group interviews to

- Diagnose your competitor's strengths and weaknesses.
- Spot the source of marketing problems.
- Spark new product lines.
- Develop questionnaires for quantitative research.
- Find new uses for your products.
- Identify new advertising or packaging themes.
- Test alternative marketing approaches.
- Streamline your product's positioning.

The key figure in a focus group interview is the moderator, who introduces the subject and keeps the discussion on the predetermined topic. The moderator could be you or someone employed by an outside marketing research firm. The job of moderator is not an easy one and much preparation is necessary, but the information obtained can be substantial and well worth the effort.

The focus group interview does not follow a strict question-and-answer format. Rather, questions presented by the moderator serve essentially as catalysts for effective group discussion. Typically, answers point out areas that merit deeper probing by the moderator through ad-lib questioning. A successful session leads to thoughts and ideas that were not anticipated. Consequently, it is crucial that the moderator create an atmosphere conducive to spontaneity and candor. This format allows for flexibility and enables the moderator to pursue leads suggested by participants.

Preparation for a Session

To make the session as productive as possible, careful planning is necessary. This planning should include:

1. **Identification of goals:** An obvious, but frequently overlooked, need is the establishment of goals for the focus group session. These goals should be clear and in writing.

2. **Development of moderator's guide:** Once the goals for a session have been established, the moderator's guide can be developed. This guide is simply a list of questions to be covered by the moderator during the session. A preformulated, balanced set of questions has the advantage of reducing possible moderator bias and improving the comparability of results from several sessions.

3. **Selection of location:** In selecting locations for focus group sessions, you should keep in mind that an informal atmosphere must be created to encourage a free and uninhibited flow of information. It is common practice to hold such meetings in hotel conference rooms, private homes, or restaurants rather than in office buildings.

4. **Selection of participants:** Recruits for group sessions should be chosen from the ranks of your company's actual and potential buyers. If you do not have records on who your buyers are, it will be necessary to compile a list of relevant characteristics—for example, nonworking married women in a given age bracket with children of a certain age group. To contact and screen potential participants, use a screening questionnaire, a list of pertinent questions aimed at determining whether the individual meets the requirements for being included in a group session. This tool also enables you to detect market researchers, psychologists, or other "experts" whom you want to eliminate because they would tend to dominate and inhibit the discussion. People who are asked to participate should be offered a small inducement, such as a meal or a nominal fee. Make sure that you invite a sufficient number of people to allow for "no-shows."

5. **Preparation of facility:** Your session should definitely assume the nature of a roundtable discussion. Place as many high-sensitivity microphones as possible on the table, all feeding into the same recorder. If your tape will not run for the entire length of the session, it would be helpful to have an assistant handle the mechanical tasks. Name cards should be placed in front of every seat. Refreshments should be available.

How to Conduct a Session

As your participants arrive, welcome them and offer them refreshments. Start punctually and refer to the moderator's guide for direction. Since focus group sessions are essentially unstructured and thus unpredictable, allow participants to talk freely. It is unwise, for example, to tell a participant to reserve a comment for a later time, because the person may become alienated or forget the comment.

Table 5-3. *Guidelines for Focus Group Moderators.*

Do	*Don't*
Keep discussion on topic	Mention company or brand name
Cover all questions, though not necessarily in sequence	Permit excuses or verbal battles
Involve all participants	Let anyone dominate the discussion
Play "devil's advocate" if none is present	Let more than one person talk at a time
Pursue worthwhile ideas of participants	Let an unclear answer stand

Be flexible enough to adapt to evolving circumstances. Your guide simply serves as a reference point and a checklist to ensure completeness of coverage. Moreover, should the discussion take a totally unexpected turn, you should possess enough adaptability to pursue a line of questioning that is not on your list but promises to offer new insights. Use diplomacy when you have to "turn off" an unproductive discussion or respond to the curiosity of participants as to the identity of the sponsor. Table 5-3 contains some guidelines that will help you avoid crucial mistakes.

Processing and Using the Results

After you have completed all your focus group interviews related to a particular marketing problem, you should listen to the tapes several times and excerpt relevant statements. Frequently, verbatim transcripts are made, with the moderator's statements capitalized for easier identification. Videotapes offer an additional benefit over voice tapes, since you can examine gestures and facial expressions as well as posture (body language). Furthermore, it is advisable to have several people study the tapes as well in order to obtain other interpretations. You should then compare notes and organize the resulting key statements into a meaningful pattern or patterns. Subsequently, a quantitative questionnaire should be developed that serves to substantiate the preliminary findings, using random selection of participants.

Image Research

The consumer and the industrial purchaser buy an image as well as a product or service. An image can be described as that complex of attitudes, beliefs, opinions, and experiences that makes up an individual's total impression of a product, service, or corporation. An image represents a "personality" with which the prospective buyer either can or cannot identify. Our purchases involve projections of our images of ourselves and the world. We want the products and services we use to reflect those images.

For example, in banking, a leading New York bank has long claimed, "You have a friend at Chase Manhattan." Studies indicate that banking customers do not believe this claim. Manufacturers Hanover Trust Company, a large competitor with a somewhat stuffy image of its own, decided that it could not meaningfully claim the personal touch, and instead elected speed and efficiency as its advertising theme.

In consumer goods, Gillette Company has long produced quality products for men. When Gillette introduced to the market a deodorant intended for both men and women, women were reluctant to consider it for their personal use. Only when the company stressed a family theme in its advertising for Right Guard did Gillette attain the top position in this market.

In the retailing field, Gimbel's, with an indistinguishable image, struggled to regain its one-time vitality but didn't succeed—and had to close its doors. Perhaps the most monumental challenge is presented by A&P's situation. It was a poorly managed supermarket giant that was fading because of more aggressive competition, until new management produced signs of revival.

The list of examples is endless and can be expanded to industrial goods, utilities, and foreign markets. But it becomes clear, even from this brief description, that familiarity with one's own image is of great importance. Toward this end, you should conduct image research.

The Importance of a Favorable Image

New York City's once precarious financial situation has affected the sale of municipal bonds. In the banking business, a "run" is a sudden withdrawal of funds by a large number of depositors because of a loss of confidence in the bank's stability. Obviously, images strongly influence consumer behavior. Manufacturers Hanover Trust was probably well advised to project a realistic image and institute a program to back up its claim rather than to promise the unbelievable. Irving Trust Co., another New York-based bank, instituted a personal banking program whereby customers are assigned their own bankers who provide continuous and complete service. The bank has been able to generate new business with this innovation. European American Bank probably would have been better off had it positioned itself as the friendly neighborhood bank and avoided any association of its name with foreign interests.

Trying to change an existing image is a slow, painful, and expensive process that requires considerable patience, skill, and commitment. Gillette's masculine image was a definite handicap in trying to introduce a family deodorant. The company might have met with less resistance by establishing a separate division or subsidiary under a different name. In introducing shavers for women, other male-oriented firms, such as Schick Inc. and Remington Products Inc., have added a feminine touch by labeling their products Lady Schick and Lady Remington. Whether a "Mr. Clairol" label would be successful in selling male-oriented products, though, is questionable.

In any case, the best insurance against an unfavorable image is prior testing of strategic and tactical marketing moves. As a manager you know that images, as intangible and elusive as they are, cannot be left to chance. Rather, they need careful and skillful management. Image affects business; a poor image means poor business. That fact is why image research is so important. It represents an essential ingredient in image management, indicating strengths to be capitalized on and weaknesses in need of correction. Image research is thus an invaluable input into your managerial decision making. It is governed by three key questions that pose themselves to every manager who is concerned with creating and maintaining a favorable image.

1. How does an image develop?
2. How can it be researched?
3. How can it be changed?

Developing an Image An image can come from a multitude of factors. It can be the outcome of a company's own efforts as well as those of its competitors. It can result from the choice of corporate or brand name, the symbolism used, or any other part of the entire marketing effort, including product design, pricing, and distribution. The symbolism may include logos, slogans, jingles, colors, shapes, or packaging.

In a packaging test, for example, housewives were presented with identical samples of a new detergent in three different experimental packages. After using the contents, the housewives reported that the product in the blue package did not possess enough cleaning power; the one in the yellow package damaged the fabric; while the one in the blue package with yellow sprinkles was just right, having enough cleaning power but gentle on the clothes. This example shows that a mere change in packaging colors can substantially influence the image of a product.

Table 5-4. *Marketing Mix and Product Image.*

Controllable Image Ingredients	What They Can Do
Design	Provides esthetic appeal
Color	Sets a mood
Shape	Generates recognizability
Package	Connotes value
Name	Expresses central idea
Slogan, jingle, logo	Create memorability
Advertising, personal selling	Communicate benefits
Sales promotion	Stimulates interest
Price	Suggests quality
Channels of distribution	Determine prestige
Warranty	Establishes believability
Service	Substantiates product support

Therefore, if you want to strategically shape your product's image, Table 5-4 offers some useful insights and guidelines. It presents a dozen image ingredients that are under your control and briefly highlights their respective roles in determining your product's overall image.

Researching an Image　Because of their largely emotional nature, images are best researched by using projective techniques that present the respondents with a stimulus (such as a cartoon situation) and ask them to interpret it. While ostensibly talking about this stimulus, the interviewees will unknowingly project their own feelings into the interpretation, thus revealing a true image that could not be obtained by straightforward questioning. The three projective techniques most frequently used in marketing research are *sentence completion, word association,* and *picture association.*

Sentence completion tests are made up of 10 to 20 sentence fragments that give only a partial direction of thought and encourage the respondents to complete the sentences in any way they think appropriate. The statements should be balanced with respect to personal ("I think Chase Manhattan is . . .") and neutral ("Aim toothpaste is . . .") direction. An equal balance should be achieved between negative ("The worst thing about the Rabbit is . . .") and positive ("The thing I like best about Jetta is . . ."). The major benefit of this technique rests in the fact that respondents express their own feelings in their own words. Sentence completion tests can be administered either by personal interview or by the pencil-and-paper method.

Word association is a high-pressure technique that presents an interviewee with key words, terms, or names one at a time and insists on the respondent's immediate reporting of whatever comes to mind upon hearing a given word. In order to avoid second-guessing, the subject is not granted any time for reflection or deliberation. A brief series of about five responses per trigger word is generally registered. The main advantage of this method is that it produces spontaneous associations. This technique must be administered by means of personal interview.

Picture association presents respondents with drawings or photographs of different people representing potential product users. The interviewees are asked to identify the respective users of products A, B, and C. The interviewer then probes for characteristics of the pictured people, thus developing a personality profile of the perceived typical user of a particular product, which is, in turn, reflective of its image. The prime payoff of this approach is that it elicits a wealth of uninhibited information that would otherwise be impossible to obtain. Like the word association test, picture associations must be administered by personal interview.

While these three projective techniques benefit greatly from professional interpretation, budget-conscious managers can attempt their own analyses using plain old common sense.

A method more suited to the do-it-yourself approach is the *semantic differential*. As illustrated in Figure 5-1, it uses pairs of adjectives with opposite meanings. Respondents are required to express the

Figure 5-1. *Semantic differential profiles of two competing products.*

	1	2	3	4	5	
Well-known	O	___	___	X	___	Unknown
Modern	___	X	___	___	O	Old-fashioned
Reliable	___	___	O	___	___	Unreliable
Expensive	O	___	X	___	___	Inexpensive
Prestigious	O	___	___	X	___	Low-class
Attractive	___	X	___	O	___	Unattractive
Economical	X	___	___	O	___	Wasteful

Legend: X _____ Product A
             O – – – – – – – – Product B

Competitive strengths and weaknesses emerge as average scores are graphically connected.

strength of their attitudes by checking off the appropriate position on the scale connecting a given pair of adjectives as it applies to the product in question. The various positions on the scale are usually assigned numerical values (for example, 1 through 5 in the figure) and the individual results for each pair of adjectives are averaged for all respondents. When these averages are connected, a product profile emerges. If this procedure is applied to other products in the same category, a graphic comparison of competitive profiles can be undertaken that highlights the strengths and weaknesses of the different products involved. This technique enables you to capitalize on your product's advantages and to correct, or at least play down, its disadvantages in your marketing approach.

Changing an Image The answer to the question "How can an image be changed?" can probably be summed up in two words: *quality* and *communication*. If you determine that your product's malady is an unfavorable image, you can correct this situation by first being concerned with quality and prepared to offer generous and uncomplicated guarantees. Chrysler Corporation achieved a tremendous improvement in image by offering a 5-year/50-thousand-mile warranty. A&P, in an unprecedented move, admitted in its ads, "We have let pride [quality] slip a little," and promised marked improvement to a wary public. (One of the best moves toward ensuring product quality is to have the quality control manager at your plant report directly to the president, thus making that individual independent of production and marketing pressures.) The issue of quality extends into every controllable image ingredient listed in Table 5-4. The product's design, color, shape, package, name, slogan, jingle, and logo all must connote this characteristic and commitment.

You must also examine the quality of your sales force and service organization to improve the presentation and quality of product performance. There have been occasional instances when an entire sales force has been replaced in an attempt to strengthen company image and sales. And the availability of reliable, competent, and friendly service is a factor that frequently makes or breaks a sale.

In addition, advertising messages and news releases can obviously go a long way toward improving an image and restoring public confidence by communicating improvements that have been made and correcting any false impressions. Some companies are getting considerable use out of the ozone-depletion controversy by communicating the fact that they have changed from the possibly harmful aerosol sprays to nonpressurized pump sprays.

A Brief Here are some of the key questions that you may want to ask yourself
Checklist with respect to your image management responsibilities and efforts:

- What do we know about the image of our company/product/service in the eyes of actual or potential buyers?
- Do we have any image at all? Are we well-enough known?
- Is our image positive or negative?
- Is the perceived image accurate or inaccurate? Are we better than our reputation?
- What does our name suggest? Is it appropriate? Have we outgrown it?
- How does our image compare with that of our competition?
- What are our perceived strengths and weaknesses?
- How can we improve our image?

Favorable images serve to attract investment, talent, and buyers. A company's image can make products stand out that are otherwise indistinguishable. Mostly, however, good images lead to a competitive edge.

Major Sources of Secondary Information

Federal Securities and Exchange Commission
Agencies Bureau of Economic Analysis (Department of Commerce)
Bureau of the Census (Department of Commerce)
Internal Revenue Service
Department of Agriculture
Civil Aeronautics Board
Patent and Trademark Office (Department of Commerce)
Consumer Products Safety Commission
Federal Home Loan Bank Board
Federal Reserve System
Department of Health and Human Services
Department of Education
Department of Labor

State Agencies Division of Banking
Department of Commerce

Department of Consumer Services
Department/Division of Economic Development
Department of Environmental Regulation
Department of Food and Drugs
Department of Insurance
Division of Labor/Industrial Relations
Department of Occupational Regulations
Division of Purchasing
Division of Securities
Bureau of Workers' Compensation

Some of the more important government publications that are issued by these various federal and state agencies are

- *Statistical Abstract of the United States:* provides summary data on demographic, economic, social, and other aspects of the American economy.
- *County and City Data Book:* presents statistical information for counties, cities, and other geographic units on population, education, employment, income, bank deposits, housing, and retail sales.
- *U.S. Industrial Outlook:* projects industrial activity by industry and includes information on production, sales, shipments, and employment.
- *Marketing Information Guide:* offers a monthly annotated bibliography of marketing information.

Other publications include the *Annual Survey of Manufacturers, Business Statistics, Census of Manufacturers, Census of Population, Census of Retail Trade, Wholesale Trade, Selected Service Industries, Census of Transportation, Federal Reserve Bulletin, Monthly Labor Review, Survey of Current Business,* and *Vital Statistics Report.*

Industry Studies   A variety of broad industry studies are conducted by organizations such as Frost & Sullivan Inc., Arthur D. Little Inc., Stanford Research Institute, and a number of Wall Street securities firms. It should be noted that many of these studies do attempt to make broad generalizations. You should carefully examine these reports to be sure of applications for your particular organization.

Trade There are a variety of directories (published by Gale Research Com-
Associations pany, for example) of trade associations covering virtually every product
or business category.

Periodicals
and
Directories

- *Business Periodicals Index:* lists business articles appearing in a wide variety of business publications.
- *Standard and Poor's Industry Surveys:* updates statistics and analysis of industries.
- *Moody's Manuals:* offers financial data and names of executives in major companies.
- *Journal of Marketing, Journal of Marketing Research,* and *Journal of Consumer Research.*
- *Advertising Age, Chain Store Age, Progressive Grocer, Sales and Marketing Management, Electronics, Architectural Record, Plastics.*
- *Business Week, Fortune, Forbes, Harvard Business Review* (general business magazines).

Suppliers of
Commercial
Marketing
Research Data

- *A. C. Nielsen Co.:* provides data on products and brands sold through retail outlets, on television audiences, and on magazine circulation.
- *Market Research Corporation of America:* provides data on weekly family purchases of consumer products, on home food consumption, and on retail drug and discount retailers in various geographic areas.
- *Selling Areas Marketing Inc.:* offers reports on warehouse withdrawals to food stores in selected market areas (SAMI reports).
- *Simmons Market Research Bureau:* provides annual reports covering television markets, sporting goods, and proprietary drugs with demographic data by sex, income, age, and brand preferences.
- *Other research sources:* Audit Bureau of Circulation; Audits and Surveys; Dun & Bradstreet; National Family Opinion; Standard Rate and Data Service, Inc.; and Starch/Inra/Hooper, Inc.

In Conclusion

There is an overwhelming amount of information available for inputting into a total marketing intelligence system. Yet, as a practical matter for many managers, there is not enough time or money to conduct all forms of marketing research. The prudent approach to determining what specific research to undertake is to look at the *strategic marketing plan* (Chapters 6 and 7) to identify what voids of information exist and what information is needed in order to make intelligent decisions.

6

Strategic Marketing Planning

Objectives:
To enable you to

1. Identify the steps in the *strategic marketing planning* process
2. Develop a long-term *strategic direction or mission* for use in a small company, a business unit, or a product line within the corporate structure of a larger organization
3. Identify objectives and strategies with *long-term implications*
4. Develop a *portfolio of products and markets* based on the mission or strategic direction

Case Example

Ralston Purina Co. Ralston Purina Co. lacked a mission—a strategic direction—within its environment of mature products in highly competitive market segments. This agricultural and grocery products company went back to the basics. After a decade of acquisitions in diverse fields (from a Colorado resort to the St. Louis Blues hockey team), the company redefined its *mission* as "a market leader serving the entire agricultural industry." CEO William P. Stiritz stated: "Our future growth will come through aggressive new product development in our core businesses." This back-to-basics approach, which occurred in 1984, meant fighting to regain or retain market share in tough markets and against hot competition. The primary strategy was new product development and market expansion within the framework of the company's mission.

An example from its product line illustrates this point. Ralston Purina produces a feed supplement that a hog farmer can mix with his own corn. The company expanded to meet the needs of a new rural market of small farmers, horse owners, and breeders of chickens, rabbits, and dogs. Since the customers in these markets are too small to order feed in bulk, Purina offers its products in small packages through lawn and garden shops. New for the company, too, is the $280-million-a-year birdseed market. Ralston Purina also markets feeders equipped with a new line of fruit-added seed.

Ralston Purina's strategy went from the broad to the specific—from the top of the organization through the functional areas—all within the framework of the strategic marketing plan. You can follow the flow of steps.

1. Management developed a clearly stated *mission* or *strategic direction* for the company with a time frame of three to five years.

2. Quantitative and nonquantitative *objectives* and *goals* were developed.

3. A *growth strategy* indicating a clear direction for new products in core businesses was defined.

4. A *business portfolio* that focused on existing and new markets and products was created. Those that didn't strategically fit were eliminated.

5. A one-year *marketing plan* was developed that generated strategies for packaging, promotion, pricing, and distribution to suit each market segment.

If you were to consider the strategic process used by Ralston Purina as a flow chart, it would appear as in Figure 6-1. Explanations for the top row of boxes, the strategic portion of the plan covering a period of three to five years, follow. The details of the bottom rows of boxes, representing the annual marketing plan, are covered in Chapter 7. Seen as a whole, the process provides you with a total strategic marketing plan that can be used for your company, business unit, product line, or single product.

Strategic Plan: Three to Five Years

The total viewpoint as expressed in Figure 6-1's top row of four boxes is known as the *strategic plan* and is a portion of the total strategic marketing plan. The strategic plan can be defined as the managerial process of developing and maintaining a *strategic fit* between the organization and changing market opportunities. It relies on developing (1) a mission/strategic direction, (2) objectives and goals, (3) a growth strategy, and (4) business portfolio plans.

Figure 6-1. *Strategic marketing plan.*

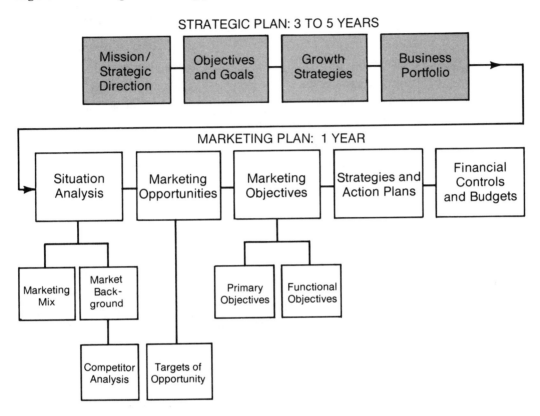

Mission/
Strategic
Direction

Think of your mission as the strategic direction of the company, marketing group, product line, and/or individual product. It is the long-range philosophy of a business unit, a strategic vision of what your product or business can and should be. As you think about the mission, consider the following:

- What are your distinctive areas of expertise?
- What business should you be in the next three to five years?
- What customers are to be served?
- What customer functions are you to satisfy?
- What technologies will you use to satisfy customer/market needs?
- What changes are taking place in markets, consumer behavior, competition, environment, culture, and the economy?

The point of this exercise is that the responsibility for defining strategic direction no longer belongs only to upper management. Managers from various departments—marketing, product development, sales—contribute to the overall strategic direction of a business

Table 6-1. *Company Identity as Reflected by Orientation Concepts.*

Product-Driven Orientation	Market-Driven Orientation
Railroad company	Transportation company
Oil company	Energy company
Baby food manufacturer	Child care business
Cosmetics company	Beauty, fashion, health company
Computer manufacturing company	Information processing company
Electrical wire manufacturer	Energy transfer business
Vacuum cleaner manufacturer	Cleaner environment business
Valve company	Fluid control company

by asking, ''What business should I be in for my individual product?''

The major work in this area of strategic thinking is attributed to Theodore Levitt, of the Harvard Business School, in his classic article, ''Marketing Myopia.''[1] Using the railroads as a prime example, Levitt shows how the railway system declined in use as technology advanced, because managers defined their product too narrowly. He explains that to continue growing, companies must determine customers' needs and wants and not rely simply on the longevity of their products.

According to Levitt, a myopic view is based on four beliefs that begin in a manager's mind and permeate an organization:

First, the belief that growth is guaranteed by an expanding and affluent population.

Second, the belief that there is no competitive substitute for the industry's major product.

Third, excessive belief in mass production and in the advantage of rapidly declining unit costs as output rises.

Fourth, preoccupation with a product that lends itself to carefully controlled scientific experimentation, improvement, and manufacturing cost reduction.

Looking out the window toward inevitable change, not into a mirror that reflects existing patterns, is the distinguishing characteristic of a market-driven, rather than a product-driven, organization. Table 6-1 gives examples of how these opposite points of view differ in their expressions of identity, which is the basis of a company's mission.

[1]T. Levitt, ''Marketing Myopia,'' *Harvard Business Review* (Sept.–Oct. 1975), p. 28.

Case Examples

Gerber The Gerber Products Co. originally defined its strategic direc-
Products Co. tion as a baby food manufacturer (product-driven). This narrow focus restricted managerial thinking to product lines. By
expanding its viewpoint to a market-driven orientation, it redefined its strategic direction to a *child care company.* The implication of that change is expressed in a product line and in a
range of businesses consisting of not only its baby food manufacturing, but of children's toys, furniture, and clothing, and
day care centers as well. Each product is consistent with Gerber's new mission, or strategic direction, as a child care business.

J.P. Stevens & In another case, J.P. Stevens & Co., Inc., a textile manufactur-
Co., Inc. ing organization for 80 years, became trapped in its narrow
self-definition as textile producer (product-driven). Its limited
vision kept it in a flat, mature market with extreme levels of
competition from Asian producers. By expanding its concept to
a market-driven orientation, management redefined the mission as the *total home environment business,* and experienced
a change in the entire structure of the organization. Translat-
ing that strategic direction into a product and market portfolio
resulted in a range of product lines in home furnishings, from
oxford-cloth sheets to crystal and sterling stemware and, even,
wood furniture. With over 2,500 items, the total line became
one of the largest designer collections ever assembled.

The Bekins The Bekins Company originally defined itself as a mover of
Company household goods (product-driven). With a more expansive strategic viewpoint, it redefined its mission as a *relocation business.* By doing so, management expanded its strategic vision
into new markets, new products, and new services that formerly were not likely to be reviewed under the myopic product-
oriented viewpoint. For example, not only does the company
continue to move household goods (its primary business), but
it now can provide a whole range of services related to moving
people: real estate, financial, and other types of services and information that its customers need.

Consider now Levitt's example: the railroad company versus the
transportation company. Viewing the basic product as railroad cars
traveling on parallel tracks down a particular path results in a shortsighted business condition. As a transportation company, however,
the strategic vision includes transportation of all types—air, water,
space, and forms still unknown. Since railroad companies own land
on either side of the tracks, a transportation viewpoint can conceivably include laying underground pipe to transport food, fluids, chemicals, and power lines.

This type of expansive strategic thinking is not limited to the private-sector, profit-making corporations. It applies equally well to the public sector. Consider the March of Dimes Birth Defect Foundation, an organization that was originally dedicated to the cure of polio. Fortunately, polio is no longer a serious threat. Does that situation mean that the March of Dimes is out of business and can serve no useful function? Not at all. By redefining its mission, or strategic direction, as *birth defects,* the organization is alive and well, using its skills and resources in a broader mandate to serve society's needs.

Even companies with strong positions in the marketplace and with profitable businesses are redefining mission statements to embrace the inevitable movement toward new technologies. For example, consider GTE Directories Corporation, the producers of the familiar telephone directories known as the Yellow Pages. Its basic business consists of selling advertising space, printing the volumes, and distributing the directories. In 1984, GTE defined its business purpose and developed the following mission:

> A worldwide integrated publishing and marketing corporation of directional hard copy and electronic advertising media and informational services.

Does the mission specifically state that the company is the producer of the Yellow Pages? Not at all. Does the statement include that product? Yes, by using the phrase "directional hard copy," it includes the product line of Yellow Pages. Yet the clear implication is that the managers can think expansively of new products that may take different forms.

Now consider the phrase "electronic advertising media." Taking into account existing and yet-to-be developed technology, GTE can link up to new media that can augment its Yellow Pages or, in time, even displace it. This portion of the mission permits managers at all levels of the company to open their minds to the new possibilities, while still being consistent with GTE's basic business.

Finally, the phrase "information services" opens the window into expansion areas as developed countries move increasingly toward service economies and information transfer, thus building "a worldwide integrated publishing and marketing corporation."

Recall Steve Harrell's previous comment that "the marketing manager is the most significant functional contributor to the strategic planning process. . . ." In an effort to implement just such thinking, Rhett W. Butler of GTE Directories Corporation made the following statement to 123 middle-level managers representing its worldwide operations at a planning orientation in June 1984:

I want each of you to put the letters CEO before your actual title. I want you to think like chief executive officers within the areas of your responsibilities.

Using the GTE mission statement as the strategic direction and giving the managers the mandate to think like CEOs provided the format for developing a strategic marketing plan in which managers could exercise the creative process. Through this approach, the strangling effect of marketing myopia is dissolved and strategic thinking is set in motion.

But how far should your thinking go toward a market-driven orientation? It is best to initially think as far toward that orientation as possible, and then come back to a more comfortable position toward a product-driven orientation. That position is usually based on the *culture* of the organization, which can range from conservative to aggressive; on the human and material *resources* available for maintaining existing business and for investing in future growth; on the amount of *risk* that management is willing to assume in going into debt; on the degree of environmental *change* that is anticipated in market behavior; and on the threat of *competitive activities* and their impact on survival and growth. Even amid these factors, your approach should be to think as expansively as possible. An approach rooted in a product-driven orientation ultimately leads to the negative effects of mature and then declining businesses.

The implications for a company's mission, or strategic direction, begin with each manager, regardless of his or her level in the organization, viewing the company, the division, or a product from a strategic marketing viewpoint. Consequently, managers are no longer restricted to the narrow focus that results in mature products, price wars, and other competitive conflicts. The broader market-driven viewpoint permits managers to think more expansively about business, market, and customer needs—not just products.

Objectives and Goals Your guidelines for developing objectives and goals are that they be strategic in makeup; that is, that they have broad impact on your business within your operating environment and that they cover a time frame of from three to five years. This time period is reasonable for most businesses: short enough to be realistic and achievable in an increasingly volatile marketplace, yet long enough to be visionary about the impact of new technologies, changing behavioral patterns, the global marketplace, emerging competitors, and changing demographics.

Specifically, your objectives and goals can be classified as quantitative and nonquantitative. For example, in quantitative statements you include performance expectations such as sales growth ($/units), market share, return on investment (ROI), and other quantitative measurements that are usually standard requirements of your general management or financial department. Nonquantitative objectives and goals cover such areas as upgrading dealer organization, expanding secondary distribution, improving marketing intelligence systems, building new specialty product lines, repositioning older commodity products, and reorganizing to become a market-driven business.

Case Examples

The diverse examples of two actual companies—an auto parts manufacturer and an electric utility company—illustrate specific ways in which quantitative and nonquantitative objectives and goals are stated. Because of the confidential nature of these statements, the names of the companies are omitted and the numbers have been altered. Furthermore, these objectives are only a sampling. The actual number of objectives ranged from 15 to 25 for each company. Other, less complex companies could realistically have as few as 5 to 10 objectives.

Auto Parts Manufacturer

Quantitative Objectives and Goals

· Attain net sales of $37.0 million by 19xx within the following categories:

	Net Sales ($ mil)	Mix (%)
Distributor	13.0	35
Corporate brand (direct)	6.5	18
Generic	7.0	19
National accounts	5.5	15
Military	3.0	8
Export sales	2.0	5
Total	37.0	100

· Launch 200 new products on a quarterly basis over the next three years, including electrical, front end, brake, air conditioning, and power train.
· Maintain 60 or more dedicated distributors strategically located worldwide to achieve sales objectives.
· Improve customer satisfaction to 94.5 percent, as measured by the Customer Service Index base period of 1985–86.

Nonquantitative Objectives and Goals

- Utilize as a marketing mix element an effective supply and distribution system for the potential launch of existing products into new market segments.
- Develop a prototype of an automated catalog information system for use with distributors by the fourth quarter of 19xx.

Electric Utility Company

Quantitative Objectives and Goals

- Achieve total revenues of 1.242 kwh (kilowatt-hours) in the following end-use categories by 19xx:

Process heat	875 kwh
Space conditioning	185
Lighting	115
Residential water heating	20
Major appliances	15
Commercial food service	32
Total	1.242 kwh (mil)

- Effectively promote process heat in targeted manufacturing markets by increasing account load of sales force from 90 to 125 over a 36-month period.
- Reestablish relationships with builders, realtors, and appliance manufacturers to take advantage of the 20 percent customer turnover each year, adding 100 kwh of electric process heat equipment.

Nonquantitative Objectives and Goals

- Change customer perceptions that electric energy is an expensive commodity.
- Improve knowledge of the marketplace, customers, and competition through a comprehensive marketing intelligence system.
- Reorganize to become a more customer-oriented, market-driven company.

While some managers resist the use of nonquantitative objectives, there are long-term market conditions or internal obstacles that need to be overcome, and numbers cannot always be attached to such objectives. Yet, for measurement purposes, dates and reporting periods can be used to show progress toward achieving these objectives. The use of quantitative and nonquantitative objectives in combination allows for the most accurate and effective planning.

Growth While objectives and goals indicate *what* you want to accomplish,
Strategies growth strategies deal with *how* you are going to achieve those objectives. Strategies are divided into two categories: internal and external. *Internal strategies* relate to marketing, manufacturing, R&D,
distribution, and pricing, as well as to existing and new products,
market research, packaging, customer services, credit, finance, sales
activities, and organizational changes. *External strategies* refer to such
possibilities as joint ventures, licensing agreements, new distribution
networks, emerging market segments, and any opportunities for diversification, if that diversification fits the company's mission.

Case Examples

Auto Parts   *Internal Strategies*
Manufacturer
- Install an internal computerized program that will link the
  top 80 distributors' inventories with independent repair
  shops' ordering requirements.
- Complete the upgrade of the Memphis depot and launch
  just-in-time delivery service to distribute within 125 miles
  of the facility.
- Execute a new warranty administration program that is
  equitable to the company, distributors, and end-user customers, with a timing of 15 days for claims disposition,
  compared with the current 21 days.
- Implement a quality improvement program consisting of
  continuing education programs, and establish indices of
  performance levels in accordance with new corporate objectives.

External Strategies
- Establish quality teams at distributors to review causes of
  errors and recommend corrective action.
- Form joint venture with (name of company) to increase total market share in selected fuel and cooling systems components, resulting in sales of $60 million and 22 percent
  market share.
- Establish an image for high-performance parts in aftermarket by establishing 125 new performance center dealers
  in key segments of the United States and Canada.
- Establish teleconferencing broadcasting sessions to the field
  to maintain competitive advantage.

Electric Utility Company

Internal Strategies

- Establish a corporate lighting group to plan marketing programs and serve as technical support for all lighting activities.
- Establish a central promotional group to develop and produce literature and sales aids; plan and coordinate trade show activities; develop advertising themes and positioning strategies; and coordinate publicity campaigns.
- Operate an ongoing training activity to introduce products and share information with company employees, contractors, dealers, realtors, and customers on equipment features, application, benefits, sales, and service techniques.
- Develop a performance-type housing construction rating system to certify and endorse properly insulated and weatherized homes.

External Strategies

- Construct and manage a network of insulation, weatherization material, and electric heating equipment distributors to support builder design and construction activity.
- Develop and implement an active call program targeted at key builders in prime market areas identified for long-term urban redevelopment.
- Develop joint working relationships with electric equipment manufacturers to work on applications involving high temperature and environmental concerns.

It is also appropriate here to distinguish between a strategy and a tactic. A strategy is a longer-term concept and has wider implications for your company than does a tactic. A strategy usually affects the functional areas of your organization, such as manufacturing, product development, and finance; it concerns the broader aspects of new markets and distribution systems. On the other hand, tactics cover a shorter time span, are action-oriented, and are usually concerned with local issues of more limited impact, such as a single product being launched in a target market segment with specific promotional activities. In practice, a single strategic objective could be accomplished through four or five strategies and, in turn, six to ten tactics.

Business Portfolio A business portfolio consists of all existing markets and products and all new markets and products that could be served in the next three to five years, and that are consistent with the company's mission/strategic direction.

Figure 6-2. *Business portfolio plan guidelines.*

	Existing Products	New Products
Existing Markets	1. Market Penetration	3. Product Development
New Markets	2. Market Development	4. Diversification

Your mission/strategic direction has meaning only if it can be translated into markets and products. Generally, the broader the mission is, the broader the range of markets and products is; the narrower the scope, the narrower the portfolio of markets and products. Gerber Products Co. again provides a useful example. The company continues to manufacture baby foods. However, a revised mission took it from a baby food manufacturer to a company in the child care business. Consequently, the expanded portfolio also includes children's clothing, toys, and furniture, as well as child care centers. All of these products are consistent with the new mission.

Referring again to the case example of J.P. Stevens & Co., Inc., we find a business portfolio including a total collection of 2,500 items in the line. The growth strategy for J.P. Stevens would identify the action needed to create the new business portfolio. For example, strategy statements include licensing seven manufacturers to produce nontextile goods. These companies include Towle Mfg. Co., which makes glass and flatware; Henredon Furniture Industries, Inc.; Motif Designs, for turning out the foulard wall coverings; and Deeth, Ltd., of Bombay, for handweaving the rugs.

Figure 6-2 illustrates how you can construct a business portfolio of markets and products. Adapting Ansoff's product–market grid to the strategic marketing planning process,[2] you can categorize markets and products to reflect the mission/strategic direction. As you view the diagram, note that you can list existing products into existing markets and the process is identified as (1) market penetration. You can also view existing products for new markets, which can be defined as (2) market development. Also look at introducing new products into existing markets, a process known as (3) product development. Finally,

[2]H. I. Ansoff, "Strategies for Diversification," *Harvard Business Review* (Sept.–Oct. 1957), pp. 113–124.

look at new products for new markets, expressed as (4) diversification. To use the grid, list products and markets in each of the quadrants. The listing will then serve as a guideline for product–market growth over three to five years.

Case Example

Lenox, Inc. To illustrate the value of the business portfolio, consider Lenox, Inc., the premier U.S. china maker. Plagued by foreign competition, in particular from Japan's Noritake Company, Lenox took command of its business through solid strategic marketing planning. Using the product–market matrix, we can get an overview of the company's business portfolio.

1. **Existing products into existing markets:** Through market penetration, Lenox went after more share of its traditional wedding trousseau market as that market showed a resurgence of growth.
2. **Existing products into new markets:** Using the market development quadrant, Lenox targeted the young, affluent, and growing population of professional women.
3. **New products into existing markets:** Expanding its product development, the company moved into jewelry and giftware.
4. **New products into new markets:** Using the diversification quadrant, Lenox sought acquisitions in such areas as leather goods, luggage, and furniture.

Marketing Plan: One Year

A review of the strategic plan makes it apparent that you can no longer think narrowly about a product; you must now think about markets and a marketing plan. The lower rows of boxes in Figure 6-1 (on page 221) make up the marketing plan, which has a time frame of 12 months. The detailed plan and actual work forms are presented in Chapter 7, but an overview, to explain the entire planning format and to provide perspective for the areas in which strategies are developed, is useful here.

Situation Analysis The marketing plan process begins with a *situation analysis* of a specific product or market. Whereas the strategic plan looks ahead three to five years, the situation analysis requires that you look *back* three to five years to obtain an historical perspective of your business.

Situation analysis is divided into three parts: marketing mix analysis, market background, and competitor analysis. For a *marketing mix analysis,* objectively and factually write your sales and unit volume by product, analyze your pricing, and assess your promotion and distribution. Market *background* deals with the nature of your audience, human factors, the image you convey, what customers think about your product, and the frequency of its use. The examination of background permits you to think extensively about your marketplace and your customers. The third part also permits you to analyze your competitors in detail.

Marketing Opportunities After you have analyzed the situation, the next step is to *evaluate opportunities.* Surprisingly, this part of the process is often neglected by managers. This planning step is exceedingly important, since the whole purpose of conducting a situational analysis is to expose opportunities. Opportunities are voids or gaps in a product, a market, or a service that can be filled to satisfy customer needs and wants. This stage of the marketing plan is best achieved by incorporating the input of various functional managers from manufacturing, R&D, product development, finance, and sales.

Brainstorming is a useful technique for identifying opportunities. For example, consider the features and benefits of your product. Study the situation analysis, including competitive intelligence, and allow the ideas to flow. Don't attempt to judge them—just record them as they emerge. The probability is that you will discard 90 to 95 percent of them. But the remaining 5 to 10 percent could be the opportunity to enter a new business, form a new product, or render a new service.

Marketing Objectives The third step in the marketing plan is to work out primary and functional marketing objectives. First, develop *primary quantitative objectives,* such as sales in dollars and units, market share, gross margins, return on investment, return on assets, and any other quantitative information required of you by your organization. Second, develop *functional objectives* as they pertain to product, packaging, services, pricing, promotion, and distribution. These functional areas are commonly referred to as the *marketing mix.* It should be evident that the marketing mix is a key part of the marketing plan in that it represents the controllable factors you can employ to achieve the primary financial and volume objectives.

Strategies and Action Plans On the basis of your marketing objectives, you can now develop the *strategies and action plans* that translate those objectives into action. Unless the objectives can be supported by firm action plans, they are useless: They are no more than good intentions until the activities that will make them happen are developed. For each objective there should be a strategy and an action plan. Each strategy should be detailed by what is going to happen, when it is going to happen, and who is responsible for carrying out the action.

Financial Controls and Budgets This step in the marketing plan involves the financial controls, budgets, and variance reports that translate into numbers the actions that you have stated in the previous steps. (See Chapter 3, under Financial Resource Analysis.)

The Total Plan

The combination of the three-to-five-year strategic and the annual marketing plans forms a total *strategic marketing plan* for any level of an organization, from corporate management down to product line. Further, for every major product and market described by the business portfolio, there is a specific annual marketing plan. Thus, there is a joining of a long-term strategic viewpoint with a one-year tactical framework to create action—something that the strategic plan by itself could not accomplish and for which the marketing plan alone is too narrow for today's competitive environment.

7

Developing
the Marketing Plan

Objectives:
To enable you to

1. Identify the steps in developing the *marketing plan*
2. Understand and explain the *relationship* between the strategic plan and the marketing plan
3. Develop a marketing plan using the *sample format*
4. Use qualitative guidelines and quantitative measures to *evaluate* a strategic marketing plan

The total framework for a strategic marketing plan consists of a three- to five-year strategic plan (Chapter 6) and an annual marketing plan. As highlighted in Figure 7-1, we now turn our attention to the formulation of specific tactical plans for products and markets.

In Chapter 6, an auto parts manufacturing company and an electric utility company illustrated how two diverse organizations write objectives and strategies. The sample marketing plan that follows uses only the electric utility company as an example. It is an actual case of a midwestern company facing extensive competition for the first time. Deregulation of the industry set a whole flow of events into movement that created a competitive environment and initiated strategic marketing planning. Consider the following events that took place in a flat-growth economy: Deregulation brought in more aggressive pricing competition from natural gas companies; lower-priced energy came from neighboring states; major industrial organizations were beginning to generate their own energy and bypass the utility company; and the utility company, after many years of development, completed a nuclear plant that had the capability of doubling the electric energy output.

Figure 7-1. *Strategic marketing plan.*

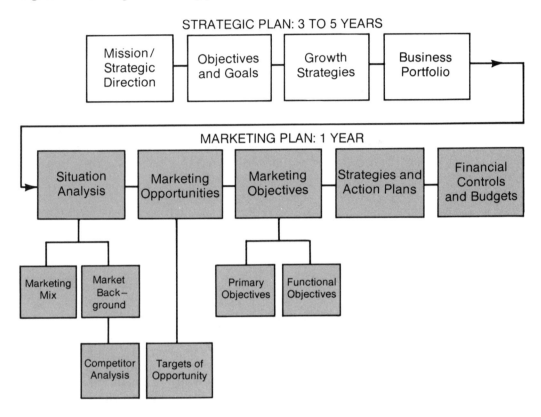

Thus, there was a need to develop a plan that would search for new strategies to penetrate existing markets. The utility also needed to increase usage of electric energy by identifying industrial, commercial, and residential users that could consume more energy through additional applications.

Sample Marketing Plan

The product produced by the electric utility is energy expressed in kilowatt-hours (kwh). It is used in a variety of end-use applications such as major appliances, water heating, space conditioning, lighting, commercial cooking, electric transportation, motor drives, and process heating. The markets for this product are residential, manufacturing, nonmanufacturing, and municipalities, but these are generally grouped as residential, industrial, and commercial.

The sample plan focuses on only one segment of the total market, *lighting*. Each section of the plan is provided with guidelines on how to fill it out and with sample responses so that you can apply the format to your own situation, regardless of your product or service. Although the term "product" is used in the guidelines, a service organization can use the same planning format, whether that service is in the financial, medical, or some other professional field.

For authenticity in using the electric utility company as an example, only the numbers from its actual plan have been disguised for confidential purposes. Also, the information provided does not constitute the utility's entire plan, but only a sampling for you to observe how an actual plan would be filled out.

Marketing Plan

Situation Analysis

PART I: A. Product/Program/Service

The Marketing Mix In this section, describe in factual and objective terms where your operation stands in relation to the total marketing mix (product/price/distribution/promotion). Compile data for a period of at least three years and determine what the future trends are for the industry, product line, or market segment.
Objectively describe the product by:

1. Sales history.
2. Position in the industry, including market share as well as less tangible aspects of relative position in the life cycle curve (introduction/growth/maturity/decline/phase-out).
3. Future trends in the industry, government, etc., that may affect product position.
4. Intended purpose of the product(s), in terms of market use, uniqueness, or positioning.
5. Features and benefits of the product(s), in terms of cost, safety, or convenience, that make for a winning proposition.
6. Other pertinent product information, such as expected product improvements and additional product characteristics (quality, size, model price). You may also wish to include recent features that enhance the product position; competitive trends in features and benefits; and required changes for improved competitiveness.

1. *Sales History*
Product: Lighting

Year	Sales (millions kwh)	Revenues ($ million)	Number of Customers (000)
Current	275	29.5	715
Year 1	265	22.7	608
Year 2	259	18.8	597
Year 3	213	12.1	359

2. *Position in Industry*

Based on an analysis of where electric energy fits into the total energy picture for the United States and the company's trading area, the following key points emerged.

- For the United States and our trading area, use of energy is declining. We are not in a growth cycle.
- Electric energy represents about 10 percent of total energy.
- Commercial and industrial customers (manufacturing and nonmanufacturing) use about 60 percent of the electric energy produced.
- The lighting market is a major one for the company: Almost one-half of total sales over the past three years went into lighting. The following table shows the approximate percentage of total energy sales for lights and lighting energy.

Market	Percentage	Billions kwh
Residential	13.0	1.25
Manufacturing	16.5	2.05
Nonmanufacturing	24.0	2.45
Street lighting	1.2	0.75

3. *Future Trends*

- Trend toward the growth of energy-saving lamps and longer-life products, with a proliferation of new products from Taiwan, Korea, Hungary, Poland, and Canada.
- Customer reluctance to spend money for the higher-cost, higher-efficiency lamps and fixtures, such as fluorescent circle lights. Initial cost is a strong consideration in determining lighting systems, particularly with manufacturing and nonmanufacturing customers.
- Ninety percent of assaults and burglaries occur at night.

4. *Intended Purpose of the Product*

The intended purpose is to provide a reliable source of energy and related products and services to safely light homes, businesses, parking lots, and roadways. The use of the energy within the lighting market is categorized as follows:

- *Residential interior lighting,* representing about 13 percent of residential customer electric energy used for lighting.
- *Commercial and industrial interior lighting,* representing 16 percent of electric energy used for lighting.
- *Street lighting,* representing 65 percent of electric energy used for lighting. It is also estimated that 40 to 55 percent of service area streets have no lighting or could use additional lighting for safety, security, crime prevention, and business merchandising.
- *Residential and commercial outdoor protective lighting (OPL),* representing 6 percent of electric energy for lighting. OPL's function is to provide all-night protection to business and residential customers. There is no information on the reliability of OPL's compared with customer-installed floodlights as a crime deterrent.

5. *Features and Benefits of the Product*
The reliable source of energy and the effective application of lighting provide safety, security, comfort, and crime prevention and are a benefit to business merchandising. The benefits and features of lighting are related to the following statistics:

- Twelve times as many crimes of violence are committed at night.
- Sixty percent of auto accidents occur at night, even though only 30 percent of all driving is done after dark.
- Four times as many fatal accidents occur at night.

B. Pricing

1. In this section, evaluate the company's and competitors' pricing policies for each market segment and/or distribution channel and their impact on market position.
2. Evaluate what the pricing trends will be on the basis of raw material sourcing; product specification changes; financial constraints, and expected market situation (customers' attitudes/competitive response, etc.).

1. *Pricing Policies and Discounts*
The pricing classifications are highly fragmented and are categorized by residential, commercial, industrial, and municipal. Within these categories prices vary by street lighting, traffic and signal lights, and ornamental lighting. Further breakdowns in pricing apply to annual charges per lamp, dusk-to-midnight service, flat rate and metered rate, and on peak/off peak usage. At the present time, the company has 23 rate classifications in the breakdowns shown above.
[*Author's note:* Information would be provided in a table of rates by classification or made part of an appendix.]

2. *Future Pricing Trends*
A 12 to 18 percent per year increase is anticipated for the next three to five years. This prediction contrasts with the no

or very low increase forecast for natural gas and oil for the same period.

C. Distribution Channels and Methods

1. The current channel of distribution analysis should include quantities sold directly, through dealers, and through points of sale (POS); as well as an analysis of physical distribution.
2. Identify effectiveness of coverage through current channels and functions they perform. Comment on effectiveness of distribution systems (direct/dealers/POS); include key activities that are being performed at each point and areas that require special attention.
3. Special functions performed by company sales force (sales activities) on the basis of distribution channel selected and market segment addressed: Specify what key jobs and/or activities need to be performed by the sales force (primarily company sales force, but also dealer outside sales reps, if applicable). Issues such as "push" and "pull" sales strategies should also be mentioned. How effectively does the sales force cover the market area? Show target accounts by district.
4. Identify future trends in distribution methods and channels. What growth is expected in each major market segment? How will this growth affect the needs for different (or existing) distribution channels or methods (physical distribution)?

1. *Current Channels of Distribution*

Distribution takes place through a multilevel channel system. At one level, lighting is specified by architects, builders, and interior designers. At another level, direct distribution takes place through representatives of major retailers, manufacturers, and municipal governments. And at still another level of distribution are the manufacturers of lighting fixtures and bulbs, including company-owned stores.

2. *Effectiveness of Coverage Through Current Change*

- The company sells through its 17 customer offices. The offices stock 61 different lamps and sales totaled $622,000. The share of the total service area lamp sales was 3.6 percent.
- General Electric has about 50 percent of the incandescent bulb market, with Sylvania and Westinghouse at about 10 percent each. There are 28 U.S. manufacturers of all types of lamps with about 17 percent of the market.
- About 13 percent of the incandescent lamps and 5 percent of the fluorescent lamps are imported primarily from Taiwan, followed by Korea, Hungary, Poland, Mexico, and Canada.

• Large firms purchase their lamps from distributors of manufacturers' reps. Contractors provide the lighting systems for new construction.

Overall, there are extremely well-developed distribution channels for lamps.

3. *Special Functions Performed by the Company's Sales Force*
  (a) Continuing personal contact is maintained by the company's sales force, with frequency of contact based on size of customer and energy usage. Frequency of contact is also determined by building activities and types of users and specifiers. Activities relate to new construction or renovation, and users and specifiers relate to builders, contractors, architects, and interior designers.
  (b) When there is direct contact with large users, company sales reps invite major retail, manufacturing, and government customers to General Electric's Nela Park Demonstration Lighting Institute to learn about the latest, most efficient lighting systems.

4. *Future Trends in Distribution Methods and Channels*
  (a) The trend in the incandescent market for energy-saving lamps and longer-life products will signal a need for technically trained lighting experts who will function as advisers at all levels of the distribution system and for various-size customers. These functions will begin with an analysis of lighting needs, followed by advice on installation.
  (b) Distribution channel representatives will be providing continuing monitoring of lighting systems to match changing layouts in offices and manufacturing organizations for efficiency and energy savings.
  (c) There will be more use of demonstration centers through joint ventures of the company with manufacturers of lighting fixtures and bulbs at key locations.

D. Advertising and Sales Promotion

  1. Analyze the advertising and sales promotion directed at each segment of the market by copy theme, expenditure, and media.
  2. What are the past and current advertising and sales promotion strategies by product and market segment?
  3. What publicity, educational, and other nonadvertising influences have been used, and with what effect?

1. *Advertising and Sales Promotion by Copy Theme, Expenditure, and Media*
  (a) General Electric spends about $10 million for light bulb advertising and about 85 percent of that is spent on network TV.
  (b) Within the street lighting segment, there are no advertising or sales promotion efforts. Promotion is limited to the use of direct mail for inviting municipal officials to a General Elec-

tric outdoor roadway lighting demonstration facility . North
Carolina.

(c) Within the outdoor protective lighting segment, there is
no space advertising and only a limited amount of sales promotion in the form of direct mail to commercial customers four
times per year.

2. *Past and Current Advertising and Sales Promotion Strategies*

Most company advertising is confined to corporate advertising directed at economic development within the company's
trading area. There are other advertising themes, such as serving the energy needs of the public and showing the company as
a responsible corporate member of the community. All media
have been used, including TV, radio, newspapers, and billboards.
However, minimal advertising has been focused in the lighting
segment of the market.

[*Author's note:* Advertising details may be included here or
shown as exhibits in an appendix.]

3. *Publicity, Educational, and Other Nonadvertising Influences*

Marketing research indicates that inviting customers and
prospects to the demonstration facilities maintained by General
Electric has a positive impact. Evidence is currently being compiled to show the direct sales impact on outdoor protective
lighting and street lighting segments.

[*Author's note:* Here, too, any lengthy quantitative information can be shown in an appendix, with a summary indicated
in this section.]

**Situation
Analysis
PART II:** This section is an extension of the basic marketing situation.
However, focus is on the behavioral aspects of customers and
Market prospects in a changing and competitive environment.
Background

The information in this section is important because it
serves as foundation material for developing the objectives and
strategies that follow. It also highlights any gaps in knowledge
about your markets and suggests the types of marketing research needed to make effective decisions.

A. Customer Profile
What is the profile of potential customers? Classify by:

1. The markets served by distributors, dealers, and other intermediaries, as well as from direct to end-user sales.
2. Overall sales by market segment and channel of sale.
3. Other classifications: describe profile of customers by type
of product they use; level of sophistication; point of purchase; sensitivity; etc.

B. Frequency and Magnitude of Product Usage
1. How often do they purchase?
2. In what volumes?
3. Is there a seasonal effect?

C. Geographic Aspects of Product Usage

Are most of the buyers in a region of the country? National? International?

D. Customer Characteristics

Age? Level of education? Degree of sophistication? Management practices? Time in the business?

1. Attitude toward the company, the products, the services, our quality image?
2. Economic factors?

E. Decision Making

Who makes the buying decisions? When and where are they made, and by whom?

F. Customer Motivations

Why do customers buy? (Quality? Performance? Image? Service: Convenience? Location? Friendliness?) What motivates them to buy the product, to select one supplier/provider in preference to another?

G. Customer Awareness

What is the level of customers' awareness of the company's product? To what extent do they?

1. Recognize a need.
2. Identify the brand/product/company.
3. Associate the brand/product/company with desirable features.

H. Segment Trends

What are the trends in the size and character of the various submarkets? A submarket or segment should be considered if it is accessible, measurable, or potentially profitable. Also identify segments that are emerging, neglected, or poorly served.

A. Customer Profile

1. *Markets Served by Distributors, Dealers, and Other Intermediaries*

- Independent building contractors: serve new residential areas and renovations in established areas; and small commercial businesses (nonmanufacturing) that represent 37 percent of lighting energy consumption.
- Architects and lighting engineers: serve manufacturing organizations as well as municipalities that represent 17.7 percent of energy consumption.
- Interior designers: serve all segments of the market.

2. *Overall Sales by Market Segment*

[*Author's note:* It is not appropriate here to indicate names of individuals. However, in the actual version of this plan, names of builders, contractors, architects, and interior designers are listed by category and by market segment along with sales, number of customers or customer size, and amount of energy consumption.]

B. Frequency and Magnitude of Product Usage

1. *Frequency*

A company survey of 375 large manufacturing firms indicates that about 12 percent of their electric energy use is for lighting; for the 7,000 nonmanufacturing firms surveyed, about 24 percent of electric energy is used for lighting.

2. *Magnitude*

Within the outdoor protective lighting segment, the lighting is controlled by photocells. There is no reliable information on the extent of use of owner-installed floodlights for all-night protective purposes.

3. *Seasonal Effect*

In the past three years, approximately 1,750 street lights were added to the company's service area, adding $560,000 to annual revenue.

C. Geographic Aspects of Product Usage

A comparative listing of county saturation by outdoor protective lighting (OPL) and floodlighting follows.

County	OPL (%)	Floodlighting (%)
Nassau	2.10	26
DeKater	0.30	19
Orange	0.54	22
Brock	1.11	24
Metro	2.72	27
Brighton	0.98	19

D. Customer Characteristics

Within the light bulb segment, demographic studies during the last 12 months indicate there are significant differences among the customer purchasers of the leading brands. For example, General Electric bulb buyers are older, upscale customers with high household incomes and are college educated. Additional market research revealed characteristics of customers from among business and government purchasers.

1. *Attitudes*

The behavioral characteristics reveal a strong and growing concern for security by both businesses and residential customers.

2. *Economic Factors*

Street lighting represents 3 to 5 percent of communities' budgets. Nassau County requires street lighting in all new subdivisions, with the expense passed along through a special assessment tax.

E. Decision Making

Buying decisions are made by government officials, with strong influences from architects and lighting engineers. A decision takes place from 8 to 12 months prior to the beginning of construction or renovation.

F. Customer Motivations

The motivational factors are based on such national statistics as the fact that 90 percent of assaults and burglaries occur at night. (See other motivational factors related to crime and accidents identified in the "Features and Benefits" section of this plan.)

G. Customer Awareness

1. *Recognize a Need*
A sharp rise in lawsuits involving improperly lit streets and walkways is heightening awareness levels of the need for more street lighting.
2. *Identify the Brand*
There is greater awareness of lighting and efficiency in all market segments. There is also increasing use of the highly efficient sodium lamps and conversion of mercury vapor lamps to sodium. All incandescent systems will be converted to high-pressure sodium in the next 18 months.
3. *Associate the Brand with Desirable Features*
While our manufacturing customers associate the features of OPL for security purposes and relate those positive factors to our company, there is a negative attitude because of the eight-week installation time, owing to inadequate company procedures in dealing with outside subcontractors.

H. Segment Trends

Within the street lighting segment of the market, the statistics cited earlier indicate a clear-cut trend toward concern for the use of additional lighting for safety, security, crime prevention, and business growth.

Situation Analysis PART III: Competitor Analysis (Process Heating)

[*Author's note:* Instead of lighting, another market segment, process heating, is used in this section to better explain competitor analysis.]

A. Market Share
List all major competitors, in descending-size order, showing relative position. List enough additional competitors to show a total minimum list of five.

B. Competitive Strengths and Weaknesses
What are the weak and strong points in comparing competitors' financial resources, management leadership, human resources, and other relevant data?

C. Product Comparison

How do the company's products compare with those of the competition with regard to:

1. Pricing, price lines, and discounts.
2. Product features and quality. What are the specific features and benefits of the competitive products? Is quality consistent according to intended design? How about product performance and value?
3. Advertising volume and effectiveness.
4. Effectiveness of distribution and sales methods. Address both distribution mix (sales through dealers or direct) as well as physical distribution of finished products.
5. Packaging. Review comparisons with competitive brands on the basis of tests for performance and preference; also review quality, size, models, and innovations.
6. Attitudes of various classes of customers by quality, service, performance, and image.
7. Trends in competitors' share of market. Specify trends of share gains in individual product and/or product lines. If possible, also relate to distribution channel.
8. Sales force effectiveness and market coverage. Review effectiveness as it relates to sales and service for each of the market segments that are critical—for example, effectiveness of sales and service with industrial accounts as well as dealers.

A. Market Share

Total overall market share is about 4.6 percent of consumption, as indicated in the following table.

Application	Total Market Size (Millions of kwh)	Our Market Share (%)	Our Customer Annual Energy Use (Millions of kwh)
Forging	142	45.0	164
Heat treating	2,685	9.5	260
Molding plastics	217	100.0	217
Kilns	286	11.5	21
Melting > 1,000° F	2,101	1.0	12
Melting < 1,000° F	971	62.0	803
Ovens > 600° F	9,088	1.0	85
Ovens < 600° F	1,934	29.0	569
Die casting	161	75.0	46
Salt bath	139	91.0	36
Drying	1,436	1.0	24
Liquid heating	18,450	0.1	25
Plating	206	66.0	236
Total	37,817		2,498

B. Competitive Strengths and Weaknesses

Gas marketing engineers are generally more knowledgeable about customers' operations than are the company's industrial marketing engineers. The competitors also have greater financial resources to offer as incentives to the customers.

C. Product Comparison

1. *Pricing, Price Lines, Discounts*

The installed cost of an electric process heating system is typically two or three times the price of similar systems using natural gas. At an average gas price of $5.50 per million BTU's and an electric cost of $0.6 per kwh:

- Electric energy is about two times more expensive than gas at temperatures below 600 degrees Fahrenheit.
- Electric energy is about equal with gas at processed temperatures in the 1,800-degree Fahrenheit range and is less expensive at the higher temperatures.

2. *Product Features and Quality*

Electric heat is much easier to incorporate into automated applications and assembly line applications. Higher production and demand for uniform product quality tend to favor electric heat. It is easily programmed for spot heating and automatic operation, which is not the case for gas process heating equipment, which requires more sophisticated maintenance.

3. *Advertising Volume and Effectiveness*

Process heat is a very diverse and not a well-defined end-use application category. As a result, no advertising has been budgeted for this market segment.

[*Author's note:* In other circumstances, comparative charts of advertising volume, media, and effectiveness would be inserted.]

4. *Effectiveness of Distribution and Sales Methods*

The sales forces of most equipment vendors are limited and target customers are not identified in an organized manner. Many process heating equipment manufacturers offer comparable electric and gas equipment.

5. *Packaging*

[*Author's note:* Not applicable in this example.]

6. *Attitudes of Various Classes of Customers*

Customers are particularly sensitive to the company's charges and are very concerned about rate increases. As rates escalate, there will be some shift to off-peak production, limited to some extent by the labor premium for second or third shifts.

7. *Trends in Competitors' Share of Market*

Natural gas is expected to maintain its price advantage over electricity during the next five years. No supply shortages are forecast and local gas companies will continue to accelerate their aggressive approach to capture more market share. This effort includes flexible rate options, financing programs, and free consulting services.

[*Author's note:* When more extensive competitor analysis is available, as suggested by the checklists in Chapter 2, information would be added.]

8. *Sales Force Effectiveness and Market Coverage*

[*Author's note:* See item 4. In typical industrial or consumer goods firms, sales managers would provide the appropriate data.]

Marketing Opportunities In light of the facts presented in the previous two sections, now examine your strengths, weaknesses, and options. Your opportunities will begin to emerge from this examination as you consider the variety of alternatives available.

Do not attempt to restrict your thinking at this time. Consider all possibilities that can expand your coverage of existing markets and lay the groundwork for entering new markets. A screening process will identify the major opportunities when you establish objectives and determine resources required. [*Author's note:* See Portfolio Analysis in Chapter 3 for three approaches to screening opportunities.]

A. Present Markets

What are the best opportunities for the expansion of present markets through cultivation of new business/new users/ competitive displacement; increasing usage by present customers; rescoping of market segments; reconfiguration of the product; new uses of present product; repositioning the product; and new market segments?

B. Buyers

What are the best opportunities for improving or expanding channels of distribution; product pricing; product promotion; enhancing customer service; and trade buying practices?

C. Growth Markets

Identify the major product growth markets in key areas (state geographic location, if applicable). Which markets represent the greatest long-term potential?

D. Product and Service Development and Innovation

What are the immediate and long-range opportunities for product development and innovation in the following areas: addition of new products to the line; diversification into new or related products, product lines, and/or new items or features; product modification (alterations); and packaging improvements? What new services should be offered (or current services improved)?

E. Targets of Opportunity

List any areas outside of your current market segment or product line (and not included in your marketing plan) that you would like to explore.

A. Present Markets

- Residential security lighting (expansion)
- Nonresidential interior lighting (increased usage)
- Induction melting (displace gas competitors)
- Dual fuel (new uses)
- Commercial cooking (reposition product)

B. Buyers

Present distribution: Provide special training to electrical contractors, sellers, and installers of all forms of lighting applications and controls.
Pricing: Provide a builder allowance for add-on outdoor lighting packages.
Promotion: Expand current advertising to mention the safety benefits of lighting.
Trade buying practices: Form better working relationships with architects, lighting engineers, and builders.
New channels of distribution: Establish a full-time field sales force specializing in lighting.
Company service: Establish a corporate lighting group to plan marketing programs and serve as technical support for all lighting activities.

C. Growth Markets

Process heat: Target specific lighting applications involving high-temperature and precise-temperature control.

D. Product and Service Development and Innovation

Evaluate current lighting equipment and change specifications to conform to new automated factories. Provide engineering assistance to manufacturing customers expanding specialized lighting operations.

Marketing Objectives Having reported relevant factual data in the Situation Analysis section and interpreted their meaning and consequences to your product line in the Opportunities section, set the goals you want to achieve during the current planning period. One part of this section focuses on your primary or overall objectives as they relate to sales, market share, profits, and return on investment. Another part is a statement of your functional objectives, which concern both product- and nonproduct-related goals.

For those goals to be realistic and achievable, you must first generate assumptions and projections about future conditions and trends.

A. Assumptions and Projections

List your major assumptions for the current planning period in relation to:

1. Economic assumptions: gross national product, industrial production, plant and equipment expenditures, activities of

competitors, costs and prices, local economics, consumer
expenditures, tendencies, changes in customer needs.
2. Technological assumptions: intensity of research and development effort, likelihood of technical breakthroughs,
availability of raw materials, plant capacity.
3. Sociopolitical assumptions: prospective legislation, probability of political tensions, tax picture, population patterns, education, consumer habits, changes in customer
needs.

A. Assumptions and Projections

1. *Economic Assumptions*
There will be no single big market that will create unusual
growth. However, significant gains can result from work on
every market segment.
2. *Technological Assumptions*
Rate increases can't be counted on to achieve corporate marketing objectives and should be considered only as a last resort.
3. *Sociopolitical Assumptions*
Within the economic environment of slow growth (1 percent
per year), deregulation, and aggressive competition, we must
become a more customer-oriented, market-driven company if
we are to achieve our objectives.

B. Primary Objectives

1. Financial objectives: state current and projected sales,
units, profit margins, market-share objectives, as well as
any other financial measurements required by the organization.
2. Entrepreneurial objectives: relate to nonmeasurable objectives for which you will not be accountable, but that are
key success factors—for example, innovative product/
price/promotion and distribution. (Optional or as required
by senior management.)

1. *Financial Objectives*
Sales and market-share objectives of the product:

Lighting Segment	Sales ($M)	Units of kwh (M)	Market Share (%)
Residential, outdoor	4.0	21	64
Outdoor protective lighting	1.7	3	29
Street lighting	1.4	3	29
Commercial	1.2	3	21
Commercial, outdoor	3.8	19	37
Total for market segment	12.1	55	

Profit and other financial objectives:

Lighting Segment	Profit Before Taxes ($000)		Return on Investment (%)
Residential, outdoor	600	(15%)	25
Outdoor protective lighting	340	(20%)	15
Street lighting	252	(18%)	20
Commercial, indoor	180	(15%)	23
Commercial, outdoor	684	(18%)	20
Total	$2,056		20.6 (avg)

C. Functional Objectives

1. Product objectives:
   a. Development
   b. Modification
   c. Differentiation
   d. Diversification
   e. Deletion
   f. Segmentation
   g. Pricing
   h. Promotion
   i. Distribution mix
   j. Physical distribution
   k. Packaging
   l. Service
   m. Other

(Functional objectives normally refer to the marketing mix: product/pricing/distribution/promotion.)

2. Nonproduct objectives:
   a. Manufacturing
   b. Marketing research
   c. Credit
   d. Sales activities (educational/informational)
   e. R&D
   f. Training
   g. Human resource development

1. Product Objectives

Development: Launch a new product line of directional outdoor residential lighting (fourth quarter, Johnson and division managers).

Modification: Reduce installation time of new outdoor protective lighting products from six weeks to three weeks (third quarter, Ludlow).

Pricing: (a) Institute a leased lighting program with a payback period of three to six years to increase market penetration (fourth quarter, Quinn); (b) rebate $100 per customer on conversions of manual lighting to automatic controls (first quarter, Brooks); and (c) offer 10 percent reduction on the first annual lighting bill for all new outdoor protective lighting industrial customers (second quarter, Lanier).

Promotion: (a) Develop and distribute a catalog showing new product line of lighting fixtures to use for mailing and for leave-behind by sales force (third quarter, Timmons); (b) develop a coordinated space advertising and direct-mail program to business owners, stressing the benefit of outdoor lighting (third quarter, Timmons); and (c) establish a dedicated sales force that specializes in lighting (fourth quarter, Johnson).

Distribution: Set up master contracts with 15 to 20 contractors covering each target area identified in the business redevelopment section of the company's trading area (second quarter, Thompson).

Packaging: (a) Add an outdoor lighting package to a building allowance program for all new construction of single or multiple housing (second quarter, Thompson); and (b) offer eight new choices of decorative lighting in the three new regional shopping malls (second quarter, Ludlow).

Service: Launch new programs to survey lighting efficiency among residential, commercial, and industrial customers (first quarter, Lange).

2. *Nonproduct Objectives*

Human Resource Development: (a) Set up a training program to train lighting specialists and service planners to design systems in cooperation with customers (second quarter, London); and (b) train a speaker corps made up of senior- and middle-level managers to present the benefits of street lighting to business and commercial groups (third quarter, Bordwin).

Strategies and Action Plans Strategy is the art of coordinating the means (money, human resources, materials) to achieve the end (profits, customer satisfaction, growth) as defined by company policy and objectives. In this section, strategies have to be identified and put into action. Responsibilities have to be assigned, schedules set, budgets established, and checkpoints determined. Make sure that the operations groups (sales, manufacturing, etc.) actively participate in this planning exercise, since they are the ones that have to implement it.

A. Marketing Strategies and Tactics

1. Product strategy: What changes are needed in product and packaging?
2. Pricing strategy: What changes are needed in prices, discounts, and long-term contracts?
3. Advertising strategy: What are the most effective benefits to feature, and how should basic copy ideas and copy themes be presented to special groups?

4. Media stragegy: What suggestions for consideration by media department of advertising agency should be made?
5. Promotion strategies: What suggestions to private label, dealers and/or distribution and/or POS consumers, and sales force (direct and dealer/distribution) should be made?
6. Other tactics.

1. *Product Strategy*
Institute new installation procedures for outdoor protective lighting in north side of city where high-crime, high-accident areas exist (third quarter, Levine).

2. *Pricing Strategy*
- Rebate $100 per customer on conversions of manual lighting to automatic controls (first quarter, Brooks).
- Offer 10 percent reduction on first annual lighting bill for all new outdoor protective lighting industrial customers (second quarter, Lanier).

3. *Advertising Strategy*
Select the most effective benefits to be featured and present basic copy ideas and copy themes to special groups.

- Employ copy themes that promote the value of lighting to architects, lighting engineers, and builders through key trade publications serving those groups.
- Focus on copy themes that capitalize on growing public concern about theft, vandalism, and crime through an aggressive campaign at least five times frequency in all local media.

4. *Media Strategy*
Produce TV and radio advertising dealing directly with the security and decorative aspects of lighting. Place in prime evening viewing over the next 12 months. Major copy theme: "You Are Not Always There to Protect Your Home. But Lights Are" (first quarter, Broderick).
[*Author's note:* Advertising agency or department promotion plans would be attached to the marketing plan.]

5. *Promotion Strategies*
(a) For OEM (original equipment manufacturer), private label dealer, and/or distributors: (1) display indoor/outdoor lighting at customer energy center; (2) develop literature that highlights themes in general advertising program for use at fairs, exhibits, and customer offices and as bill enclosures that target the value of residential outdoor lighting for safety and beautification (second quarter, Lutt); and (3) conduct six contractor/builder information meetings during next 12 months to educate them on the value of lighting and on the technical aspects of installation (first quarter, Thomas).

(b) For the sales force: (1) redeploy sales force to high-potential industrial parks now under construction; and (2) install salary/commission package and eliminate former salary-only compensation plan.

6. *Other Tactics*

Compile, publish, and distribute reports, case studies, magazine articles, and press releases that describe successful installations (first quarter, Thompson).

Establish a corporate lighting group to plan marketing programs and serve as technical support for all lighting activities.

Summary Statement of Final Strategy Include the highlights of your basic strategies aimed at achieving your primary objectives. Show the market segments, characteristics, barriers, and the strategies.

You may also include alternative and contingency plans if situations occur whereby objectives cannot be reached. Make sure they relate to the overall marketing plan (not just product or product-line plans) as well as the corporate objectives.

Summary of Final Strategy for Lighting Product

Market	Characteristics	Barriers	Strategies
Residential interior lighting	High growth New energy-saving products available Represents 14% of electric energy consumed	Customer resistance to spending for high-efficiency lamps Resistance to increased costs of lighting energy	Use price incentives on usage of energy Introduce a new product line of energy-saving fixtures
Commercial/ industrial interior lighting	Represents 16% of electric energy Energy savings are big considerations Worker productivity is related to lighting	Initial cost of new lighting systems high Inadequate staff to provide consultation on energy savings	Create a special sales force to reach new industrial parks Conduct lighting seminar featuring safety, improved merchandising results, esthetics, and productivity

(continued)

Summary of Final Strategy for Lighting Product (*continued*)

Market	Characteristics	Barriers	Strategies
Street lighting	High growth 40–55% of service areas have no street lighting Safety, security, crime are strong motivational factors	Difficult for service areas to fund project Slow purchase decision, average two years	Help communities develop street lighting master plans Assign lighting specialist to speed-up purchase Institute new installation procedures by priority areas
Residential/ commercial outdoor protective lighting	High growth 90% of assaults and burglaries occur at night Served by industrial contractors High priority for residential and commercial customers	Long lead time for installation Lack of control over contractors	Conduct technical seminars for contractors Promote the value of out-door lighting to business owners through general advertising, direct mail, and business meetings

Financial Controls and Budgets   Having completed the design phase of your marketing plan, you must decide how you will monitor its execution. Therefore, before implementing it, you have to develop procedures for both control (comparing actual and planned figures) and review corrective measures taken.

[*Author's note:* These budgeting and controlling aspects generally conform to the procedures established by the financial department.]

Item	Current Year Budget ($000)	Current Year Actual ($000)	Budget Next Year
Total sales (lighting)	11.2	11.4	12.1
Units kwh (M)	50.0	52.0	55.0

Item	Current Year Budget ($000)	Current Year Actual ($000)	Budget Next Year
Market share (average, all segments)	34.0	34.2	36.5
Field selling (allocation $)	1.2	1.4	2.5
Administration ($)	.5	.5	.7
Advertising and promotion ($)	1.5	1.8	2.0
Workshops ($)	.1	.1	.2
Other	.2	.2	.3
Total marketing ($)	3.5	4.0	5.7

Guidelines for Planning

You have just reviewed an abbreviated version of an actual marketing plan for a midwestern utility company. While the terminology may differ from yours, the conditions are the same as for any other business, product, or service. There are sales to be achieved, a product to be delivered, a service to be provided, market segment opportunities to be reached, competitor activities to be monitored, and environmental factors to be dealt with.

The plan has a logical progression: where you have been, where you want to go, how you want to get there, and how you know when you have arrived. More specifically, Figure 7-2 outlines an eight-step process for reaching the ultimate outcome of any marketing plan: the development of competitive marketing strategies.

Schedule for Marketing Planning The purpose of a planning schedule is to demonstrate that effective planning is a participative process requiring input from all levels of management. While Figure 7-3, a calendarized schedule, displays an optimum situation, the activities and units of responsibility may vary within each organization. In practice, many organizations with formalized planning systems will take a six-month period to develop an operating plan. If a company is working on a calendar year, the process begins in July and is usually submitted to top management by November or early December.

Figure 7-2. *The marketing planning process.*

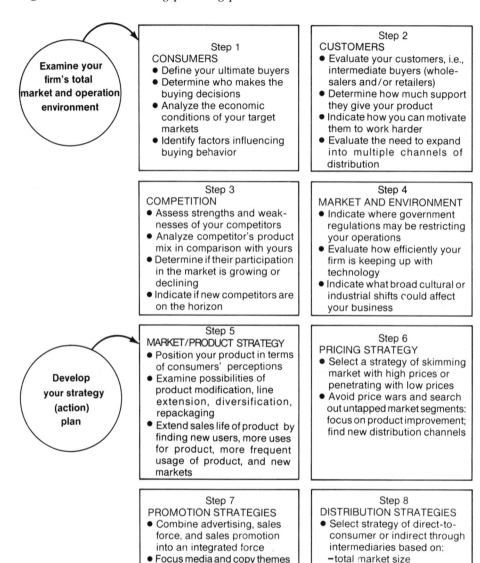

Examine your firm's total market and operation environment

Step 1
CONSUMERS
- Define your ultimate buyers
- Determine who makes the buying decisions
- Analyze the economic conditions of your target markets
- Identify factors influencing buying behavior

Step 2
CUSTOMERS
- Evaluate your customers, i.e., intermediate buyers (wholesalers and/or retailers)
- Determine how much support they give your product
- Indicate how you can motivate them to work harder
- Evaluate the need to expand into multiple channels of distribution

Step 3
COMPETITION
- Assess strengths and weaknesses of your competitors
- Analyze competitor's product mix in comparison with yours
- Determine if their participation in the market is growing or declining
- Indicate if new competitors are on the horizon

Step 4
MARKET AND ENVIRONMENT
- Indicate where government regulations may be restricting your operations
- Evaluate how efficiently your firm is keeping up with technology
- Indicate what broad cultural or industrial shifts could affect your business

Develop your strategy (action) plan

Step 5
MARKET/PRODUCT STRATEGY
- Position your product in terms of consumers' perceptions
- Examine possibilities of product modification, line extension, diversification, repackaging
- Extend sales life of product by finding new users, more uses for product, more frequent usage of product, and new markets

Step 6
PRICING STRATEGY
- Select a strategy of skimming market with high prices or penetrating with low prices
- Avoid price wars and search out untapped market segments: focus on product improvement; find new distribution channels

Step 7
PROMOTION STRATEGIES
- Combine advertising, sales force, and sales promotion into an integrated force
- Focus media and copy themes to match market and sales obstacles
- Determine sales force size, design territories, and select compensation methods based on overall objectives
- Use sales promotion to encourage more product usage, induce dealer involvement and stimulate greater sales force efforts

Step 8
DISTRIBUTION STRATEGIES
- Select strategy of direct-to-consumer or indirect through intermediaries based on:
  - total market size
  - type of customer services provided or replacement rate of product
  - amount of control you want over channel
  - extent of market coverage

Figure 7-3. *Schedule of marketing planning.*

Planning Activity	Unit Responsible	Week(s) No.
1. Marketing research conducts situation analysis and generates background data.	Marketing research	
2. Marketing research develops assumptions about future environment and identifies current position.	Marketing research	
3. Top management sets corporate objectives.	Top management	
4. Marketing vice-president interprets corporate objectives and derives marketing objectives with input of strategy team or product manager.	Vice-president marketing	
5. Sales and expense forecasts are established.	Marketing research controller	
6. Product managers develop optimum strategies for their assigned lines and review with marketing vice-president.	Product managers, vice-president marketing	
7. Product managers design detailed action programs and review with general sales manager.	Product managers, general sales manager	
8. Product managers write up their proposals and submit them to marketing vice-president.	Product manager	
9. Marketing reviews and coordinates individual product plans.	Vice-president marketing	
10. General sales manager assigns district volume objectives.	General sales manager	

(continued)

Figure 7-3. *Continued.*

Planning Activity	Unit Responsible	Week(s) No.										
11. District managers develop district sales plans in consultation with sales people.	District sales managers											
12. General sales manager reviews and integrates district sales plans.	General sales manager											
13. Product managers prepare financial summaries.	Product managers											
14. Controller prepares operating budget.	Controller											
15. Top marketing reviews and approves marketing plan.	Top management											

Getting Started: Form a Strategy Team One of the best approaches for gaining participation in the marketing plan, and in the total strategic marketing plan, is to form a *strategy team* made up of individuals from different functions of the organization. For example, include individuals from finance, product development, sales, promotion, manufacturing, distribution, and research and development (or the equivalent). The members of the team are not meant to take passive roles, but to be totally involved in the development of the plan, from analyzing the opportunities to creating objectives and strategies. For it is through this participation that new markets and new product opportunities are developed, which, in turn, help secure the future of the organization. Specific responsibilities of a planning team are presented in Chapter 13.

Evaluating a Marketing Plan The following *qualitative guidelines* serve as a checklist to evaluate the marketing plan and the total strategic marketing plan. This checklist is particularly useful in determining whether there are specific actions and action plans that evolve from the plan.

1. Are there strategies for enlarging current markets?
2. Are there strategies for developing new markets?
3. Are there strategies for defining the position for the product?
4. Are there strategies for protecting existing sales volume?
5. Are there strategies for launching new products?

For *quantitative measures* of overall planning performance, use the following:

1. Total sales and profits: compare with preceding years.
2. Market share: measure performance relative to that of competitors.
3. Sales analysis: compare sales variations from plans by breakdowns such as geography, salespeople, customers, and products.
4. Distribution cost analysis: determine the relative profitability of present ways of doing business through various channels.
5. Measures of customer satisfaction: use surveys, customer panels, and other market feedback.

Still another approach to evaluating a marketing plan, and the total strategic marketing plan, is being undertaken by a number of progressive organizations: creating an additional planning team to act as if it were your competitor. The intention is to view your company from a different perspective, from a competitor's perspective. By doing so, you often uncover weaknesses that you could not identify from the more narrow perspective of developing your own plan. The approach also identifies areas of product and market vulnerability that can be points of entry by competitors. This planning technique can prove invaluable in developing a product that would prevent entree into a specific market segment.

Develop Your Own Strategic Marketing Plan

The planning format presented in this chapter and in Chapter 6 represents an application of the total strategic marketing planning process. It is practical and workable and is currently being used by well-known organizations with domestic and international operations. With slight modification, you can use it for a specific product, for a service, for a division, or for the entire company. Use it with judgment by either increasing the detail in the sections or decreasing the content to suit the requirements of your business.

To get started:

1. Review the content of the strategic marketing plan in the last two chapters.
2. Make necessary changes so that the format and terminology conform to your business.

3. Assemble a small planning group and give it a name, such as "Product Management Team" or "Strategic Team." (The team approach is covered in more detail in Chapter 13.)

4. Brief the group on the planning format and stress the reasons why its input is imperative if full advantage is to be taken of new market and product opportunities. Also emphasize that maintaining a competitive advantage is everyone's responsibility.

5. Set up a calendar of meetings and activities, and then *get started.* Don't attempt to abbreviate the planning process. Go through the plan step by step and box by box and you will be rewarded with a structured and well-developed strategic marketing plan.

FOUR

Specific
Competitive Strategies

This part is designed to provide you with a practical working guide for developing specific competitive strategies, including the use of strategy teams for doing so.

Chapters 8 through 12 focus on the components of the marketing mix: market, product, pricing, promotion, and distribution. They include strategy applications and action steps; show the relationship of the marketing mix to the competitive analysis; use the marketing mix to isolate marketing problems and to develop marketing solutions; and identify strategies along the product life cycle. Chapter 13 discusses the use of strategy teams as the most effective means for blending human factors with the marketing concept to achieve competitive advantage.

8

Market Strategies

Objectives:
To enable you to

1. Recognize the *five major areas* concerned with developing a market strategy

2. Identify and initiate the steps needed to convert market strategies into *action*

You need to look at your market in its totality. Consider market dimension and segments, market entry procedures, amount of commitment, level of product demand, and opportunities to diversify. Determine if you want to be in a particular market; how much of it you want; how you are going to hold on to it; and how you are going to manage it for long-term profitable growth.

Market Dimension

Select the size of market you can handle successfully against competition. Concentrate selling power into markets that offer a greater chance of success. Avoid spreading out the marketing efforts and thereby becoming vulnerable to competitors. When growth opportunities become available, branch out to additional markets.

Strategy Applications
- Segments (geographic, demographic, life style)
- Single market
- Multimarket
- Total market

- Regional market
- National market

Commentary Refer to Chapter 2 for a detailed discussion of segmentation. Review how to segment a market and how to apply segmentation criteria.

Figure 8-1 illustrates the various strategy applications from single-market concentration, to product specialist, to market specialist, to selective target niches, to total market coverage. For example, in *(a)* you may have identified a poorly served, neglected, or emerging market niche and introduced a dedicated product or service. Having established a foothold in a niche (a fragment of a segment), you have a series of choices. You can consider *(b)* and become a product specialist and expand your product line. Or you can consider *(c)* and become a market specialist serving, for example, the banking industry with a total commitment consisting of a diverse grouping of products and services. If you choose *(d)*, you can employ a highly selective niche strategy concentrating in areas of most favorable opportunities. Where expansion continues, *(e)* reflects a full market–

Figure 8-1. *Market dimension strategy applications.*

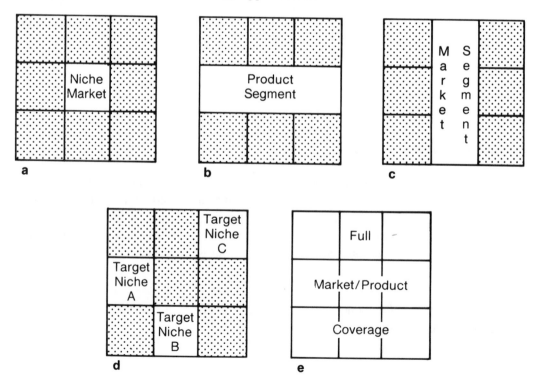

product coverage. The evolution of the process is exemplified by Seiko watches, which started in a single niche and spread into full market coverage with 400 models of watches.

An example of the reversal of the process, from full market to niche strategy, is the banking industry. Deregulation of banking in the early 1980's phased out interest-rate ceilings and permitted the tightly regulated banks to compete aggressively. As a result, many banks began to change over from full service and to pursue a strategy of segment marketing. Chemical Bank (New York) pushed its automatic teller machines to increase share of *consumer* deposits. Bankers Trust Co. (New York) concentrated strictly in *wholesale* banking. Republic National Bank (Dallas) specialized in the *energy* business. Madison Bank & Trust Co. (Chicago) specialized its services for the *commuter*. Riggs National Bank of Washington, D.C. geared its services to *trade associations* based in the Capitol. These examples illustrate a radical change in strategy from offering full service to dominating a market segment and competing vigorously for market share within a confined specialty.

Market Entry

A first-in strategy has the advantage of identifying you as the market leader. Often, follow-the-leader and last-in strategies must conform to the market leader. In the latter situations, create a competitive advantage using product, price, promotion, or methods of distribution to overcome the leader's advantages.

Strategy Applications
- First-in strategy
- Follow-the-leader strategy
- Last-in strategy

Commentary In some instances there are persuasive arguments in favor of pursuing a follow-the-leader strategy. Coca-Cola was not the first in the no-caffeine cola category; Procter & Gamble was not first in soft soap; nor was IBM the first in personal computers. Yet these organizations have significant market shares in those categories. The chief argument for a follow-the-leader strategy is that you leave all the costly product development, market research, and initial market entry—as well as the major risks—to someone else.

Ultimately, the decision in market entry depends on your resources, your ability to sustain a competitive edge (particularly if you are first in), and your long-term objective as it relates to amount of market share and your position in the market.

Case Example

Lance, Inc. To illustrate market entry strategy, consider Lance, Inc., the largest and most profitable independent marketer of snack foods in the United States as of 1987. Lance reversed its previous strategy of being first to enter a market because of excessive losses on new product introduction and its constant head-on confrontation with its major competitors in the industry, such as Anheuser-Busch's Eagle snacks and Frito-Lay. Lance decided to hold back and let the competition do the market research for new product introduction. When a new product succeeded, Lance followed into the market with a similar product at a lower price.

But a one-dimensional strategy of following in at a lower price is seldom the whole story. Market entry is but one consideration of a market strategy, which, in turn, is but one portion of the entire marketing mix. For example, Lance took an indirect approach to its market by not competing head to head in supermarkets with its formidable competitors, preferring to sell through small convenience stores that generated 50 percent of its sales. Another 30 percent of sales came from 70,000 company-owned vending machines situated mostly in noncompetitive locations. And 12 percent of revenues came from selling snacks to restaurants and schools.

Lance's follow-the-leader market strategy and indirect approach avoided the fight for shelf space, the related deep discounts, and expensive promotions.

Market Commitment

The degree of commitment to a market is determined by company priorities and resources. Consider if heavy involvement should be the major thrust of your growth strategy, or if less involvement is best to protect other market commitments.

Strategy Applications
- Major commitment
- Average commitment
- Limited commitment

Commentary There are two dimensions to market commitment: yours and your competitors'. As discussed in Chapters 2 and 3, competitive strategy requires that you use your strengths against the weaknesses of the competitor. Therefore, the commitment is determined through a side-by-side analysis of how much commitment will be given to key areas such as extent of new product development, amount of market share desired, and willingness to sustain an aggressive promotional effort against competitors. You also need to determine your competitors' pattern of behavior and how they are likely to respond to your major or limited commitment. (Checklists in Chapter 2 are provided for this analysis.) And, finally, you need to consider how and what you communicate to the marketplace (your customers and competitors) about the amount of commitment you will make—that is, major, average, or limited.

Market Demand

Managing market demand is a key factor to successful performance. You need to know to prune markets when demand slackens; to concentrate on key markets when demand increases; and to harvest profits when sales plateau and cash flow is needed.

Strategy Applications
- Pruning strategy
- Key-market strategy
- Harvesting strategy

Commentary Managing market demand requires flexibility, good timing, and extensive use of competitive analysis. For example, Chrysler Corp. used a pruning strategy during its period of revitalization in the early 1980's. It pulled out of European markets and then selected key markets with the successful K cars, while harvesting profits during the succeeding years. Though obviously simplified, the execution of the strategy through a five-year period can be recorded as one of the greatest turn-arounds in business history. Thus, the applications of market demand strategy are offshoots of the concepts and strategies of concentration and segmentation as they relate to selectively expanding or contracting your presence in a market.

Market Diversification

You should be aware of opportunities to add new businesses that relate to existing production or distribution capabilities (horizontal); to add another stage of production or distribution to existing operations: one that either precedes or follows in the ultimate path to the consumer (vertical); and to diversify into unrelated businesses using new technology and marketing strategies (lateral).

Strategy
Applications
- Horizontal diversification
- Vertical diversification
- Lateral diversification

Commentary Market diversification presents many opportunities for middle- and upper-level managers to exercise innovation and entrepreneurial thinking.

Horizontal Diversification

Procter & Gamble and Borden are experts in horizontal diversification. Originally a soap company, Procter & Gamble has long since expanded horizontally into such diverse products as cake mixes, potato chips, coffee, paper products, toothpastes, deodorants, and detergents. Borden's product mix ranges from American cheese and reconstituted lemon juice to glue and adhesive tape.

What these companies have discovered is that great economies can be derived from using the same sales force to sell new product categories to the same retail outlets, simply by applying already developed marketing skills. Because it involves building on an existing strength, either in technology or in marketing, horizontal diversification is the most promising and least risky of the market diversification strategies.

Vertical Diversification

Hart Schaffner & Marx, the manufacturer of such famous clothing brands as Hickey-Freeman and Christian Dior, acquired a chain of retail stores in the early 1980's to add to its existing stores. This type of vertical diversification is common. Another form of vertical diversification is practiced by some large retailers that produce some of the goods they sell: Sears makes some of its own appliances, or has large ownership interests in manufacturers. A&P makes much of its own baked goods. In the industrial sector, Ford has long owned its steel-making facilities.

Vertical diversification (or integration) increases risk because the management of one level of business (retailing) may not have enough expertise at another level (manufacturing).

Lateral Diversification

Lateral diversification is the most extreme form of diversification because it usually represents a complete departure from current operations. The only connection is that diverse businesses are owned by the same parent. The resulting group is called a conglomerate and was made popular in the 1960's by such corporate names as Ling-Temco-Vought, ITT Corporation, Litton Industries, Inc., and Gulf + Western, Inc.

While this form of diversification still occurs through holding companies, the current trend is more restrained, and portfolios of businesses are put together with a more cohesive strategic direction. (The frameworks for strategic direction and developing a business portfolio are discussed in Chapter 6.)

Action Steps

Market strategies must eventually be converted into actions. Keep in mind that you need to concentrate on a market that has long-term growth potential. If competitors throw obstacles in the way, assess their weaknesses and focus your strengths against them (remember the indirect approach). Their vulnerabilities will usually be apparent in areas such as product, service, pricing, channels of distribution, sales force, and promotion.

To identify strategies and initiate action:

1. List market segments representing your best opportunities.
2. Evaluate the strengths and weaknesses of the segments.
3. Identify the points of entry.
4. Consider the amount of commitment needed.
5. Monitor progress in entering and penetrating a market, or in defending existing market share.
6. List immediate strategies and tactics that can be implemented.

9

Product/Service Strategies

Objectives:
To enable you to

1. Recognize the *seven major areas* of product considerations
2. Learn five steps for developing a *positioning* strategy
3. Identify the phases of a product's *life cycle* and the life-cycle extension strategies for application to your own products
4. Gain an understanding of the four steps involved in the evolution of a *new product*
5. Learn to use the *product audit* for sustaining product profitability
6. Identify and initiate the steps needed to convert product strategies into *action*

Reviewing your products and/or services presents a dual opportunity.[1] First, you can become aware of the changing needs and wants of customers on which you can base the development of new products. In addition, you can determine how and when to remove losing and marginal products. The seven major areas of product considerations—positioning, product life cycle, product competition, product mix, product design, new products, and product audit—provide a systematic framework for developing strategies.

Positioning

Find out how customers perceive your product by examining the image it projects and the needs it satisfies. Monitor these perceptions

[1] For the sake of simplicity, the word *product* is used to cover services as well. Today, banks, insurance companies, and many other organizations that traditionally used the term *services* now refer to what they provide as products.

270

through observation and research. If they are undesirable, change them. Then, locate an open position in the market and in the customer's mind. Occupy that new position and protect it against competitive inroads.

Strategy
Applications
- Positioning a single brand
- Positioning multiple brands
- Repositioning older products

Commentary A product's position in a customer's mind is the result of three groups of influences:

1. The company's total effort, including its marketing mix.
2. Environmental influences, including competitive efforts.
3. The customer's own perceptual processes, including internal influences.

Positioning can be described as the location of a product on the perceptual map of the customer with respect to a set of coordinates representing the two major attributes customers use to evaluate products in a particular category (gentleness of a detergent versus its cleaning power, for example); competitive offerings; and the customer's conception of an ideal product in this category. Consequently, your competitors' positions are as important as your own, especially since you can relate to them in your communications efforts. The goal of positioning, then, is to create a desired position for your product and against your competition in the customer's mind.

Perceptual Mapping

But how can these aspects of positioning be investigated and illustrated? A technique known as perceptual mapping is often used to identify relative positions of competing brands. Consumers are asked to express the strength of their attitudes regarding a list of attributes in comparing a number of competitive brands. The resulting scores are entered onto a diagram that depicts the comparative ratings of the different brands involved.

Perceptual mapping can be explained best by using an example, as illustrated in Figure 9-1. In a survey, 500 male beer drinkers in Chicago were asked to rate 35 characteristics of four national (A, B, C, D) and four local (M, N, O, P) brands of beer. With the help of

Figure 9-1. *Actual positions of competing brands of beer on consumers' perceptual map.*

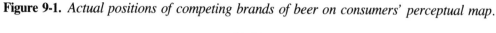
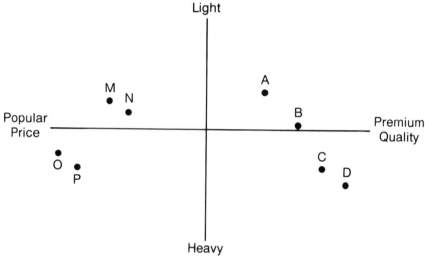

In a survey of 500 male beer drinkers in Chicago, the respondents considered the relative lightness and price/quality ratio of a beer the most important criteria in evaluating and selecting a brand. The four national brands (A, B, C, D) were perceived as being of considerably higher quality than the four local brands (M, N, O, P), which seemed to rely mainly on low-price appeal.

modern statistical methods (multidimensional scaling), the two attributes that best distinguished between the relative positions of the participating brands were selected: the price/quality ratio on the one hand, and relative lightness of the beer on the other. The price/quality ratio is reflected by the horizontal axis of the system of coordinates ranging from popular price (and accordingly low quality in the eyes of the consumer) on the left end of the scale, to premium quality (at an appropriately higher price level) on the right end. The vertical axis represents relative lightness, with the upper end signifying a light beer and the lower end a heavy beer.

The illustration reveals that national Brand A is considered to be relatively light and of premium quality, while local Brand O has a cheap image and is viewed as being about medium in lightness. While such results are quite interesting, their informational content is somewhat limited. The positions of the brands are indicated, but sufficient data for strategic decisions are not provided. Rather, to be able to develop an optimum strategy, the respondents' *ideal points* have to be indicated in the graph. An ideal point is defined as each consumer's personal description of attributes that he is looking for in a given

Figure 9-2. *Actual beer brand positions and ideal clusters on consumers' perceptual map.*

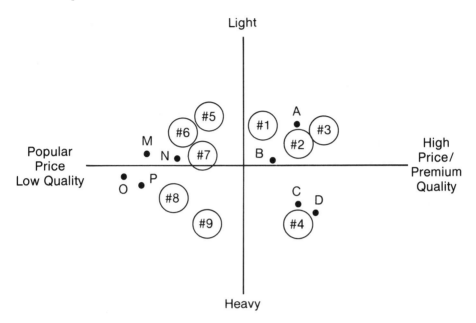

When asked to describe their ideal beers, respondents indicated preferences that combined into nine clusters. These clusters represent market opportunities and indicate that all but one of the local brands M-P are on shaky ground because they are perceived to be at some distance from any ideal cluster.

product category. These ideal points are entered into the diagram individually and not as averages. Subsequently, they are combined into *clusters* wherever a sufficient number of ideal points happen to congregate. The location and size of the clusters reflect the positions and frequencies of the ideal perceptions of consumers on the perceptual map (see Figure 9-2).

Perceptual mapping can also be used in a variety of situations, such as high-ticket purchases and business-to-business marketing. For example, Chrysler conducted a positioning study using responses to customer surveys.[2] The surveys asked owners to rank their autos on a scale of 1 to 10 for such qualities as "youthfulness," "luxury," and "practicality." The answers were then worked into a mathematical score for each model and plotted on a graph that shows broad

[2] "Car Makers Use Image Map as Tool to Position Products," *Wall Street Journal,* March 22, 1984, p. 33.

Figure 9-3. *A perceptual map of brand images.*

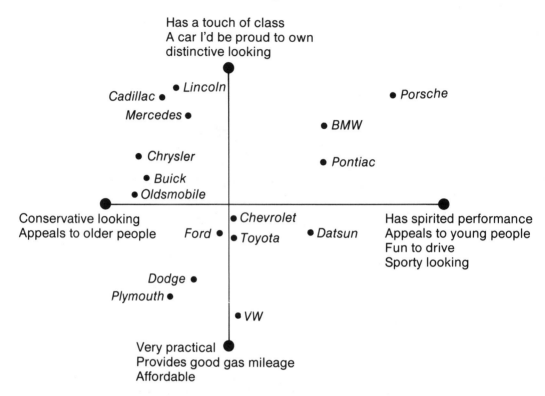

criteria for evaluating customer appeal. Figure 9-3 illustrates the results. Chrysler concluded that Plymouth, Dodge, and Chrysler all needed to present a more youthful image. It also decided that Plymouth and Dodge needed to move up sharply on the luxury scale. The advantage of the map is that it presented the cars from a consumer perspective.

Another interpretation can be made from the perceptual map shown in Figure 9-3. In viewing the results, General Motors might identify the close proximity of its Buick and Oldsmobile cars, almost on top of each other in the upper left-hand quadrant. That positioning would suggest the two divisions are waging a marketing war more against each other than against the competition.

Developing a Positioning Strategy

If the picture of your market (refer to Figure 9-2) reveals an undesirable position for your brand, the following procedure may help you improve your situation in the marketplace:

Step 1. Identify actual product position.

Step 2. Determine ideal product position.

Step 3. Develop alternative strategies for achieving ideal product position.

Step 4. Select and implement the most promising alternative.

Step 5. Compare new actual position with ideal position.

Step 1: Identification of your product's actual position invariably requires individual consumer interviews, generally in the form of a self-administered questionnaire. (Marketing research techniques are presented in Chapter 5.)

Step 2: The easiest way to select an ideal position is to accept your brand's current position, if it commands a strong position in its field, or if your brand's position coincides closely with the location of one or more major ideal clusters. A second way to determine the ideal product position is to select a position that nobody else wants.

When you consider repositioning your brand to a more favorable location on the customer's perceptual map, you should generally try to position it in the center of a major cluster. In the case of the beer survey (Figure 9-2), however, Brands C and D are leading, well-entrenched brands and Brand O would have a difficult time overtaking them. Rather, Brand O would be better off repositioning itself on the lower right periphery of cluster 8, through a combination of re-formulation (heavier flavor), modest price increase, and appropriate advertising. In this way, Brand O could hope to attract purchasers from both clusters 8 and 9 who are dissatisfied with all currently available brands. If handled properly, Brand O could be well established in its new position before any competition could enter this field.

Step 3: In attempting to achieve an ideal product position, your firm has two principal options. It can (1) move its current product to a new position, with or without a change in the product itself, or (2) introduce a separate, new product with the characteristics necessary for new positioning (leaving the current product untouched or even withdrawing it from the market).

Once you discover that your product's position is far from ideal, your advertising has its job cut out for it. Together with the other elements of your promotional mix—namely, personal selling, publicity, and sales promotion—your advertising will have to shoulder the burden of creating a new position for your product.

If you take the option of moving an existing product to a new position, you might find yourself in the situation of having to explain that your product is really different from the consumers' original perception of it. This task can be formidable unless it is facilitated by either new applications of an unchanged product or a modification of some significant product feature. Church & Dwight Co., Inc., the manufacturer of Arm & Hammer Baking Soda, relied on creating a new image for its product to stimulate sales. This product was subsequently promoted as a refrigerator and litter-box deodorant and as a drain cleaner, which revitalized its somewhat lackluster sales curve. In addition, Church & Dwight introduced a line of soda-based products, including a deodorant and a laundry detergent, all capitalizing on the well-recognized Arm & Hammer trademark.

When formulating positioning strategies, you may want to consider offering your product as an alternative to the leading brand in its category. It is generally unwise to attack a leader head on (as RCA and Xerox found out when they tried unsuccessfully to enter the computer business against IBM), unless this leader does not hold a share of mind commensurate with its share of market. In fact, your brand may benefit from being strongly related to the leader in the prospect's mind.

Step 4: After developing several alternative strategies for achieving your ideal product position, and determining their likely consequences, you are faced with the necessity of selecting one of them to implement in the marketplace. In making the decision, you should be guided by your company's overall objectives, resources, and capabilities, as well as by the specific objectives and conditions applying to your particular brand. You must consider how long and how firm a commitment your company is willing to make, and how much money it is ready to put behind such a commitment.

Achieving a lasting and favorable position is an expensive, time-consuming proposition. Success will not come overnight. Unless your company's management is firmly committed to this strategy, it is best not to tamper with your brand's position. You might do more harm than good if the effort is half-hearted, or is terminated halfway into the program.

Assuming that an appropriate commitment has been made and the most promising alternative has been selected, you have to put it into effect as rapidly as possible. Wasting time could give your competition a head start. You should carefully monitor competitive activity; it may be necessary to modify or revise your original concept in order to optimize your position in reaction to changes in market conditions.

Step 5: While tracking your competition, you also have to monitor the impact of your positioning on the customer's mind, where it counts most. Follow-up research must examine and compare your product's actual position with its desired ideal position. After all, it is possible that your program will not produce the intended results. In this event, a review of your strategy may be necessary.

Depending on how much time has elapsed since your initial study, it might be advisable to reexamine your customer's ideal points to determine whether the relevant clusters have drifted. If the clusters have shifted, appropriate changes in your approach may be required. You have to ask yourself two questions at this point: (1) Has the ideal position been achieved? (2) Is it still ideal? Periodic reexamination along these lines will ensure optimization of your product's market position and should result in substantial rewards.

Product Life Cycle

The various strategies that extend the sales life of products are the pillars of successful growth (Figure 9-4). These life-cycle extenders are the safest and most economical strategies to follow. Identify the best extension opportunities, then gain the cooperation of product developers, manufacturing, finance, distribution, marketing, and sales.

Strategy Applications
- Promote more frequent usage
- Find new users
- Find more uses for product
- Find new uses for product's basic material

Figure 9-4. *Strategy application for extending a product's life cycle.*

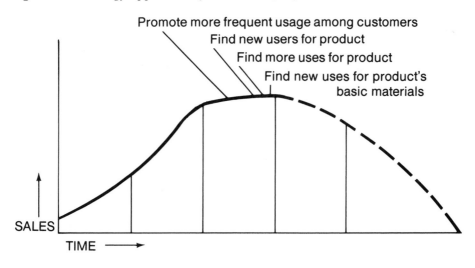

Commentary

Examples abound of organizations successfully extending the sales life of their products. The classics are nylon, Jell-O brand gelatin desserts, and Scotch brand tape. All have average life cycles of more than 50 years and are still going strong. Du Pont nylon was initially used for parachutes in World War II. The social necessity for women to wear hosiery promoted the use of nylon. It was introduced in a variety of textures and colors and its use extended to rugs, tires, clothing, and a variety of applications in the consumer and industrial markets. Jell-O expanded its assortment of flavors, promoted the product for use in salads as well as desserts, and focused on the weight-watching market. Scotch brand tape introduced tape dispensers to encourage more usage; developed colored, patterned, waterproof, and write-on tape; and developed new uses for the basic material with double-coated tapes that competed with liquid adhesives for industrial applications.

More current examples include the strategies of Chevron Chemical Company, which manufactures and distributes agricultural insecticides, pesticides, and herbicides for large-scale commercial use. Yet it extends the life of those basic products through its leading line of Ortho products for the home market. The product line varies by application: aerosol and mechanical spray, foliage protection, soil protection, insect killer, weed killer, and insect control for the home, flowers, and plants.

Measuring the Product Life Cycle

The product life cycle is divided into the stages of introduction, growth, maturity, saturation, and decline. If the product life cycle is to be of any strategic value to you and your firm, you have to determine where in the life cycle your product is at any given time. This identification of the product life cycle phase can be carried out by computing a combination of three factors that characterize your product's status, and comparing the results with a typical pattern. Before discussing the process, though, it is important to clarify that the product life cycle can be examined at three different levels—with totally different results. You can analyze the market trend for a *specific item*—for example, a specific brand of detergent. Or you can look at a *product line,* a group of related products such as powdered laundry detergents. Finally, you can refer to an entire *product category* or *market*—for instance, laundry detergents.

While a meaningful investigation is possible on any of the three levels, discussion continues with a focus on life cycles for *product categories* in order to present a complete picture of competitive strategy and interaction at the various stages of market development.

The stage of your product category's life cycle can be determined by identifying its status on the three curves shown in Figure 9-5. These curves are:

1. Market volume, expressed in units to avoid any distortion resulting from price changes.
2. Rate of change of market volume (a more complicated way of saying growth rate, because few people can conceive of negative growth rates).
3. Profit/loss, illustrating the differences between total revenue and total cost at each point in time.

Successful management of your product's life cycle requires careful planning and thorough understanding of its characteristics at the various points of the curve. Only then can you respond quickly and advantageously to new situations, leaving competitors in your wake.

Figure 9-5. *Curve trends used to measure life cycle position.*

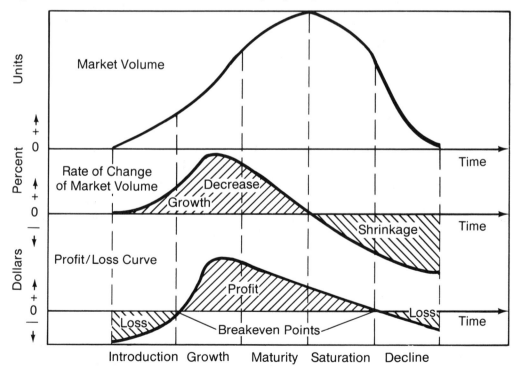

Source: Marketing Update, Issue 7 (1977), p. 3. Published by Alexander-Norton Publishers, Inc.

Introduction

During the introduction phase, market volume is expanding slowly because of high market resistance. The rate of growth is increasing faster than the market volume itself, because at this point each additional dollar represents a higher growth percentage than at any later stage of the cycle. Assuming that your company is the pioneer, and recognizing that the initial outlay for product and market development is often quite substantial, the introduction stage is generally characterized by costs exceeding revenues, by a loss. Toward the end of this phase, though, your firm should break even on its innovation; that is, its total revenue should at least equal its total cost. This break-even condition will make you more flexible when competitors appear on the scene.

Growth

The growth stage is characterized by booming sales. While the growth rate will also increase, it peaks about halfway through the stage. Thereafter, further growth occurs at a decreasing rate because of the steadily expanding base. Although profits reach their highest levels in this phase, the trend reverses in the middle of the stage as dwindling prices and rising costs generate downward pressure.

Maturity and Saturation

Market volume grows at a slower pace in the maturity stage, and the quickly decreasing rate of change reaches the stagnation level at the end of the stage. Profits diminish but are still healthy. As the market enters the saturation stage, all three curves show a negative change rate. Costs and competitive pressure reduce profits further until they cross the break-even line once more at the end of the stage.

Decline

In the decline stage, finally, all signals are for abandonment. The shrinking of market volume is accelerated by booming substitute markets. The rate of change becomes increasingly negative. Costs exceed revenue, thus creating a loss.

Table 9-1. *Identifying Your Product's Position in the Life Cycle.*

Life Cycle Stage	Sales Volume	Rate of Change of Sales Volume	Profit/Loss
Introduction	Slow growth	Increasing	Loss
Growth	Rapid growth	Increasing/ decreasing	Very high profit
Maturity	Growth	Decreasing	Decreasing profit
Saturation	Stagnation	Negative	Decreasing profit
Decline	Decrease	Negative	Loss

Strategies Throughout the Life Cycle

Obviously, the stages of the product life cycle are characterized by different conditions (Table 9-1). This fact suggests continuous monitoring and appropriate changes in your strategic approach, if you are to optimize results. These changes include adjustments in your marketing mix—that is, the particular combination of marketing tools that you use at each stage (see Table 9-2).

Introduction

In the introduction stage, it is the task of the pioneer to *create primary demand*—namely, demand for the new product category. Creating primary demand is an educational process that involves activating people's needs and focusing them on the product in question. It also means breaking old habits and forming new ones. After all, most new products don't fill a previously unfilled void, but rather displace other products that have served the same or similar purposes.

Even if the innovation is clearly superior in performance, it is a monumental task to dissuade consumers from their current loyalties. A great deal of "noise" is necessary just to attract the innovators and cross the fine line between success and failure.

The initial product mix should be kept small to provide a clear focus and keep costs under control. It should be confined to just a few variations of the underlying concept. (Baby food, for example, was launched with a mix of five products.) It is, after all, not the breadth of choice but the new approach to the satisfaction of a need

Table 9-2. *Strategies Throughout the Product Life Cycle.*

Life Cycle Stage	Marketing Mix Elements			
	Product	*Pricing*	*Distribution*	*Promotion*
Introduction	Offer technically mature product; keep mix small	"Skim the cream" of price-insensitive innovators through high introductory price	"Fill the pipeline" to the consumer; use indirect distribution through wholesalers	Create primary demand for product category; spend generously on extensive and intensive "flight" advertising
Growth	Improve product; keep mix limited	Adjust price as needed to meet competition	Increase product presence and market penetration	Spend substantially on expansion of sales volume
Maturity	Distinguish your product from competition; expand your product offering to satisfy different market segments	Capitalize on price-sensitive demand by further reducing prices	Take over wholesaling function yourself by establishing distribution centers and having your own sales force call on retailers	Differentiate your product in the minds of prospective buyers; emphasize brand appeal
Saturation	Proliferate your mix further; diversify into new market	Keep prices stable	Intensify your distribution to increase availability and exposure	Maintain the status quo; support your market position
Decline	Prune your mix radically	Carefully increase prices	Consolidate your distribution setup; establish minimum orders	Reduce advertising activity to reminder level

or the solution to a problem that attracts the innovators. A wide selection would only confuse them and increase costs unreasonably.

Channel Decisions. Your channel decisions are crucial because they lock your firm into long-term commitments to a chosen group of middlemen that cannot be changed easily, if at all. The degree of your ability to secure maximum availability of your innovation in the right outlets can make or break the creation of a new market. Getting your product on the shelf is at least as much of a challenge as getting it to move off the shelf. Obtaining the support of middlemen and "filling the pipeline" to the consumer are essential to the success of your marketing effort.

But, unless your choice of channel is predetermined through your current relationships, choosing the right intermediaries can be a difficult decision in itself. Your decisions determine the character and size of the market that you can reach. If you do not have an established trade network covering the desired target market, it is frequently useful to employ the services of wholesalers. Since they have close business connections with numerous retailers (or end users) in their respective areas, they can achieve fast, widespread distribution at a cost far below what you would have to spend if you had your own sales force calling on individual accounts.

If, however, you have an established sales force and ongoing business relationships with prospects, you still have to sell them on the merits of your innovation—which is no easy task. To this end, you have to motivate your sales force with a dramatic show that gets the adrenaline flowing. Every salesperson likes to have something new to talk about when calling on a buyer. To sustain this enthusiasm, though, you should offer a contest or a more broadly conceived incentive program that will give every individual on the sales force a personal reason to move substantial volumes of merchandise.

Advertising. Also essential is the support given your product in the form of advertising. Anything less than generous funding and an all-out advertising effort will reduce the product's chances for survival. No matter how it will perform, retailers, for example, are unlikely to carry an item for any length of time unless it produces traffic and satisfactory sales and profits. This kind of rapid acceptance and turnover is impossible without massive initial—and substantial continuing—advertising. Giving a new product lukewarm advertising support is generally tantamount to signing its death warrant.

Introductory Price. Since potential buyers are hardly in a position to develop their own ideas about price, you are relatively free to decide on your introductory price. You can set it fairly low—a strategy called penetration pricing—aiming to create a mass market and discourage competitive imitation through low unit profits and large investment requirements. Or you may consider a skimming strategy that starts out with a comparatively high price aimed at recovering your initial outlays for development and market introduction before competitive pressure erodes your temporary advantage.

Subsequent price reductions are then used to tap successively more elastic segments of consumer demand. This latter approach is most commonly employed for breakthrough-type innovations. The high price

at the outset skims the cream of the market that is relatively uncon-
cerned about price. (The innovation is not sufficiently well known to
gain in attractiveness through price reductions at this point.)

Growth

In the growth stage, you will want to modify your basic product to
take care of any problems discovered through initial consumer reactions. But since the product category is selling so well, the product
mix can remain small. With respect to channels of distribution, your
goals will be to have current channel members buy more and to sign
up new channel members. This drive is greatly aided by booming
demand, which strains the industry's supply capability and has dis-
·tributors scurrying for merchandise. Your salespeople will continue
to sell along the same lines as before, building upon the emerging
success story of your innovation. Your advertising emphasis is likely
to shift somewhat from creating product awareness to expanding market volume. Prices soften as price-cutting competitors enter the market.

Maturity

Moving into the maturity phase can be traumatic, because the peace-
ful coexistence of competitors now turns into a fight for market share.
At this time, it pays to redesign your product to make it more distinctive and easier to *differentiate* from competitive offerings. Because product technology is fairly well developed, changes tend to be
more cosmetic than functional. But discriminating customers also demand more variety and a choice of products designed specifically to
meet their particular needs and desires. Thus, it is advisable to adopt
a strategy of *market segmentation:* dividing the entire market into
smaller submarkets or segments in order to satisfy the unique needs
of these fairly homogeneous groups within the market.

   With regard to channel strategy, you may well find yourself recon-
sidering distribution structure, cost, and control. If you employed the
services of wholesalers in your introductory thrust, it may now be
sensible to eliminate them in order to push your product harder and
cut costs. Your product is now well known, and its sales volume is
high enough to justify your own retail sales force, supported by the
establishment of regional warehouses and service centers. Your own
sales force can be better trained and motivated to do an aggressive

job of promoting your product. You exercise better control over the sales effort and improve your market feedback system.

Your advertising has to communicate and enhance your drive to differentiate your product. It should put heavy emphasis on brand appeal to presell the product, so that the prospect recognizes and prefers your product even in a competitive environment. The effectiveness of your promotional efforts, however, is likely to decrease sharply as demand becomes less responsive to promotion because of growing brand loyalty, and resultant market resistance.

Since actual differences between substitute products are very slight and price sensivity (elasticity) of demand is high, price variations between your firm's products and those of your competitors gain in importance, opening up the last sectors of market capacity. Prices will tend to drop further, but stabilize toward the end of the stage as a result of cost pressures. Insofar as your company has been able to create brand loyalty among its buyers, it will have pricing discretion that permits price adjustments when necessary without losing a substantial amount of sales.

Saturation

As your product enters the saturation stage of its life cycle, a no-holds-barred fight develops for market share. Because market volume has ceased to grow, the growth of individual firms' sales volume is achieved at the expense of competitors. In your product strategy, you will find yourself compelled to differentiate further by offering even more choice. Because of the limited growth potential, it will pay to pursue a strategy of *diversification*. Entering another field could reduce your risk by decreasing your exposure to the fate of a particular product and could thus add stability, as well as potential revenue and profit, to your business.

Your channel strategy remains unaltered in the saturation phase. You should attempt to gain even more intensive distribution and, thus, maximum availability and exposure. Toward this end, your salespeople will have to make a well-planned, concerted effort to obtain more trade cooperation.

The function of advertising at this point is primarily to maintain the status quo. Little new ground can be broken, so advertising of the reminder or reinforcement type is needed. Elasticity of demand reaches its highest point at this stage. This fact is of little strategic consequence, however, since most possibilities for cost reduction have been exhausted.

Decline

With consumer interest in the product waning in the decline phase, competitors drop out of the market in droves. If you are still in the market, you will trim your product offering to the bone, rigorously weeding out weak products and concentrating on a few unchanged items. You will similarly attempt to reduce distribution cost by consolidating warehouses and sales offices, as well as establishing minimum orders to discourage small shipments. Your sales effort will tend to be low key, with an emphasis on retaining as much of your market as you can. Advertising support will be of the low-budget, infrequent-reminder type. Your prices will stay right about where they are.

How to Avoid the Decline Phase

Studies have shown that the classic product life cycle pattern just described conforms reasonably well to reality. Although some products ultimately reach the stage of decline, sales remain at relatively high levels without any permanent decline expected in the foreseeable future. In fact, two variants of this situation have been noted:

- *Stability:* Having attained a certain level, sales remain virtually unchanged over an extended period of time.
- *Increase:* After arriving at an initial peak through relatively fast growth, sales continue to grow at a rate much greater than the growth of the population. For example, cake mixes and cars are products with essentially stable saturation phases. Continuing increases in sales volume at the saturation stage that result from inherent market dynamics can be found in the markets for peanut butter, salad dressings, and cooking oils.

But, as a marketing strategist, you will not want to leave the continued success of your efforts to chance. Two major ways of altering your product's fate are at your disposal: substitution and extension. Life cycle extension is discussed in detail at the beginning of this commentary.

Substitution is a planned process whereby an old product is replaced by an innovation. A new product that will eventually take the old one's place is brought to market while the recently introduced product is still in its growth stage. This overlapping activity enables the innovation to build up sufficient volume by the time sales in the existing market have shrunk.

With a substitution strategy, profits tend to remain at fairly high levels, because old products are withdrawn from the market as soon as new products have achieved sufficient momentum to pick up the slack. The result is a series of consecutive cycles overlapping with and replacing each other.

Substitution is commonplace in the auto and fashion industries, where annual model changes and seasonally changing collections, respectively, introduce an element of psychological obsolescence. This approach, however, requires a substantial continuous development and engineering effort, since only a very small percentage of new product ideas lead to successful new products.

Product Competition

To gain a larger share of a total market, consider introducing additional products as competing lines or as private labels. The additional products provide a solid front against competitors. Overall, the strategy aims at generating higher revenue than does the use of only a single product.

Strategy Applications

- Competing brand
- Private label

Commentary Procter & Gamble, with its array of brands of detergents and other product categories, is the master at executing a product-competition strategy. Likewise, Becton Dickinson, the large health care firm, produces its famous brand of Ace bandages as the premium brand. It also makes a competing brand, the lower-priced line of Bauer & Black bandages. You have to be careful with competing brands, though, to be sure there is a minimal amount of cannibalizing of sales from one product to another. The intent is to *segment* and *position* your product with as much precision as possible.

Another strategy application of product competition, private labeling, is quite prevalent, as shown by examples such as The Coca-Cola Company supplying Minute Maid orange juice to A&P supermarkets along with A&P's private brand. There are some organizations that private-label only. And in some cases they private-label exclusively to one large customer, such as Sears. Care must be taken because the supplier is in a high-risk position should the relationship deteriorate. In its worst case scenario, such a firm could be out of business overnight. One possible remedy is to have a long-term supply contract with the customer, or to open an alternative channel of distribution.

Product Mix

Evaluate the profit advantage of a single product concentrated in a specialized market. For growth and protection from competitors, consider a multiple-product strategy, which could include add-on products and services.

Strategy Applications

- Single product
- Multiple products
- Product system

Commentary The product mix strategy overlaps with other considerations, such as those already discussed for market dimension, market entry, and market commitment strategies. As always, you should also orient your competitive thinking to your competitors' product mix and how you intend to position your product line to them.

Case Example

Ryder System, Inc. Ryder System Inc., the truck-leasing giant, maintains its strong presence as a low-cost producer in its basic (single-product) business of one-way truck rental with a 30 percent market share. It applies product mix strategies in a variety of approaches. Consider the following examples of multiple products and product systems:

A contract with Emery Air Freight Corp. to manage a 100-truck fleet in Chicago. Ryder provides drivers in Emery uniforms and in Emery painted trucks. It also handles maintenance and even helps plan routes.

A just-in-time delivery service that can deliver automotive parts to midwestern automotive plants to meet rigid schedules.

A business that transports school students in its 3,700 buses.

A service that provides full-line maintenance to airlines that are looking to shed that service to release operating capital.

Product Design

The demands of the marketplace, the intensity of competition, and the flexibility of your company will dictate whether a standard, customized, or modified product is the optimum strategy.

Strategy Applications
- Standard products
- Customized products
- Standard products, modified

Commentary Standard products are most appropriate for the large companies that can take advantage of the economies of scale. They are also suitable for those organizations where computer integrated manufacturing (CIM) has been installed or low-cost labor has been found. However, standard products, if easily duplicated by low-cost producers, can quickly fall into an undifferentiated or commodity category. For example, INTEL Corporation, one of the leading microchip producers, fell victim to low-cost, offshore competitors that turned its product into a commodity. INTEL switched to a customized product strategy by creating differentiated chip designs that are more difficult to clone.

In another instance of product design application, Vista Chemical Company survived in a basic business of plastics and cleaning agents. In 1986, operating income had grown five times to $90 million over the previous year. Vista moved away from dependence on high-volume, low-margin standard products to selling higher-margin customized or specialty products. For example, it shifted emphasis from polyvinyl chloride (vinyl) to higher-grade production, which required greater quality in chemical purity and temperature stability, for those customers willing to pay for such differentiation.

New Products/Services

Strategies related to product innovation, modification, line extension, and diversification require changing the product either slightly or extensively. However, don't overlook the opportunities of remerchandising and market extension, strategies that don't alter the product but permit a perception of a "new" product. Also use promotion, image, positioning, and market segmentation as strategic tools to forge new impressions—and create differentiation.

Strategy Applications	• Innovation
	• Modification
	• Line extension
	• Diversification
	• Remerchandising
	• Market extension

Commentary Since new products and services are the heart of any business that seek to sustain growth and competitive advantage, extensive coverage of this topic is required.

New Products/Services

The pace of new product introduction and obsolescence is so fast and rigorous that only one out of five innovations survives long enough in the marketplace to become a commercial success. When the stakes are so high, it pays to improve your odds by gaining a better understanding of the new product process in all its ramifications. Sensitivity and adaptability are prerequisites for success in a dynamic marketplace where needs are constantly changing.

Defining a New Product

Before defining what a *new* product is, you must first understand what a *product* is. It may seem perfectly obvious, since we deal with many products every day: A product is a thing. But that definition hardly suffices in today's environment. It reduces the concept of product to a combination of physical and chemical attributes in line with the old product-oriented concept of marketing. This emphasis on tangible characteristics neglects the fact that intangibles—such as quality, color, prestige, and service—can make a significant difference to a prospective buyer. A consumer perceives a product as a source of potential satisfaction, and may be buying your offering to satisfy a particular want or desire rather than for its functional value. Charles Revson, the late founder of Revlon, in his now classic statement put it succinctly when he said: "In the factory, we make cosmetics; in the store, we sell hope."

A *new* product can best be defined as a product *perceived as new* by a customer. A product can be many things to many people. This definition places the emphasis on perception rather than on objective facts, and leaves much room for interpretation. There is a reverse side to this emphasis on perception, though. If you have a product that has never before been offered for sale but is perceived by customers as more of the same, then you really do not have a "new" product from a marketing point of view.

If you can make a customer *believe* that you are offering a new product, it is new from the customer's point of view. But you cannot claim newness either indiscriminately or indefinitely. You have to be able to prove reformulation to the Federal Trade Commission, and federal law prohibits use of the expression "new" in packaging and promotion for more than six months. Legal limitations aside, it is really a question of convincing your target market that you have something different to sell.

Categories of New Products

New products come in many different forms. This diversity can be reduced to varying degrees of technological and marketing newness. In terms of increasing degrees of technological change, you may want to distinguish among modification, line extension, and diversification. For increasing degrees of marketing newness, you can differentiate between remerchandising and market extension. Table 9-3

Table 9-3. *Categories of New Products.*

Category	Definition	Nature	Benefit
Modification	Altering a product feature	Same number of product lines and products	Combining the new with the familiar
Line extension	Adding more variety	Same number of product lines, higher number of products	Segmenting the market by offering more choice
Diversification	Entering a new business	New product line, higher number of products	Spreading risk and capitalizing on opportunities
Remerchandising	Marketing change to create a new impression	Same product, same markets	Generating excitement and stimulating sales
Market extension	Entering a new market	Same products, new market	Broadening the base

presents the differences among these five categories of new products and points out the benefits of each.

Combined Approach for New Product Categories

Rarely will the five categories of new products presented here be used separately. They lend themselves perfectly to combined application for maximum impact, and you will probably want to avail yourself of a package approach to maintain steady growth in a rapidly changing environment. Line extension, for example, is often used with remerchandising or market extension. Diversification is often combined with market extension. The use of one category does not preclude the application of other approaches at the same time, possibly within the same market. What remains essential, though, is that the prospective customer *perceives* a difference worthy of consideration.

Steps in the Evolution of a New Product

The genesis of an innovation occurs in a process called new product evolution. It takes place in a cyclical fashion with a four-stage format, as shown in Figure 9-6. These stages break down into a number of steps that detail the activities involved in bringing about a successful new product. The steps are presented in Table 9-4, together with their respective results.

Initiative

New products don't emerge from thin air. Rather, the process resulting in a profitable addition to your product mix is triggered by an

Figure 9-6. *The cycle of new product evolution.*

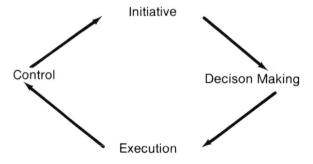

Table 9-4. *The Process of New Product Evolution.*

Process Steps	Results
Initiative	
1. Initiating forces	Get action under way
2. Perception and identification of problem or opportunity	Realize and pinpoint nature of challenge
Decision Making	
1. Definition of objectives and criteria	Set frame of reference
2. Start of comprehensive marketing research program	Feed decision maker relevant information on continuous basis
3. Examination of market data	Provide factual input
4. Idea generation	Map out alternative courses of action
5. Screening	Weed out unpromising alternatives
6. Business analysis	Subject surviving proposals to in-depth scrutiny
7. Product development	Convert ideas into products
8. Market testing	Examine market acceptance
9. Finalization of marketing program	Prepare for rollout
10. Pilot production	Fill the pipeline
Execution	
1. Full-scale launch	Begin market introduction
2. Product life cycle	Analyze sales and profit changes
Control	
1. Continuous feedback of results	Compare planned and actual figures
2. Corrective action	Keep on course

initiating force that some astute manager within your organization perceived and identified correctly. Numerous external or internal factors can cause such a new product initiative. They may be reflections of market, technological, competitive, or company developments. In any case, they constitute the motivating forces behind the evolutionary process.

Considering the rapid changes occurring in your environment, early indications of potential threats have to be watched and analyzed as carefully as the emergence of new market opportunities. Forecasting, therefore, plays a crucial role in new product evolution by predicting alternative future environmental conditions or events, as well as the likelihood of their occurrence. Some companies even retain the services of an elite group of planners to speculate about such future scenarios. But there are more basic approaches for obtaining significant insights into market trends. One is the careful examination of consumer preferences and life styles, of competitive new product activity, of distribution patterns, and—most basic of all—of sales data.

Technological developments can be just as stimulating. New applications of lasers, glass fibers, semiconductors, and now superconductors offer a host of opportunities for the imaginative manager. Within this decade, lasers have been used in industry, in surgery, and in communications. Glass fibers are used in telecommunications. Semiconductor chips have brought us microcomputers, electronic calculators, and digital watches. Increasingly, we are availing ourselves of the potential of technology transfer, that is, applying to one field the technology developed in another. For example, Rockwell International Corp., a major space contractor, used technology developed for the U.S. space program in designing antiskid devices for truck braking systems. Similarly, microwave ovens are an outgrowth of the space program.

Finally, events within your firm may also be the source of a new product initiative. Such events may be suggestions by employees concerning improvement of existing products or development of entirely different ones. Purchasing problems involving limited availability of key materials or price increases may trigger a rethinking process. Innovations in your research and development department could lead to important discoveries, which, in turn, may stimulate new product evolution processes. Sales trends can and should bring about a reevaluation of your current and future situation, often resulting in new product programs.

While there are numerous environmental clues, your firm will not profit from them unless there is someone in your organization sensitive enough to respond selectively to them. Typically, this person will be the product manager of a given product line. More than any other, this person is called upon to scan facts and developments and identify those that represent a true problem or opportunity. This task requires considerable insight and judgment, since it involves "separating the wheat from the chaff." Only someone with vision can perform this job well.

Elgin Watch Company knew in the mid-1950's that significant changes were occurring in the U.S. watch market, but completely misjudged their impact on its operations. The company is still alive, but marginally, while Timex has become a leader in this industry. But even Timex lost much of its leadership position to Seiko, because it overlooked the full impact of digital watches and other innovations.

In contrast, Pfizer Inc. assessed the market facts correctly and had the courage to make a bold decision when it saw itself simultaneously threatened with a decline in its traditional business and favored by a new opportunity of internal origin—namely, its first home-grown drug, Terramycin. Pfizer decided to market the new drug itself and subsequently became an industry leader. The importance of placing individuals sensitive to market opportunities in responsible positions can hardly be overstated.

New Product Decision Making

The sequence of new product evolution begins with goal setting and ends with initial production. In between is a series of crucial steps that will determine the success of your venture in the marketplace. Close attention to each of the following steps is essential.

Defining Objectives and Criteria. Harvard Professor Theodore Levitt once stated: "Unless you know where you are going, *any* way will take you there." This statement emphasizes the significance of objectives. They not only give direction and orientation to your effort, but they serve as a measure of actual achievements. Typically, new product objectives involve growth targets of increased sales and market share. But they often remain nonoperational, since they are interpreted by criteria. The latter are instruments of measurement that translate objectives into operational form.

Research and Examination of Market Data. While it is the role of objectives and criteria to guide the evolutionary effort and keep it on course, it is the job of a continuous marketing research program to supply the decision maker with the relevant facts. The task of such a comprehensive marketing research program is to reach the consumer and establish communication in order to keep the evolutionary process going efficiently and on course.

The body of data generated in the first round of this marketing research program is then subjected to careful analysis in order to develop usable information capable of triggering dynamic thinking.

Creativity that is divorced from the developments in the marketplace often ends up being misguided and ill-fated.

Idea Generation.   Once a data base has been established, idea generation can begin. At this early stage, many ideas are necessary for an ultimate yield of one successfully commercialized product. A study by management consultants, Booz, Allen & Hamilton Inc. puts this ratio at 58:1. Scrutiny becomes more and more rigorous as a product idea advances from its genesis. All the more reason to generate or collect as many ideas as possible at the outset. The search for alternative courses of action would be limited only by any previously cited facts (which could also act as stimulants) and should not in any way concern itself with such issues as feasibility or profitability.

A wide range of sources should be tapped: internal sources such as top management, research and development people, marketing personnel, and other employees; but also a variety of external sources such as consumers, middlemen, competitors, scientists, inventors, research labs, and suppliers. The techniques employed in activating these sources range from brainstorming to various surveying methods.

Screening.   Assuming you have generated a wealth of new product ideas, they should then be subjected to a screening procedure. This step aims to weed out unpromising ideas before they become costly in time, effort, and money. Thus, the goal at this step is to eliminate from further consideration as many ideas as possible. Two-thirds to three-quarters of the original ideas vanish at this point.

The focus now is to examine questions of feasibility and profitability. Neither of the two, after all, can exist without the other: Feasible products that are not profitable are simply giveaways; profitable products that are not feasible are fiction. The issue of feasibility may be general (whether appropriate technology exists) or specific (whether your R&D and production departments can handle the job). Profitability, on the other hand, involves projections of anticipated price levels and unit costs to decide whether there is enough money in a deal to warrant your attention.

Business Analysis.   The few chosen ideas that pass the screening test enter the business analysis stage. They now receive in-depth scrutiny. The purpose of this step is to advise top management whether it should authorize certain proposals as development projects. Therefore, a careful *impact statement* has to be developed for each concept, with thorough projections of what would happen if it were adopted and converted into a real product.

Management must know the consequences to your firm in terms of required technological know-how, production and sales-force utilization, image, morale, and—most of all—finances. A concept test is likely to help you in assessing consumer reaction and preference at this point.

Your financial analysis also has to be much more thorough at this step than during screening, relying on tools such as break-even analysis (to determine the sales volume needed to cover costs) and differential accounting (to compute the return on investment).

Product Development and Market Testing. Once a particular idea has tested out well and has received top management's blessing, it is assigned to personnel for conversion into a tangible product. Here, your technical and production people go to work with clear-cut specifications spelled out by you on the basis of several rounds of marketing research. They will develop rough drafts that will then be laboratory tested and refined, until they have developed a product that is completely debugged and ready for full-scale production.

Of course, before you begin full-scale production, you have to test a sample quantity among users, asking them to try your product at your expense and then to tell you what changes they would suggest to improve its performance or enhance its appeal. This procedure, product testing, is intended to help you touch up and finalize the design of your product. The most popular approach to product testing involves matching your (unidentified) product against the product (also unidentified) of a major competitor to find out which one your audience prefers and why. The results cannot be taken as conclusive evidence, however, since *you* select the participants and give them the product.

The outcome should not be mistaken for a true indication of your innovation's market potential, which can be meaningfully explored only by means of test marketing. This activity involves introducing your product in a number of test cities (or market segments) to see how well it will sell under real market conditions. It is important that these test markets be representative of your overall market and that you run the test long enough to establish repurchase patterns. After all, it is relatively easy to sell somebody something for the first time. The real test is whether the customer buys it again. This determination cannot be made through sales audits alone, but requires customer interviews as well.

Interviews are costly, thus making test marketing expensive and controversial. Another reason for controversy is that your competitor's intelligence system may detect your findings and attempt to blunt your efforts if you decide on a rollout with full market coverage.

Final Marketing Program and Pilot Production. Completion of market testing enables you to put the finishing touches on your marketing program by adjusting certain elements of your marketing mix for maximum effectiveness. This adjustment permits you to get ready for a full-scale rollout. Of course, you first have to go through pilot production, that is, a production run designed to get enough merchandise on the shelves to satisfy initial demand. This step completes the decision-making phase of new product evolution.

Execution and Control

Once you complete the internal development and external testing of your new product, you are ready to launch its full-scale market introduction. Your revised introductory program should now be set in motion to start your product's life cycle, which goes from introduction through growth and maturity, and then to saturation and decline.

Because no one is all-knowing and even the best planning cannot foresee all possible events, continuous feedback of the result of your strategy in the marketplace is necessary. This feedback enables periodic comparisons between planned and actual figures, which, in turn, may lead to corrective action designed to keep your program on course. Ultimately this action may result in initiating another evolutionary process that could displace the current product.

Product Audit

Knowing when to pull a product from the line is as important as knowing when to introduce a new one. Consider such internal requirements as profitability, available resources, and new growth opportunities. Examine external factors of sales-force coverage, dealer commitment, and customers' needs to determine if a comprehensive line is required.

Strategy Applications
- Line reduction
- Line elimination

Commentary Efficient use of the product audit is one of the procedures for sustaining product profitability.

Case Example

Cooper Tire & The strategy application is demonstrated by Cooper Tire & Rub-
Rubber ber Company. During the early 1980's, it was running its
Company plants near capacity, versus an industry average of 75 percent.
Utilizing a product audit, Cooper maintained a profitable mix in
sufficient depth and width to match market needs, competitive
strategy, and buyer behavior.

For example, it decided to produce tires for the replacement
market exclusively. This decision to use a product audit to focus
its product line was significantly timed because consumers
were keeping cars an average of seven years, up from five and a
half years in 1970. Also, Cooper capitalized on a buyer trend
toward its less expensive tire and its private brands rather
than the more expensive, heavily advertised competitive
brands. Further, Cooper gained an advantage from the trend by
placing the bulk of production in the lower-priced bias-ply tires
rather than the premium radials that averaged 90 percent
higher prices.

Establishing a Product Audit Program

Just as regular physical examinations are essential to maintain the
body's good health, likewise, products require regular examination to
determine whether they are healthy, need repromotion, or should be
allowed to phase out.

The first step in establishing a regular product evaluation program
is the creation of a Product Audit Committee. This core group, com-
prised of the top people in the marketing, finance, engineering, and
purchasing departments, should possess ultimate decision-making authority regarding the composition of the company's product mix. Depending upon the dimensions of the product mix and the significance
of the products or developments involved, the Product Audit Committee should meet monthly, and every product should have at least
an annual review.

How does such a committee discharge its responsibilities? To do
justice to each product and to have an objective basis for interproduct
comparisons, a common rating form should be used. For products
that appear dubious, and thus demanding careful evaluation, a form
(Figure 9-7) suggested by Philip Kotler, professor of marketing at
Northwestern University, requires the assignment of values with respect to seven criteria. Some of these values will necessarily be subjective in nature, with 0 in each case representing strong grounds for
eliminating the product, and a score of 1 suggesting continuance. In

Figure 9-7. *Product rating form.*

PRODUCT NO. _____ MODEL NO. _____ DATE _____

WEIGHT (W)	**RATING (R)**

1. What is the future market potential for this product?

.0 .2 .4 .6 .8 1.0 $W_1R_1 =$
Low   High

2. How much could be gained by product modification?

.0 .2 .4 .6 .8 1.0 $W_2R_2 =$
Nothing   A Great
                            Deal

3. How much could be gained by market strategy modification?

.0 .2 .4 .6 .8 1.0 $W_3R_3 =$
Nothing   A Great
                            Deal

4. How much useful executive time could be released by abandoning this product?

.0 .2 .4 .6 .8 1.0 $W_4R_4 =$
A Great   Very
Deal   Little

5. How good are the firm's alternative opportunities?

.0 .2 .4 .6 .8 1.0 $W_5R_5 =$
Very   Very
Good   Poor

6. How much is the product contributing beyond its direct costs?

.0 .2 .4 .6 .8 1.0 $W_6R_6 =$
Nothing   A Great
                            Deal

7. How much is the product contributing to the sale of the other products?

.0 .2 .4 .6 .8 1.0 $W_7R_7 =$
Nothing   A Great
                            Deal

                                      _____
                                      Product retention index

Source: Philip Kotler, ''Phasing Out Weak Products,'' *Harvard Business Review* (March–April 1965), p. 116.

each case, the score reflects the majority opinion or consensus of the committee.

Depending upon the company's circumstances and objectives, each scale can be given a different degree of importance or weight. These weights *(W)* are then multiplied by the appropriate ratings *(R)* and totaled to form the specific product's retention index *(WR)*. In the event that all criteria are given equal weight, this sum can range from a maximum value of 7 for a sure winner to a minimum of 0 for a definite loser.

Phasing out weak products, following the decision to drop them, requires careful consideration of the company's obligations to the various parties affected by the decision. Supplier and customer notification and an adequate stock of replacement parts may be necessary.

As an example of how a product audit works, Figure 9-8 gives a summary comparison of the ratings for two dog food products. The weight of each criterion is determined by corporate policy and does not vary with the products to which it is being applied. The ratings themselves reflect the committee's judgment as to the prospects for the given product. While the soft–moist category in the figure scores high in three crucial areas—market potential, executive time, and contribution—the canned food shows a somewhat bleak outlook.

Although the maximum overall score is 10.0 (total weight of 10 times maximum score of 1.0), a product retention index of 4.2 does not necessarily mean automatic dismissal of the product in question. It is, however, definite cause for careful investigation and continuous monitoring to prevent problems from mushrooming. It is apparent that the canned product seems to have little life left, and closer ex-

Figure 9-8. *Applying the product rating form.*

Product: Dog Food		Canned		Soft-moist	
(W) Weight	Criterion	(R) Rating	(WR) Weight Rating	(R) Rating	(WR) Weight Rating
2	Market Potential	.4	.8	1.0	2.0
1	Product Modification	.2	.2	.4	.4
1	Marketing Modification	.4	.4	.4	.4
2	Executive Time	.8	1.6	1.0	2.0
1	Alternatives	.4	.4	.8	.8
2	Contribution	.4	.8	.8	1.6
1	Sales Support	.0	.0	.4	.4
	Product Retention Index	4.2		7.6	

Multiply the Weight (W) by the Rating (R) to obtain Weighted Rating (WR). Weight of 1 = important, weight of 2 = very important. See Figure 9-7 for rating scale.

Source: Philip Kotler, "Phasing Out Weak Products," *Harvard Business Review* (March–April 1965), p. 116.

amination might reveal that resources, facilities, and talent could be more profitably employed elsewhere. The soft–moist product, with a product retention index of 7.6, shows a strong and healthy picture, although it could benefit from changes in several areas.

Overview Necessary

Rating forms are useful for pinpointing weaknesses. Just like thermometers, they indicate the existence of problems but do not supply diagnoses. Quantitative data contained in these forms have to be supplemented and amplified by qualitative information. In order to obtain a complete picture, and make meaningful decisions, the Product Audit Committee must solicit input from all major functional departments of the company.

Product Mix Vital

Every business firm has products and/or services to sell. The mix of these products, as well as the vitality of the individual elements, is crucial to the survival and growth of the firm. But does the company have a regular, rigid program for examining the contribution that each product has made, is making, or will make to its overall success? Is each product constantly challenged and the product mix rejuvenated by weeding out losers and adding winners? Every firm needs a systematic review program in order to ensure long-term growth.

Product audits represent regular, systematic assessments of the strengths, weaknesses, and future prospects of a company's products, as well as their profit contributions. Such audits can be carried out meaningfully only on a product-by-product basis, requiring a team effort in which the marketing manager assumes a key role with ultimate performance responsibility.

In contrast to accounting audits, product audits are conducted strictly for internal purposes. They should be part of a regular program, practiced consistently and continuously. Products that are no longer earning their keep should be eliminated without delay or sentimentality, provided that such a move has no negative repercussions for the remaining members of the product family. Such pruning frees valuable resources that provide the basis for growth through new products.

Action Steps

Anticipate a competitor's move into your marketplace by developing a competing product or service. Recognize early the potentials of new technology, particularly in areas where competitors may choose not to invest. Use life-cycle extensions as the mainstay of your strategy. Whenever possible, preempt competitors' strategies and blunt their efforts to take market share from you.

To identify strategies and initiate action:

1. List product strategies that represent the best opportunities.
2. Indicate what action is to take place and who is assigned the task.
3. Relate feedback to the objective(s) desired and the strategies selected.
4. List immediate plans and future courses of action.

10

Pricing Strategies

Objectives:
To enable you to

1. Recognize the five strategy options for *new products*
2. Learn the six strategy applications for *established products*
3. Identify and initiate the steps needed to convert pricing strategies into *action*

The third major component is pricing strategy. However, it is important that pricing not be dealt with as an isolated item. Consider the goals of the company, which could be high return on investment or high market share. Consider the product's life cycle stage—new, growing, mature, or ready for phase-out. Above all, in tough pricing competition, examine all possible alternatives, such as product improvement, promotion, and distribution strategies, before getting involved in pricing wars. Pricing must work in harmony with all of these strategies.

New Products

Skimming a market with high prices, penetrating with low prices, using odd or even prices, and following the market leader are strategies determined by such factors as market share, speed of market entry, time needed to recover your investment, and how far behind your competition is with its product entry.

Strategy Applications
- Skim pricing
- Penetration pricing

- Psychological pricing
- Follow pricing
- Cost-plus pricing

Case Example

Michelin Tires The full impact of pricing strategy was demonstrated by Michelin during the early 1980's. As the second-largest tire producer in the world, it was fighting hard to overtake the world leader, The Goodyear Tire & Rubber Company. Michelin's strategy was to "buy" market share through price reductions. This strategy was in direct contrast with its historical pricing pattern of maintaining a 30 percent premium over its competitors. Some of Michelin's approaches included:

- Winning a major original equipment contract from Ford for two car models and pushing out traditional competitors (even though profit margins were reported as almost nonexistent).
- Signing up Montgomery Ward & Co. Inc., May Department Stores Co., and Federal Mart Corporation to a growing list of large retail chains.
- Establishing itself as the largest newspaper advertiser of radial tires in the country and using low price as the lure.

Thus, Michelin used price to fight its way to market leadership. However, profit reduction was also the immediate penalty for using price as a weapon to "buy" market share rapidly. The long-term benefits would be the possible economies gained through larger production runs, administration consolidation, distribution savings, and the effect of high market share on profitability.

Commentary The primary lesson of the example is that pricing strategy is never derived in isolation of other marketing mix factors. Another major consideration in pricing is its effect on the *image* of the product in the customer's mind. Michelin had built a market niche through product quality at a premium price. Can low price and high price be compatible? Is a conflict created in the customer's mind? Careful consideration should be given to such questions when positioning a product into a new category and devising a pricing strategy counter to traditional patterns. Some organizations recognize image as a precious factor and will create a new name brand for a low-price category to avoid conflict rather than run the risk of damaging the image of its upscale product. In general, it is difficult to regain a premium price position for the same brand once it has been diluted by low-price promotions through mass merchandising outlets.

Skim Pricing

Skim pricing involves pricing at a high level to hit the "cream" of the buyers who are less sensitive to price. The conditions for considering this strategy are:

- Senior management requires that you recover R&D and other developmental costs rapidly.
- The product or service is unique. It is new (or improved) and in the introductory stage of the product life cycle. Or, it serves a relatively small segment that is price-inelastic.
- There is little danger of short-term competitive entry because of patent protection, high R&D entry costs, high promotion costs, or limitations on availability of raw materials, or because major distribution channels are filled.
- There is a need to control demand until production is geared up.

The electronics industry usually employs skim pricing at the introductory stage of the product life cycle to the point that consumers and industrial buyers expect the high introductory-pricing pattern. There are exceptions, however. One was Texas Instruments' introduction of a much-touted bubble memory, a solid state magnetic storage device for computers that has high capacity and the capability of not losing stored data when power is cut off. Even with the impressive technology, sales were initially disappointing because potential users were not willing to pay the high introductory price.

Case Example

The Timken Company The Timken Company manufactures tapered roller bearings. The 1980's were devastating for the industry; such formidable companies as International Harvester, Schatz Federal Bearings, and KuBar Bearings were driven out of the business because of Asian imports. Timken survived—even with skim pricing—by sticking to the solid principle of meeting customer needs at all times. It provided product support with sales engineers who were intensively trained in an 18-month program that emphasized customer service. Timken adamantly refused to accept the notion of product maturity, but chose to innovate through research, new facilities, and fresh ideas. Most important, Timken managed to envelop a market segment by concentrating entirely on tapered bearings. Competitors found it difficult to penetrate that segment, since none came close to offering this Ohio-based company's 26,000 bearing combinations. Thus, such factors as product availability, service, innovation, and technical sales were used together to permit skim pricing in an intensely competitive market.

Penetration Pricing

Pricing below the prevailing level in order to gain market entry or to increase market share is known as penetration pricing. The conditions for considering this strategy are:

- There is an opportunity to establish a quick foothold in a specific market.
- Existing competitors are not expected to react to your prices.
- The product/service is a ''me too'' entry and you have become a low-cost producer.
- You adhere to the theory that high market share equals high return on investment, and management is willing to wait for the rewards.

One of the most striking examples of penetration pricing occurred in the early 1980's in the fast-growing market for computer printers, a market pioneered by U.S. manufacturers. But the Japanese seized the opportunity and targeted the segment for printers selling for less than $2,500. Such companies as Ricoh, Okidata, Shinshu, and Seiki attacked the segment by offering printers at rock-bottom prices and short delivery times. From virtually no U.S. sales in 1979, the Japanese shipped 75 percent of all units selling for less than $1,000 by 1982.

Psychological Pricing

Psychological pricing means pricing at a level that is perceived to be much lower than it actually is: $99, $95, $19.99, $1.98. Psychological pricing is a viable strategy and should be experimented with to determine its precise application for your product. The conditions for considering this strategy are:

- A product is singled out for special promotion.
- A product is likely to be advertised, displayed, or quoted in writing.

- The selling price desired is close to a multiple of 10, 100, 1,000, and so on.

While psychological pricing is most likely to be applied to consumer products, there is an increasing use of the strategy for business-to-business products and services, as in the example of a machine priced at $24,837.00. Note in this example that the traditional "9" is not used. Tests by such organizations as Sears reveal that the "9" doesn't have the psychological impact it once had. In various combinations the "7" has come out on top.

In instances where a prestige product or service is offered, a psychological price may be expressed as "one hundred dollars" to give an elitist impression.

Follow Pricing

Pricing in relation to industry price leaders is termed follow pricing. The conditions for considering this strategy are:

- Your organization may be a small or medium-size company in an industry dominated by one or two price leaders.
- Aggressive pricing fluctuations may result in damaging price wars.
- Most products offered don't have distinguishing features.

The most visible example of follow pricing is found in the computer market, in which IBM holds the dominant worldwide position. IBM usually sets the pricing standards by which its competitors price their products. However, this situation turned out to be a two-edged sword. The clones of IBM-compatible computers priced at 20 to 40 percent below IBM reached such high proportions that IBM was forced to reverse its role and use follow pricing against smaller competitors as a means of protecting its share of the market. However, IBM's use of follow pricing was a holding action in its broader strategy of maintaining price leadership with the introduction of its new line of personal computers in 1987.

Cost-Plus Pricing

Cost-plus pricing entails basing price on product costs and then adding on components such as administration and profit. The conditions for considering this strategy are:

- The pricing procedure conforms to government, military, or construction regulations.

- There are unpredictable total costs owing to ongoing new product development and testing phases.
- A project (product) moves through a series of start-and-stop sequences.

Cost-plus pricing, unless mandated by government procedures, is product-based pricing. Such an approach contrasts with market-based pricing, which takes into consideration such internal and external factors as:

Corporate, divisional, or product-line objectives as they relate to profits, competitive inroads, market share, and market stability.

Target-market objectives related to desired position in the market, profile of customer segments, current demand for product, and future potential of market.

Marketing mix strategy (for example, how pricing fits together with product and promotion) and distribution components of the mix.

Established Products

Price wars can be avoided or postponed by locating untapped market segments and focusing on product improvements. You can also preempt and discourage new competitors by gradually sliding down prices, thereby making the market seem unprofitable. You should always price according to the flexibility of demand and your production economies.

Strategy Applications
- Slide-down pricing
- Segment pricing
- Flexible pricing
- Preemptive pricing
- Phase-out pricing
- Loss-leader pricing

Commentary Price wars are always a danger for established products. While there are pricing strategies to be used for such products, it is best to apply marketing creativity to avoid the possibility of pricing wars. For example, American Hospital Supply Corporation, the medical products distributor, tied its pricing strategy into long-term contract commitments from hospitals. Once a hospital signed a contract, it became part of ASAP (Automated Systems Analytical Purchasing), the company's computerized system. The system benefits the hospitals by reducing inventory requirements and paperwork, improving cash flow, providing 24-hour delivery, and offering *price protection.* American Hospital Supply benefits by keeping out price cutters.

Slide-Down Pricing

Moving prices down to tap successive layers of demand is known as slide-down pricing. The conditions for considering this strategy are:

- The product would appeal to progressively larger groups of users at lower prices in a price-elastic market.
- The organization has adopted a low-cost producer strategy by adhering to learning curve concepts and other economies of scale in distribution, promotion, and sales.
- There is a need to discourage competitive entries.

Slide-down pricing is best utilized in a proactive management mode rather than as a reaction to competitors' pressures. If you anticipate the price movements and do sufficient segmentation analysis to identify price-sensitive groups, you can target those groups with specific promotions to preempt competitors' actions.

Skim pricing, as previously noted in regard to the electronics industry, begins with high pricing and then evolves to slide-down pricing. The downward movement of price usually coincides with such events as new competitors entering to buy market share through low price and when economies of scale begin to take effect.

Segment Pricing

Segment pricing involves pricing essentially the same products differently to various groups. The conditions for considering this strategy are:

- The product is appropriate for several market segments.
- If necessary, the product can be modified or packaged at minimal costs to fit the varying needs of customer groups.
- The consuming segments are noncompetitive and do not violate legal constraints.

Examples of the use of segment pricing abound. The most visible ones are airlines that offer essentially one product, an airplane seat between two cities. Yet this "same" product may serve different segments, such as businesspeople, clergy, students, military, senior citizens, each at different prices. Then, there is further segmentation according to time of day, day of week, or length of stay at one destination.

To best take advantage of this pricing strategy, search out poorly served, unserved, or emerging market segments.

Flexible Pricing

Pricing to meet competitive or marketplace conditions is known as flexible pricing. The conditions for considering this strategy are:

- There is a competitive challenge from imports.
- Pricing variations are needed to create tactical surprise and break predictable patterns.
- There is a need for fast reaction against competitors' attacking your market with penetration pricing.

The case example of Cummins Engines (Chapter 2) illustrates how that company used flexible pricing as part of its strategy to counterattack the Japanese manufacturers moving in on its diesel engine market. CEO Henry Schacht reduced prices rapidly to meet the penetration pricing attempts of the Japanese engine entries.

As organizations reduce staffs and eliminate organizational layers to become more competitive, there is also a movement to give greater authority and responsibility to product and field managers who are closer to the market situation. The intent is to allow a flexible pricing strategy to be employed when appropriate. In contrast, the long chain of command from field managers to executive levels often consumes excessive time and the opportunity to react is missed.

It is incumbent upon middle managers to identify competitive situations where flexible pricing may be used. However, you should remember that flexible pricing, as in all applications of pricing strategy, is not a license to reduce prices to meet competitors' levels in all circumstances. Pricing is still but one component of the marketing mix and is to be viewed within that total framework of marketing strategy options.

Preemptive Pricing

Preemptive pricing is used to discourage competitive market entry. The conditions for considering this strategy are:

- You hold a strong position in a medium to small market.
- You have sufficient coverage of the market and sustained customer loyalty (that is, customer satisfaction) to cause competitors to view the market as unattractive.

IBM used preemptive pricing to protect its dominant position in the typewriter market when it cut prices on its electronic and electric models. In the early 1980's, IBM had 85 percent of the electric typewriter market and about 70 percent of the fast-growing electronic typewriter market in the United States. Facing increased competition in the latter market from a dozen companies announcing entries, IBM reduced prices as an early line of defense to discourage as many product entries as possible.

Preemptive pricing, as with flexible pricing, requires close contact with the field. Customer intelligence and competitor intelligence networks are issues critical to the correct timing of the strategy.

Phase-Out Pricing

Phase-out pricing means pricing high to remove a product from the line. The conditions for considering this strategy are:

- The product has entered the down side of the product life cycle, but it is still used by a few customers.
- Sudden removal of the product from the line would create severe problems for your customers and create poor relations.

Phase-out pricing does not mean dumping. Rather, it is intended for use with a select group of customers who are willing to pay a higher price for the convenience of a source of supply. For example, Echlin Inc., the producer of auto and truck parts, stocks nearly 150,000 different parts for every auto from the Model T to a Rolls Royce. Customers with old or rare auto models are only too pleased to pay the price for product availability.

Loss-Leader Pricing

Pricing a product low to attract buyers for other products is called loss-leader pricing. The conditions for considering this strategy are:

- Complimentary products are available that can be sold in combination with the loss leader at normal price levels.

- The product is used to draw attention to a total product line and increase the customer following. The strategy is particularly useful in conjunction with impulse buying.

Loss-leader is one of the most common forms of pricing strategy. It is prevalent in all ranges of businesses, from department stores to auto dealers to industrial product lines. You should remember, however, to consider the profitability of the total product line.

Creative financing can be combined with loss-leader pricing to use interest-rate financing as an incentive to move products, and as an alternative to cutting prices. For example, Xerox advertised in the early 1980's, ''We've lowered the prime rate; we're now financing many copier purchases at just 15.9 percent.'' And Digital Equipment Corp. offered a three-year, 10.9 percent lease on equipment with a list price of $30,000 or more. Lanier Business Products Inc. and other small and medium-size companies have set up their own financing operations to provide more *marketing flexibility*.

Action Steps

Before converting your pricing strategies into action, remember: Price wars are like fire. Those who persist in such actions are ultimately consumed by them.

To identify strategies and initiate action:

1. List pricing strategies that represent the best opportunities and that will avoid price wars.
2. Indicate what action is to take place and who is assigned the task.
3. Relate feedback to the objective(s) desired and the strategies selected.
4. List immediate plans and future courses of action.

11

Promotion Strategies

Objectives:
To enable you to

1. Follow the guidelines for forming a *total promotion strategy*
2. Develop a successful *advertising* campaign
3. Use *sales promotion* to stimulate sales
4. Identify and initiate the steps needed to convert promotion strategies into *action*

To develop an effective promotion strategy, you need to shape a program that *combines* advertising and sales promotion into a totally integrated force. Keeping these activities separate leads to vague advertising and ineffective sales support.

Advertising

Know the job you want advertising to accomplish. For example, it can support personal selling; inform a target audience about the availability of your product; or persuade prospects to buy. Then, choose media and copy themes to match those objectives. Your advertising thus becomes realistic, measurable, and results-oriented.

Strategy Applications
- Advertising objectives
- Media selection
- Advertising copy

Commentary Advertising is but one part of the communications mix; communications is but one part of promotion; promotion is but one component of the marketing mix. Thus, advertising—as with all the other components—is never created in isolation.

Case Example

Interstate
Bakeries Corp. Interstate Bakeries Corp. made heavy use of promotion to change from an old-line baker into a successful consumer marketer of pastries, breads, stuffings, and similar products. From 1985 to 1987, the Kansas City (Missouri) company moved from a $4.2 million operational loss to earnings of $13.4 million on sales of $729 million.

But not all was rosy for Interstate during the transition from failure to success. There were heavyweight competitors flexing their marketing muscles with such strong brands as Wonder Bread, Hostess snack cakes, Colonial, and Rainbo. Realizing the need to devise aggressive promotion strategies, Interstate took the following steps:

1. Strong brand promotion was introduced in contrast to its traditional pattern of a little-advertised commodity competing primarily on price.
2. New products were promoted with themes in keeping with changing consumer taste and shifting trends with products such as honey-wheat breads, pudding pies, and pecan rolls.
3. Image-building advertising focused on promoting Interstate as a "bakery" with all the favorable connotations associated with the word, such as purity, good taste, value, and warm home feelings.
4. Promoting its 3,000 route distributors as a large pipeline, Interstate pushed its highly advertised brands through the distribution network.

How to Develop a Successful Advertising Campaign

The case illustrates the integration of promotion with company image, product development, positioning, and distribution. Imagine that you are responsible for developing an overall advertising strategy that would be implemented through an advertising department or an outside advertising agency. You need to know, first, that advertising is aimed at informing your target audience about the availability and features of your product or service. Second, once that audience has been informed, advertising should persuade your prospects to buy your offering. In this process, advertising interacts closely and continuously with the other elements of your marketing mix, such as

Table 11-1. *Developing an Advertising Campaign.*

Campaign Step	Advertising Activities	Research Activities
Precampaign Phase		
1. Market analysis		Study competitive products, positioning, media, distribution, and usage patterns
2. Product research		Identify perceived product characteristics and benefits
3. Customer research		Conduct demographic and psychographic studies of prospective customers; investigate media, purchasing, and consumption patterns
Strategic Decisions		
4. Set advertising objectives	Determine target markets and market targets (user profile, exposure goals)	
5. Decide on level of appropriation	Determine total advertising spending necessary to support objectives	Investigate competitive spending levels and media cost necessary to reach objectives
6. Formulate advertising strategy	Develop creative approach and prepare "shopping list" of appropriate media	Examine audience profiles, reach, frequency, and costs of alternative media
7. Integrate advertising strategy with overall marketing strategy	Make sure that advertising supports and is supported by other elements of marketing mix	
Tactical Execution		
8. Develop detailed advertising budget	Break down overall allocation to spending on media categories and individual media	
9. Choose message content and mode of presentation	Develop alternative creative concepts, copy, and layout	Conduct concept and copy tests
10. Analyze legal ramifications	Have chosen copy reviewed by legal staff or counsel	
11. Establish media plan	Determine media mix and schedule	Conduct media research, primarily from secondary sources
12. Review agency presentation	See entire planned campaign in perspective for approval	

Campaign Step	Advertising Activities	Research Activities
	Campaign Implementation	
13. Production and traffic	Finalize and reproduce advertisement(s), buy media time and space, and deliver ads	
14. Insertion of advertisements	Actually run ads in chosen media	Check whether ads appeared as agreed and directed
	Campaign Follow-Through	
15. Impact control		Get feedback on consumer and competitive reaction
16. Review and revision	Adjust advertising execution or spending levels to conditions	Check whether changes made yielded desired results

your product policy, pricing, and distribution. More specifically, it prepares the way for, and reinforces, personal selling efforts. In turn, its impact is enhanced by sales promotion activities.

Obviously, then, advertising cannot be developed in a vacuum. Your advertising plan is but one component of the marketing plan. Accordingly, planning an advertising campaign is quite similar to other business planning activities. It requires, as does all planning, anticipating conditions and developing, within the context of those conditions, objectives, implementation plans, and controls designed to achieve the objectives.

Table 11-1 details the steps involved in developing an advertising campaign. It shows clearly that continuous marketing research is the foundation of a sound campaign.

Situation Analysis in the Precampaign Phase

Planning tradition calls for a careful assessment of overall market conditions before formulating an advertising campaign. In other words, you should conduct a market analysis that surveys the competitive field as a first step in the precampaign phase. This analysis should include an examination of the range of competitive offerings and their recent market trends, their positioning and media choices, and their distribution and usage patterns. You will want to find out who competitors' customers are and when, where, and for what purpose they make purchases. This background information will provide the necessary perspective for choosing appropriate promotion strategies.

As a second step, subsequent product research should focus more intensively on your own product. Its principal purpose is to ascertain from actual or potential users of the product which features they consider desirable and what benefits they associate with its use. This information will be extremely helpful in making the right positioning decision and in formulating effective appeals. In this context, usage patterns must be studied in depth.

The third, and final, step of the precampaign research concentrates on the customer. It attempts to develop demographic and psychographic profiles of actual or prospective buyers. It is essential for you to know who are the frequent and infrequent users of your product, how old they are, where they live, how much money they have at their disposal, their educational backgrounds, their occupations, their marital status and family size, and so forth. You will also want to know how they think and act. Research provides answers regarding their attitudes, interests, and opinions (AIO), which should help determine what motivates them.

You must then analyze their media habits. Knowing who your customers are and how they behave is of little value unless you know what they watch, listen to, and read. You need to know how to reach them. It is also helpful to find out where they purchase, how much, and how often, and who does the purchasing. Additional insights can be gained from a look at consumption patterns. You can ascertain who ultimately consumes your product, when, how much, how often, and under what circumstances.

Only after all of this preliminary information has been gathered, interpreted, and internalized should the advertising planning be initiated.

Making Strategic Decisions

Once the relevant data base has been assembled and examined, you have to make a number of strategic decisions that will guide the subsequent detail work. As in all planning activities, the first major decision is to set advertising objectives.

Advertising Objectives.   Objectives are guidelines for action that spell out what you want to achieve. It could be said that the basic objective of all advertising is to sell something—a product, service, idea, or company. Thus, the means to that end in advertising is effective communication, resulting, ideally, in positive attitudes and/or behavior on the part of the receivers of the message.

However, the objective of increasing sales is too broad to be implemented effectively in an advertising program. Rather, you should formulate more specific and limited aims that can be addressed aggressively and whose achievement can be meaningfully measured. For example:

- Support a personal selling program.
- Achieve a specific number of exposures to your target audience.
- Address prospects who are inaccessible to your salespeople.
- Create a specified level of awareness, measurable through recall or recognition tests.
- Improve dealer relations.
- Measurably improve consumer attitudes toward your product or company.
- Present a new product and generate demand for it.
- Build familiarity and easy recognition of your package or trademark.

The list is truly endless and as varied as companies and situations. It illustrates some of the possibilities, pinpointing the need for precision to derive maximum guidance from objectives and the need to compare results against them. Because objectives imply accountability for results, they often lead to an evaluation of individual or agency performance.

Advertising Appropriation. Having determined where you want to go, you must now decide how best to get there. Marketing executives can choose from a number of alternative approaches for setting the level of total advertising spending.

The *affordable* method: ignores your objectives and is simply an expression of how much you think you can afford to spend. This viewpoint makes your level of appropriation subject to whim and may grossly over- or underestimate the amount in relation to your needs.

The *percentage of sales* approach: probably the most widely used because of its simplicity; that is, it ties your advertising allowance to a specified percentage of current or expected future sales. This procedure, with its built-in fluctuations, not only discourages long-term advertising planning but also neglects current business needs and opportunities.

The *competitive parity* method: proposes that your company match competitive spending levels. This simplistic outlook is no more sophisticated or justifiable than the two preceding approaches.

The *objective and task* method: the most meaningful approach. You proceed in three steps: (1) define your advertising objectives as specifically as possible; (2) identify the tasks that must be performed to achieve your objectives; and (3) estimate the costs of performing these tasks. The sum total of these costs represents your level of appropriation. While this approach does not examine or justify the objectives themselves, it nevertheless reflects your perceived needs and opportunities.

Devising a Conceptual Framework

After the spending level for your prospective advertising campaign has been decided, its conceptual framework must then be established. The evolution of your basic creative approach to the campaign is dependent to some extent on the choice of media.

At this point, strategic decisions are concerned with selecting those appeals most likely to stimulate prospects' purchasing decisions in your favor. Product appeal is defined in terms of price, importance to the consumer, frequency of purchase, competitive edge, and utility. While the creative process at this stage involves a considerable amount of intuition, the quality and reliability of the data available to copywriters and art directors significantly affect the outcome of their efforts. Besides selecting appeals, you must, of course, choose the basic method by which you want to convey your message. This requires a consideration of audience profiles, style, and costs of alternative media.

Advertising is not an end in itself; it has to support and be supported by the other elements of the marketing mix. Therefore, a logical last step in the strategic phase of planning is to confirm that what you intend to do not only is compatible with your overall marketing strategy but enjoys an outright synergistic relationship with your entire marketing plan.

Making Your Advertising Investment More Productive

Advertising is a key element in a total communications package. In terms of creating widespread awareness and exposure of your product, it certainly is your best buy. But remember, no matter how good your agency or advertising department is, you bear the ultimate responsibility for results. Therefore, it pays to be skeptical, to be more independent, and not to be intimidated by the creators of your advertising.

Also remember that advertising can run into a significant sum of money in terms of total outlay, so you will want to make sure that your ads are working hard for you. You can work more intelligently and effectively with your advertising people, and offer more precise guidance as to what they should stress, if you follow a few simple guidelines:

1. Be aware of your product's *positioning* in the marketplace. Offer it as an alternative to an exciting way of doing things or to the leader in the field. Emphasize a major customer benefit that is unique, meaningful, and competitive, and truly and convincingly delivered by your product.

2. Maintain a *personality* for your brand. Use your advertising to make a positive contribution to the brand image. If you want your ads to command attention and to produce results, they need to be characterized by a certain singularity that makes them stand out from the flood of competing messages. It is helpful to use a symbol or other repetitious element that will be remembered by customers.

3. Don't bore your audience and don't be impersonal. *Innovate.* Start trends instead of following them. The risks are high but so are the potential rewards.

4. Be *factual* rather than emotional. One powerful way to present factual material is to use a problem-solving approach. Choose a problem that your customer can relate to and show how your product can solve it.

5. Formulate *effective headlines.* Use simple, understandable language. Department store advertising research has shown that headlines of ten or more words sell more merchandise than do shorter ones. Understandably, recall is best for headlines of eight to ten words.

6. Visually reinforce your advertising with *illustrations,* particularly of demonstrations. Also, pictures with story appeal awaken the curiosity of the readers and tempt them to read the text. Photographs almost invariable pull better than drawings. They attract more readers, generate more appetite appeal, are more believable, result in higher recall and coupon redemption, and produce more sales.

7. Use *captions,* the capsule explanations beneath pictures, to sell. Include your product's brand name and the major benefit you promise.

8. Generate an informative atmosphere. Giving your ads an *editorial appearance* is often more successful than using elaborate, "creative" layouts.

9. Be aware that *readership* falls off rapidly in ad copy of up to 50 words but shrinks only insignificantly in copy of 50 to 500 words. Although long copy is read by relatively few people, those people generally represent genuine prospects. Studies show that industrial ads with more than 350 words are read more thoroughly than shorter ones. (However, avoid long-winded TV commercials. Let the action speak for itself.)

10. Don't replace your advertisements before they have a chance to develop their full potential. The most basic learning theories stress the importance of *repetition* in affecting behavior. Repeat your winners until their effects start to wear off.

Sales Promotion

Integrate sales promotion with your advertising and sales-force objectives and strategies. Use sales promotion to encourage more product usage, induce dealer involvement, and stimulate greater sales-force efforts.

Strategy Applications

- Support sales force
- Support dealers
- Stimulate consumer action

Commentary

Case Example

American Hospital Supply Corporation

American Hospital Supply Corporation (now part of Braxter Travenol) was cited earlier as a case example for pricing strategy. Another aspect of that organization's marketing skills is demonstrated in its use of sales promotion, covering such areas as:

- Setting up advisory services to entice hospitals to buy more thermometers, bed pans, and other supplies from among the 117,000 products that AHS handles.
- Placing a full-time representative at a customer's location to manage its supplies efficiently. The result is that AHS can equip hospitals with almost 70 percent of their supply needs within 24 hours.

- Providing a range of incentives—from cash bonuses for hospitals to free coffee makers, blenders, and even flashlights for physicians—as a means of encouraging supply purchases.
- Offering various management control systems to help hospitals cut inventory. In one case a hospital cut inventory by $420,000, or 65 percent, and saved $400,000 in supply purchases.
- Using direct-mail catalogs to targeted segments of the health care market and using different gift incentives for purchases at various dollar levels.

How to Use Sales Promotion to Stimulate Sales

Although a great deal of money is spent on it, sales promotion rates relatively little attention from either marketing management or advertising agencies. Within most marketing managers' tools, sales promotion exists as a poor relative—grudgingly acknowledged but unenthusiastically integrated into the total promotion effort. Given such neglect, this potentially powerful tool is often poorly understood, planned, and applied, leading to considerable waste and inefficiency. It can be an effective component of most any promotion mix, ranging from consumer goods to industrial goods and even services, dynamically supplementing and complementing the more sophisticated advertising and personal selling efforts.

What is sales promotion? It is all those promotional efforts of a firm that cannot be grouped under the heading of advertising, personal selling, publicity, or packaging. More precisely, sales promotion refers to activities or objects that attempt to encourage salespeople, resellers, and/or ultimate buyers to cooperate with a manufacturer's plans by temporarily offering more value for the money or some other special incentive related to a specific product or service.

While somewhat lengthy, this definition points up a number of essential features:

- Sales promotion includes both *activities*—such as demonstrations and contests—and *objects*—such as coupons, premiums, and samples.
- It may be directed at one or any combination of *three distinct audiences:* a company's own sales force; middlemen of all types and levels, such as wholesalers and retailers (for simplicity's sake, they will be referred to as "dealers"); and consumers or industrial buyers.

- In contrast with the continuous, long-term nature of the other elements of the promotion mix (David Ogilvy has, for instance, said that "an advertisement is a long-term investment in the image of a brand"), sales promotion campaigns are *temporary* measures that should be used with discretion.

However, unless it is used wisely, sales promotion can easily become self-defeating and counterproductive. While there are no hard and fast rules, a brand, for example, that is "on deal" one-third of the time or more is likely to suffer image problems. In fact, if yours is a leading brand in a mature market, you should use sales promotion most sparingly because it is improbable that you will gain any lasting advantage from a more generous application. It is important to remember that sales promotion is costly and should thus be judged from a cost/benefit point of view. So, don't overuse it—even if the temptation is great to yield to internal pressures or external competitive challenges.

Nevertheless, sales promotion has experienced a phenomenal growth that can be expected to continue to increase rapidly. Both internal and external factors have been contributing to this impressive record. Among the internal propellants are (1) senior management, which, in many cases, has come to view sales promotion as an acceptable and effective means of stimulating sales, abandoning the long-held premise that hawking one's wares cheapens the brand; (2) a more professionalized approach to sales promotion that seeks to employ better-qualified individuals and upgrade their status within the organization; and (3) product managers who tend to be more receptive to the "quick fix" aspects of sales promotion that help them achieve fast and impressive results, which, in turn, may lead to personal advancement.

Some important external reasons for the increased use of sales promotion are as follows:

- The number of products in the industrial and consumer marketplace has proliferated, leading to intensified competition and the need to create more "noise" at the point of purchase (POP).
- There is a need to respond to competitive increases in promotion spending, although clearly accompanied by the danger of escalation into a "war" in which all sides lose.
- In a recessionary economy, manufacturers are more willing to use rebates to shrink inventories and improve liquidity, just as consumers are more responsive to sales stimulation measures (in 1980, two-thirds of U.S. families used coupons as part of their regular shopping).
- The growing power of and pressure from the trade produce more promotional allowances and support from suppliers.

• There is a certain degree of disenchantment with advertising, which many managers feel has declined in efficiency and effectiveness owing to a disproportionate rise in cost and in competing messages.

Beginning a Sales Promotion Campaign

If you favor a planned approach to sales promotion over a haphazard one, you will find it advantageous to follow a series of logical steps for maximum impact and efficency. The latter can, however, be achieved only if a *sales promotion campaign* is undertaken not in isolation but, rather, as a part of a long-term plan, carefully coordinated and integrated with the other elements of a firm's promotion mix and, ultimately, with its marketing mix. As already stated, sales promotion complements, supplements, and, often, amplifies other promotional tools, and it should always be *used in concert* with them. For example, displays that tie in with TV commercials produce more sales than unrelated ones.

The following steps are involved in the evolution of a sales promotion campaign:

1. Establish your objectives.
2. Select appropriate techniques.
3. Develop your sales promotion program.
4. Pretest your sales promotion program.
5. Implement and evaluate your campaign.

This sequence contains all four major elements of the marketing management cycle: analysis, planning, execution, and control. Following this pattern slows down the process in comparison with "shooting from the hip," but it makes success considerably more likely.

Establish Sales Promotion Objectives

While the main purpose of sales promotion is to increase the sales volume of a product or to stimulate traffic in a retail outlet, more specific objectives can be identified, depending upon the type of audience and the nature of the task involved. Sales promotion efforts directed at your *company's own sales force* aim to generate enthusiasm and zeal. It is vital that you give your salespeople special incentives to excel and provide the desired support. A second targeted group is your *company's dealers* or distributors, without whose active cooperation your entire marketing effort, and (more specifically) a sales promotion campaign, would be futile. Lastly, while the support and loyalty of your sales force and dealer/distributor network are certainly crucial, a sales promotion campaign would, nevertheless, hardly be complete if it failed to *stimulate buyer action.*

Specific objectives abound:

- Identify and attract new buyers.
- Encourage more frequent and varied usage of current products.
- Motivate trial and purchase of new products.
- Educate users and nonusers about improved product features.
- Suggest purchases of multiple and/or larger units of your product.
- Win over buyers of competitive products.
- Reinforce brand loyalty and purchase continuity.
- Create customer enthusiasm and excitement leading to word-of-mouth recommendations and referrals.
- Diminish fluctuations by encouraging off-season usage.
- Counter competitive raiding.
- Generate more traffic at your dealers' outlets.

Although sales promotion campaigns represent short-term stimulative and corrective instruments, they are most effective when used in a long-term framework. Further, sales promotion objectives cannot and should not be developed in a vacuum, but rather should tie in with overall marketing strategies—in particular, with the sales promotion program. In addition, your sales promotion objectives should be audience-specific and should be spelled out in quantitative form to facilitate later evaluation.

Select Appropriate Techniques

Once you have decided which market segments you want to address, you can select specific techniques for motivating the dealer, introducing new products, and promoting existing products.

Motivating the Dealer. With dealers (any intermediary in the industrial, consumer, or service sector), the most powerful language to speak is still money, that is, profit. Among many available techniques, sales promotion for motivating dealers can include buying allowances, cooperative advertising, dealer listings, sales contests, specialty advertising, and exhibits at trade shows.

Introducing New Products. Another meaningful way to break down the variety of approaches is to group them according to their major application area. Sales promotion techniques particularly well suited to the introduction of new products include free samples or trial offers, coupons, and money refunds.

Promoting Existing Products. You may want to use one or more different tools when attempting to promote established brands: premiums, price packs, contests and sweepstakes, trading stamps, and demonstrations. These tools aim to attract competitors' customers and build market share, introduce new versions of established brands, and reward buyer loyalty.

Table 11-2 will aid your selection process by presenting the pros and cons of these sales techniques.

Develop Your Sales Promotion Program

Having selected the techniques most suitable for accomplishing your objectives with respect to one or more of your prospective audiences—sales force, dealers, and consumers—you must now work out the operational details of your campaign. This activity includes *determining the budget* for your program, which has to take into account three types of costs:

1. The *administrative cost,* covering creative aspects, production of the promotional material, mailing, and advertising.
2. The *incentive cost,* which includes the cost of the premium, coupon, price pack, and sales force or dealer incentive and reflects, of course, the likely rate of redemption (which can vary greatly, depending upon the method of delivery).
3. The *marginal product cost,* such as the cost of a different package or imprint, of business quantities (unless accounted for as incentive cost), or of overtime or supplementary purchases necessitated by the temporary increase in output.

Of necessity, the budget for a specific campaign will have to be set in accordance with the promotional needs of the product during the remainder of the year as well as with the needs of other elements of the product mix. The budget is obviously constrained by the size of the overall annual appropriation for sales promotion, which is usually spelled out as a *percentage of a company's advertising and sales promotion budget* and may run anywhere from 20 percent for industrial firms to 60 percent for consumer goods.

Table 11-2. *Advantages and Disadvantages of Various
Sales Promotion Techniques.*

Technique	Advantages	Disadvantages
Free samples	Induce trial Attract new customers Speed up adoption	Expensive Lacks precision Cumbersome
Free trial	Overcomes market resistance	Costly to administer
Door-to-door couponing	Very selective High redemption rate	Time-consuming Needs careful supervision
Direct-mail couponing	High targetability At-home coverage High redemption rate	Lead time needed Costly Dependent upon list quality
Newspaper couponing	Quick and convenient Geographically targetable Low cost	Low redemption rate Retailers may balk Requires careful planning
Magazine/supplement couponing	Targeted audience Effective coverage Increases in readership	Can become expensive Consumers neglect to clip Slow redemption rate
Money refund	Generates new business Reinforces brand loyalty	Results can be slow Modest impact
In-or-near-pack premiums	Increases product sales Modest distribution cost	Bonus to loyal buyers Pilferage problem
Self-liquidating premiums	Low cost Boosts brand image	Modest sales impact May be too popular
Price pack	Moves merchandise Keeps up visibility	Not selective May cheapen brand image
Contests/sweepstakes	No purchase required Increases brand aware- ness	Expensive Modest participation
Trading stamps/ promotional games	No extra expense for consumer Creates store preference	Consumer boredom Expensive
Point-of-purchase displays	Effective stimulation	Requires dealer cooperation

When deciding on the *length of your campaign,* you will find yourself at a critical point. If the promotion is too short, neither you nor your target audience will derive sufficient benefit from it. On the other hand, if it is too long, your brand's image is likely to be cheapened and your campaign's "act now" urgency will be diluted.

A related issue is, of course, frequency—that is, how often you should promote a given product. Generally, the rules are: not too often, not too short, not too long.

Pretest Your Sales Promotion Program

Having further determined *when to run your campaign,* making sure your schedule ties in smoothly with the other elements of your marketing plan as well as with the plans of your purchasing and production departments, you should now proceed to *pretest your campaign* on a limited scale. This activity will help to reassure you that you have chosen the most appropriate device and incentive, and are delivering it in the most effective manner.

Implement and Evaluate Your Campaign

Once your campaign has been fine-tuned and fully orchestrated, you can put it into effect. If you are introducing a new product, you may want to hold a giant national *sales meeting* to motivate your sales force to go out and excel. For an established product, you may instead send your salespeople *kits* that spell out the objectives of your campaign and its operational details, as well as the nature and size of the incentives offered to them, your dealers, and your consumers.

It will be helpful to equip your salespeople with audiovisual aids and samples of the promotional materials to be used. They also need arguments to support their effort and a schedule specifying dates for sell-in, shipping, advertising, mail-drop, and expiration of the deal. A well-informed, enthusiastic sales force is vital to the success of your program.

As an astute manager, you should closely and continually monitor the progress of your campaign. Poor execution can cause it to backfire by creating frustration and ill will. You should therefore make every effort to achieve the objectives of your campaign. The degree of goal attainment or effectiveness can be measured in various ways, in accordance with the nature of your objectives—for example, in the form of product movement or market-share figures. But it is here that the limitations of sales promotion must be considered. *Sales promotion is a short-term tool that can support long-term goals only in a supplementary capacity.* It cannot build a consumer franchise. To the contrary, if it is used too often, it can destroy the image of a brand. Thus, it should be used not as a substitute for advertising, but rather as a complementary endeavor.

Action Steps

Consider the following points: Speed is the essence of promotional success. There are few cases, if any, of a profitable campaign that was prolonged. A campaign may lack ingenuity, but it has a chance for success if delivered with extraordinary speed. Effective use of promotion can force competitors to react to your moves on your terms. For example, the timing of your promotion can weaken competitors by making them use additional resources after they have completed a major sales promotion effort.

To identify strategies and initiate action:

1. List the promotions that represent the best opportunities.
2. Indicate what action is to take place and who is assigned the task.
3. Relate feedback to the objective(s) desired and the strategies selected.
4. List immediate plans and future courses of action.

12

Distribution Strategies

Objectives:
To enable you to

1. Recognize the primary strategies for *moving a product* to its intended market

2. Learn the criteria for *choosing* channels of distribution

3. Identify ways to *evaluate* distributor performance

---

*M*uch of this decade's fight will be waged at the wholesale and field levels.

August Busch III, CEO
Anheuser-Busch Companies, Inc.

The fifth major component of your competitive strategy is distribution. The ultimate success of your business strategy depends on moving your product to its intended market. Accordingly, you need to take great care in selecting distribution strategies and to consider the far-reaching impact of channel decisions. Such decisions involve (1) the long-term commitment to the distribution channel; (2) the amount of geographic coverage needed to maintain a competitive advantage; and (3) the possibility of competitive inroads.

Channel Dimension

Review the categories of products being sold by your company and their market coverage. Determine if existing channels provide adequate market coverage and if there are expansion possibilities. Consider these criteria: Specialty products do best with exclusive (restricted) distribution; convenience products do best with intensive (widespread) distribution; and shopping products do best with selective (high sales potential) distribution.

Strategy Applications
- Exclusive distribution
- Intensive distribution
- Selective distribution

Case Example

Alco Standard Corporation

Alco Standard Corporation manufactures or distributes everything from paper products to pharmaceuticals. The organization was started in 1965 with acquisitions of over 200 small companies. Most of them were family-owned and had less than $10 million in sales. These individual family businesses became corporate partners and Alco Standard provided accounting, legal, and other services. The total business, nearly 180 companies as of 1987, is divided into eight segments, including paper products, pharmaceuticals, and food equipment.

The 1984 acquisition of Saxon Industries Inc., a distributor of industrial paper products, indicated a shift in Alco Standard's focus away from manufacturing and toward *distribution*. It also demonstrated its distribution strategy in the pharmaceuticals market. Alco Standard managers saw the market expanding as new drugs were introduced. They also detected changes in market behavior whereby manufacturers were selling more pharmaceuticals through wholesale channels to avoid the high cost of using their own sales force. Thus, Alco Standard shrewdly acquired pharmaceuticals wholesalers.

The acquisition of the drug wholesalers triggered a distribution strategy that was applied in the following ways. The company set up a plan to attract small, privately held pharmacies and merge them into the distribution network by offering such services as advertising support and access to Alco's computers to manage inventory. Initially, 300 members signed up and short-term projections indicated 1,500 of some 25,000 nationwide independent pharmacies would join the plan.

Alco's strategy of using distribution as a focal point has paid off in sales and profit growth. As of the mid-1980's, the company continued to view the strategy of acquiring distributors and expanding its distribution expertise as a way to propel itself into the future. At this point in time, distribution accounted for 87 percent of its sales.

Channel Dimension: Choosing Channels of Distribution

There are at least three reasons why distribution channel dimensions are of great importance to your firm:

1. They involve long-term commitments to other firms.
2. They delimit the portion of the market that you can reach.
3. They affect all other marketing decisions.

Channel dimensions involve long-term commitments to other firms. Once chosen, distribution channels typically develop a great deal of inertia against change. Your choice of a channel type associates your brand in the consumer's mind with a certain kind of store or outlet, thus creating an image that is difficult, if not impossible, to alter.

Signing up individual wholesalers or retailers often involves substantial up-front outlays. This money is needed for factory training of service personnel; workshop and field training of counter and other sales personnel; granting of easy terms for initial stock; advertising and promotional support; field sales support through missionary salespeople; and many other investments and commitments that would be wasted if you were to abandon these channel partners.

Remember, too, that it would hardly sit well with the trade if you walked away from your commitments. Your channel partners would also resent and resist any infringement on their franchise by your adoption of a multiple-channel strategy for the same brand.

Channel dimensions delimit the portion of the market that you can reach. Your selection of channel members restricts the kinds and numbers of ultimate buyers that can be reached through them, effectively cutting you off from that part of the market that does not patronize those outlets. Of course, your selection of outlets may coincide with your desired target market, in which case your neglect of the remainder of the market is deliberate.

But what if you can't attract the kinds of stores or outlets that cater to the group of consumers you wish to reach? Then you have to settle for what you can get. To avoid this trap, your product, your price, and your support must satisfy the intermediaries you want to win over.

Channel dimensions affect all other marketing decisions. The interdependence of marketing mix decisions is most evident when choosing distribution channels. If you choose a pattern of exclusive distribution, your product becomes a luxury item requiring high prices and high dealer margins. If, on the other hand, you go after intensive market coverage, you characterize your product as mass merchandise, which, in turn, necessitates a low-price policy.

Choice of advertising approaches, themes, messages, and media will vary with your product's distribution channels. Also, product and packaging design must reflect the characteristics of your chosen channels; merchandise suited for self-service outlets has to be presented differently from goods requiring the advice and explanation of knowledgeable sales personnel. Obviously, channel decisions cannot be made in a vacuum, since they have repercussions on every other marketing decision you make and thus affect your entire marketing effort.

Distribution and Market Exposure

Adequate market coverage is relative to the product being promoted. Depending on the degree of market exposure desired, you can choose from exclusive, intensive, and selective distribution strategies (see Table 12-1).

Exclusive.   If you have a prestige product to sell, you will grant the exclusive right covering a geographic area to a specific wholesaler or retailer, protecting this firm against territorial encroachments by other companies carrying your products. This policy severly limits

Table 12-1. *Considerations in Choosing Your Degree of Market Exposure.*

	Distribution		
Consideration	*Exclusive*	*Selective*	*Intensive*
Degree of coverage	Limited	Medium	Saturation
Degree of control	Stringent	Substantial	Virtually nil
Cost of distribution	Low	Medium	High
Dealer support	Substantial	Limited	Very limited
Dealer training	Extensive	Restricted	None
Type of goods	Specialty	Shopping	Convenience
Product durability	Durable	Semidurable	Nondurable
Product advertising	Yes	Yes	No
Couponing	No	No	Yes
Product example	Automobile	Suit	Chewing gum

the number of middlemen handling your products and should be adopted only if you want to exercise substantial control over your intermediaries' prices, promotion, presentation, and service. It results in a stronger commitment on the part of your dealers and, thus, in a more aggressive selling effort.

Frequently practiced in the automobile business, exclusive distribution, however, can lead to a number of legal problems:

An exclusive dealer contract, signed between your firm and a specific retailer, prevents the middleman from selling competitors' products. Such a practice violates Section 3 of the Clayton Act of 1914 if it may have the effect of "substantially lessening competition or tending to create a monopoly."

Closed sales territories, a term referring to a vertical territorial restriction between your company and an intermediary, frequently come under scrutiny. Ever concerned with maintaining competition, the courts have, however, generally gone along with such arrangements when the manufacturer in question is not a market leader.

Tying contracts, which require your exclusive dealers to carry other of your products, violate the Sherman Antitrust Act and Clayton Act if they preclude competitors from entering major markets.

Intensive. Intensive distribution is the direct opposite of exclusivity. Popular among producers of convenience items, this policy aims to make these goods available in as many outlets as possible. As the category name suggests, buyers of such products expect them to be conveniently accessible and will not expend much shopping effort. Products in this category are frequently purchased, low-ticket nondurables, such as cigarettes and chewing gum.

Selective. Between the extremes of exclusive and intensive distribution falls selective distribution. This policy involves setting up selection criteria and deliberately restricting the number of retailers that will be permitted to handle your brand. More than one, but less than all applicants in an area will be selected. This approach implies quality without the restrictions of exclusivity.

Selective distribution is far less costly than intensive distribution and affords greater control. In particular, it is suitable for such retail goods as name-brand clothes, which fall into the semidurables category (in contrast to the expensive durable specialty goods that are best handled through exclusive distribution). Selective distribution lends itself to cooperative advertising, in which manufacturer and retailer share the cost.

Direct Versus Indirect Distribution

A very basic distribution decision that you have to make relatively early in your planning is whether you want to handle the distribution of your product alone or you want to enlist expert help. The former method is called direct distribution and the latter, indirect distribution.

Direct distribution, as the name suggests, involves a direct transfer of ownership from the producer to the consumer. As Figure 12-1 shows, this method does not preclude various types of facilitators from entering into the picture. As long as they do not assume title separate and distinct from the manufacturer, the channel still remains direct. Thus, producers can sell through the mail, over the phone, door to door, through a factory outlet, through their own retail stores, or even through an independent agent, and still be involved in a direct transaction. Direct distribution obviously involves a greater degree of control than indirect distribution, but it cuts a producer off from the widespread coverage that the latter approach can offer.

Indirect distribution, on the other hand, always incorporates middlemen or resellers, who are basically of two types: wholesalers and retailers. Figure 12-1 presents a graphic comparison of the direct and indirect approaches.

Figure 12-1. *Direct and indirect distribution approaches to alternative channel designs.*

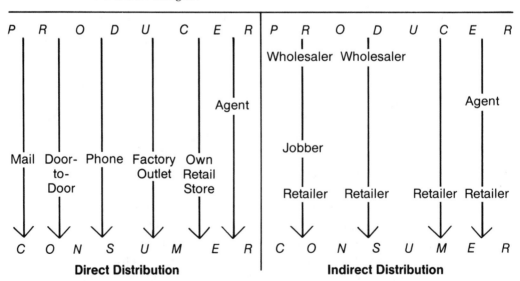

Source: *Marketing Update,* Issue 10 (1978), p. 4. Published by Alexander-Norton Publishers, Inc.

What you see in Figure 12-1 is typical of the most frequently encountered channel designs. It is evident that in the direct distribution channel there is never a third party who takes title to the goods in question. For indirect distribution, the opposite situation is clearly the case, even though the manufacturer is likely to have a sales force to call on intermediaries of the middleman variety.

The illustration does not propose to exhaust the variety of channel structures. Instead, it abstracts the most frequently used designs. As can be readily seen, multiple channels are entirely possible and are often adopted to increase exposure and impact in the marketplace. However, selecting more than one route to the consumer can lead either to complementary or to competing and, thus, conflicting channels. Where it results in conflict, this growth policy can defeat its own purpose.

Function versus Institution. In differentiating between direct and indirect distribution, a basic distinction ought to be made between the functions and institutions of wholesaling and retailing.

The function of wholesaling is to sell those items necessary for use in the conduct of a business (for example, typewriters) or for resale. The function of retailing, in contrast, is to sell for personal, non-business use. In a retailing transaction the buyer of an item is a consumer who intends it for private use or consumption.

The respective institutions are business firms specializing in each particular type of transaction. An institution of wholesaling—a wholesaler—is a firm whose primary business is buying merchandise in large quantities at substantial discounts and reselling it in unaltered form at a relatively modest markup to industrial or institutional users, or in somewhat smaller, but still sizable, quantities to other wholesalers or retailers.

An institution of retailing—a retailer—is a firm whose primary business is buying merchandise in medium-size quantities (cases versus the wholesaler's truckloads) and reselling it in small quantities (frequently individual units) to consumers, often at substantial markups.

The reason for drawing these distinctions between function and institution lies in the fact that *institutions can be eliminated, but their respective functions cannot.* When you first enter a new market, it is generally advisable to go the indirect route, involving wholesalers who can deliver quick and widespread coverage at a reasonable cost. Later, though, as your product moves into the maturity stage of the life cycle, you may want to eliminate your wholesalers in order to gain more immediate access to your retailers and better control over the selling effort. It is at this point that you often discover that one can eliminate the institution but not the function of wholesaling (or retailing, for that matter). The question, therefore, is not whether to perform these functions, but who is to perform them.

Case Example

Kelly-Moore Kelly-Moore Paint Co., a regional manufacturer of paint, has
Paint Co. Inc. shown remarkable performance by producing 10 percent on its sales over a 10-year period (1977–87), as compared with the giants Sherwin-Williams and du Pont, each of which averaged only 2.5 percent net on sales for the same period. What made Kelly-Moore's success remarkable was that its primary focus was on contractors, a customer group in the distribution chain that buys less than one-third of the paint sold in the United States.

The essence of Kelly-Moore's strategies can be summarized as follows:

- It provided maximum service to contractors who generally worked out of their homes. For example, Kelly-Moore's 86 paint stores served as *free warehouse* space for the contractors who could not buy paint in any volume.

- It maintained ongoing market intelligence. Because the stores doubled as contractor warehouses, Kelly-Moore knew exactly what customers' usage and color patterns were at any given time. Such feedback made for tighter corporate planning and helped in anticipating the changing needs and wants of the marketplace.

- Kelly-Moore moved further down the distribution chain into the consumer end of the business by building on its contractor base. For example, when contractors left touch-up cans behind them after completing a job, Kelly-Moore used those samples as a means of selling to consumers directly. The approach was complimentary, not conflicting, since the direct-to-consumer sales were generally for the do-it-yourself segment of the market.

Why Use Intermediaries?

There are a number of reasons for using middlemen. The majority of manufacturers lack the financial wherewithal to perform effectively at both levels, production and distribution. They have to rely on middlemen to provide the financing for an aggressive, widespread selling effort. But even companies with adequate financial means might find investment in vertically integrated channels unattractive because of a relatively low return on investment. Thus, they might pursue higher-yielding opportunities at the production end, leaving the distribution function to specialists.

Finally, producers going into the distribution business themselves often find that they must carry complementary products of other manufacturers to help defray the high cost of distribution and get maximum yield from their effort.

Making the Decision

When the time comes to make the channel decision for your product, several factors need to be considered. An important initial consideration is: Where does the customer expect to find your product or service? The industry's prevailing distribution pattern can thus be a powerful guide in making such a channel decision. If your current sales force has related experience and appropriate business contacts, you may want to follow established routes.

Other factors to be taken into account can be grouped as company, competitive, and customer factors. Companies that are strong financially have the option of direct distribution, while weaker firms have to use middlemen. If your product line is broad, you are in a better position than a specialized supplier to consider going direct. The more control you desire, the fewer intermediaries you will want to have. Competitive practices will often encourage you to meet competitors head on in the very same outlets they use. Customer characteristics include the number of buyers, their geographic location, and their buying patterns. You are better off going direct when you have a limited number of prospects. Again, if they are concentrated in only a few areas, you can send your own sales force out to do the job. Should they buy often and in small quantities, you had better let others handle the selling.

Channel members are a vital link in your effort to satisfy distant customers. By making them your partners and serving their best interests, you will find that they will help you achieve your goals.

Channel Control

Channel control considers four sets of circumstances that dictate the search for new distributors:

1. New marketing efforts, for example, introduction of a new product or entry into new markets.

2. Desire to intensify market coverage.

3. Need to replace existing distributors.

4. Industry changes or your strategy changes in methods of distribution.

Strategy
Application

• Identify prospective outlets

• Evaluate distributors

• Select the best distributors

Case Example

Blue Bell, Inc. An innovative approach to channel control is illustrated by the strategy of Blue Bell Inc., maker of Wrangler jeans. Since 1980, garment imports doubled to $20 billion a year, and forecasts show imports grabbing 80 percent of the U.S. market by 1990. To counter the threat, Blue Bell forged a cooperative distribution relationship with Wal-Mart Stores, Inc. For example, Wal-Mart used a computer hook-up through which it could get orders filled in *one day*, instead of the five weeks it took in 1984. Blue Bell developed similar plans for its own suppliers. According to both Blue Bell and Wal-Mart, those link-ups resulted in more efficient control of the distribution channel and have saved millions of dollars since 1982. Within the textile industry in general, other companies along the distribution chain demonstrated that better coordination and control between makers of apparel and distributors or retailers are cutting lead time for new products to an average of 17 weeks from the normal time of well over six months. By developing such cooperative relationships within the distribution channel, companies are developing a competitive advantage over imports.

Within the distribution channel, the distributor is the key success factor in your strategy. After you've developed a channel control strategy, you need to know how to select and evaluate distributors.

Selecting Distributors

Since few companies are in a position to sell directly to their ultimate users, the success of a marketing effort is largely dependent upon the effectiveness and motivation of the distribution network. Accordingly, great care should be taken in selecting the group of intermediaries on which a firm relies for the execution of its marketing program. Given the high degree of specialization found among distributors, your firm's management must decide how selective or comprehensive it wants to be in its market coverage. Only with the appropriate distribution mix can your company's marketing goals be satisfactorily accomplished.

Your distributors will deliver the performance that you expect of them only if you carefully manage and constantly update your relationship with them. Therefore, you have to develop and consistently apply well-thought-out criteria for selecting the right distribution partner in a given area.

As you introduce new products, you may find that your current distributor team is ill-equipped to sell and service them, or that it already handles competitive products by other manufacturers. Or, you may be addressing a new kind of clientele not serviced by your current network. If you enter into new geographic markets, the need for appropriate representation is self-evident. To help determine how many and what kinds of distributors you need, and to facilitate the selection process, you will generally want to conduct a market analysis of the respective territory to estimate its sales potential. Fortunately, however, you rarely have to choose a completely new set of distributors. Most innovations can adequately be handled by your own firm's present distributors.

As you review your share of the business in a given area, you may well come to the conclusion that your firm is underrepresented or that your present outlets are not going after the business aggressively enough. This may cause you to add more distributors in the territory, based on population, sales, buying potential, or other relevant considerations. Or, perhaps an area is growing so quickly that your current distributor is simply no longer in a position to service the market adequately. However, the addition of new distributors in existing territories needs considerable thought and diplomacy. The desire for maximum coverage can prove to be counterproductive by demoralizing your current distributors.

By far the most frequent reason for appointing new distributors is the turnover of existing outlets. These changes may be due to natural attrition, caused by the death or retirement of principals or the sale or demise of a distributing firm. The recent trend toward more specialization or limited-line selling has also led many distributors to drop a certain manufacturer's line.

More often than through attrition, changes in your distributor mix are brought about by inadequate distributor performance that leaves the manufacturer, or even both sides, dissatisfied. But such a move can be painful and disruptive and should be undertaken only in extreme cases. It is often better to try to rekindle an existing relationship. As one producer put it: " 'Old dogs' can learn new tricks faster and perform sooner than 'new dogs'." However, when you have a chance to move from a lesser to a leading distributor in a market area, you'll find yourself likely to take the plunge.

Rarely should you have to revamp your entire distribution structure. In such a restructuring, you may add or eliminate an intermediary step in the distribution of your company's products, necessitating the selection of new distributors. If, on the other hand, you should decide to make the dramatic changeover from direct to indirect distribution, you will have to build a national distributor network from scratch—a formidable challenge, requiring years of analysis, search, and organization.

Once you have determined that you need new or additional distributor representation, your next task is to develop a list of candidates to be considered. You usually have a number of sources for this list, including your own field sales force, your manager of distributor sales, trade associations, and present distributors and dealers.

The intelligent selection of distributive outlets for your firm requires more than the good judgment of a few key people, based on their personal impressions. Since so much is at stake, the selection process should be directed by a set of carefully chosen guidelines consistently applied. These selection criteria have to be customized to suit the particular conditions and goals of your firm. Table 12-2 highlights the distributor selection criteria most often mentioned by some 200 leading U.S. manufacturers in a study on this subject. As is evident, the numerous considerations employed can be classified and summarized into a limited number of categories within which further breakdowns or adjustments are then possible to accommodate your unique situation. The broad framework, however, is applicable to any distributor selection task.

It is a monumental task to both formulate and apply a set of selection criteria suited to your particular circumstances. But it is well worth the effort, since it should lead to satisfying and lasting relationships.

Selecting a distributor is by no means a one-way street. Rather, it is a matter of both sides choosing to work with each other. Thus, once you have made a selection, you have to persuade the prospect to join your team. It may well be that your firm is being scrutinized just as carefully by your prospective distribution partner. You should welcome that and be willing to supply information as freely as you expect to receive it. A well-analyzed commitment is bound to last longer than a hasty decision.

Table 12-2. *Criteria for Selecting Distributors.*

Criterion (Category)	Reasoning
Financial aspects	Only a distributor of solid financial strength and practices can assure you of adequate, continuous representation
Sales organization and performance	The sales strength and record of a prospect is essential to your potential relationship
Number of salespeople (in the field and on the inside)	The rule is simple: the more salespeople, the more sales and the more effective the market coverage
Sales and technical competence	Salespeople with inadequate technical and sales skills are a liability
Sales performance	A track record speaks for itself
Product lines carried	Pick your bedfellows carefully
Competitive products	Generally disdained, sometimes OK
Compatible products	Tend to be beneficial
Quality level	The higher, the merrier
Number of lines	Will your line get enough attention?
Reputation	You are judged by the company you keep
Market coverage	Exposure means sales
Geographic coverage	Avoid overlap and conflicts
Industry coverage	Major user groups must be covered
Intensity of coverage	Infrequent calls mean lost business
Inventory and warehousing	Ability to deliver is often crucial
Kind and size of inventory	You want the right mix and a willingness to maintain adequate stock
Warehousing facilities	Storage and handling must be appropriate
Management	Proper leadership spells success
Ability	You want competent leadership
Continuity	Succession should be assured
Attitudes	Look for enthusiasm and aggressiveness

Evaluating Distributors

Once you have secured the services of a sought-after distributor candidate, you must then ensure that your association brings maximum benefit to both parties. You need to perform periodic evaluations designed to keep you continually informed about the relative performance of your various distributors. These evaluations may be in the nature of current operating appraisals or may take on the form of overall performance reviews. If they are simple and limited in scope, you could conduct them monthly. Thorough analyses, however, should be undertaken only at infrequent intervals: annually, biannually, or even triannually.

If you engage in selective rather than exclusive distribution, the amount of evaluative input that you can readily obtain from your distributors is quite limited, forcing you to rely mostly on your own records, observations, and intelligence. If your product is a high-volume, low-cost item with little need for after-sale servicing, you can restrict yourself to a more limited evaluation than in the case of complex systems installations.

If your team is composed of many hundreds of multiline distributors, you will tend to take a closer look at a particular reseller only if its sales trends are way out of line; this procedure has been referred to as "evaluation by exception." If, in contrast, your firm employs only a moderate number of outlets, you can be much more thorough in your analysis. There may not even be a need for formal evaluation if you have a close, continuous working relationship.

Whatever you conclude from your evaluation, it will rarely result in the termination of a particular distributor's services. Elimination is truly the last step, after all attempts to reestablish a satisfactory relationship have failed. The expense, time, and trouble involved in dropping a distributor and appointing an established outlet or even appointing an additional distributor are considerably less appealing alternatives.

Action Steps

Before converting your distribution strategies into action, remember that excessive distance and time between your product and its availability to customers adds a burden to an operation. Shorten the length of the distribution channel and reduce communication time between the customer and the home office to assure profitable market conditions.

To identify strategies and initiate action:

1. List the distribution strategies that represent the best opportunities.
2. Indicate what action is to take place and who is assigned the task.
3. Relate feedback to the objective(s) desired and the strategies selected.
4. List immediate plans and future courses of action.

13

A Global Marketing Perspective and Strategy Teams

Objectives:
To enable you to

1. Identify five entry strategies for considering a *geographic expansion* into global markets
2. Acknowledge the need to learn to *coordinate* individual talents into a cohesive force for developing competitive strategies

3. Understand the roles and responsibilities of *strategy teams* in developing competitive strategies
4. Help the team to identify *opportunities* for creating action

Defining a Global Perspective

A global, or *comprehensive,* marketing perspective goes beyond only geography and, in its broader dimensions, focuses on applications of competitive strategies. A global perspective requires the mind of a strategist and the scope of thinking of a general manager. It means opportunistic thinking, which may be expressed in targeting markets and then going for maximum penetration. For example, Atlantic Richfield Company (Arco) converted 600 of its service stations in the western United States into 24-hour minimarkets, called AM/PMs, that offer everything from bread and milk to fast foods. By 1990, projections indicate that a network of 1,000 AM/PM stores will saturate those markets.

A global perspective means overcoming obstacles of timing, market position, and competition, as Abbott Laboratories did in the medical testing market. Consider the following events. In the late 1970's, Abbott was not even among the top 20 companies in the medical testing field; now it is twice as large as its nearest competitor. Although late in entering the market for a diagnostic test for the AIDS virus, it got to the market first and, by 1987, managed to hold on to 60 percent of that fast-growing business. It snared more than 50 percent of the doctors' office market for quick pregnancy tests. And, in one year, it launched 70 new diagnostic tests in its effort to be number 1 in market share.

A global perspective means reacting soon enough to stop aggressive competitors, such as Otis Elevators did by constructing a $20-million, 29-story experimental building that contains a lobby, 11 elevators—and little else. Otis wanted to protect its 25 percent share of the $10-billion elevator market by developing faster, computerized, "smart" elevators. The reason: Japanese manufacturers, such as Mitsubishi, are beginning to push elevators into the California market as the first stage to a national rollout.

Achieving a Global Perspective

Let's look at how a customer-oriented philosophy, introduced in Chapter 3, can help achieve a global perspective.

Case Example

Sony Corp. Sony Corp. embodies the successful attributes for managing today's customer-oriented business: (1) expertise in competitive strategies; (2) sound marketing planning; (3) innovation; (4) entrepreneurship; (5) product quality; (6) product differentiation; (7) target (niche) marketing; and (8) a global perspective. The applications of those attributes are played out against tough barriers, including aggressive competition from other Far East countries such as Taiwan, South Korea, and Singapore; fighting back attitudes from U.S. and European companies; growing protectionist feelings from world governments that account for 70 percent of Sony's sales outside Japan; and the dramatic rise of the yen, which put extra pressure on price competitiveness.

Yet the internal strengths of Sony and its devotion to a customer-driven mentality continue to find ways to break through the formidable barriers in an effort to retain market leadership. Let's examine Sony's strategies:

1. Refocus strategic objectives by reducing dependence on the fiercely competitive consumer electronics market to attain as much as 50 percent of its revenues from nonconsumer products, up from a recent level of 15 percent.
2. Accelerate cost reduction procedures to accommodate the rising yen.
3. Expand manufacturing operations overseas to deal with increasing protectionist sentiments.
4. Share technology, for the first time, with other companies (and competitors) in an effort to create unified industry standards and thereby gain faster market acceptance of new product systems.
5. Adopt an aggressive marketing mentality and push harder for larger market shares even at the expense of lower profit margins initially. (For example, a Walkman selling for $32 was developed to penetrate more of the U.S. market.)
6. Continue to search for new markets where large, well-entrenched companies are not threats, or where there are major opportunities, as in the office-of-the-future or image-processing markets.

A Global Perspective on the Worldwide Market

Overseas Markets Offer Attractive Potential
There is no denying that international markets present a challenging and steadily growing opportunity for global expansion of your business base. It is likely that there are many people around the world who need what you have to offer, regardless of the industry you belong to. More and more, the world is becoming a global marketplace. To stop your marketing activities at the borders of the United States is not only arbitrary, but shortsighted.

Developed countries, such as the industrial nations of Western Europe, usually place few restrictions on international marketing activities. They also provide an easier place to break into international markets, because they usually have fully developed communications, distribution, and transportation systems, to name but a few facilitating factors.

In developing countries, on the other hand, you will need a more flexible approach, since they tend to be more jealous of their national prerogatives and less advanced in their infrastructure. But their sales potential is, nevertheless, quite substantial. It can be tapped successfully if you are willing to adapt.

The entry strategies that follow show the choices available to your firm in its attempt to penetrate markets abroad and to establish a presence in them. While representing alternative possibilities, they can also be thought of as stages in a sequential process of increasing commitment.

Case Example

Reebok International Ltd. A truly global perspective can move a company from niche markets to national coverage to international expansion. Reebok International, Ltd., the athletic shoe company, is a resounding success story of just such a perspective. In only four years (1983–87), it grew to a $1-billion international organization. Focusing on Reebok's primary success strategies, the following points emerge:

Internally. There was a successful transformation from a one-product designer sneaker company to a multiproduct, multimarket, complex organization. That complexity, however, was well managed. One organizational approach used the acquisition of the rival Avia Group to create *internal competition.* For example, an order was given to Avia, "Hit all of Reebok's soft spots. If you don't, somebody else will."

Externally. There was a major thrust into international markets. In addition to footholds in Italy and Britain, Reebok moved into Canada, France, and Germany. The Canton (Mass.) company projected that international sales would provide up to 50 percent of its revenues in five years, up from current levels of 5 percent.

Entry Strategies for International Markets One of the strategies for Reebok's growth—and perhaps yours—is through international expansion. Strategies for entering foreign markets can be classified into five basic categories: exporting, licensing, joint venture, wholly owned subsidiaries, and management contract.

Table 13-1 presents these approaches in a systematic form for comparison. These alternatives differ from one another in intensity of commitment, amount of investment, extent of control, and degree of profitability. The choice from among them is often dictated by circumstances such as insufficient funds, inadequate knowledge of a foreign environment, and host country restrictions on ownership. The intent here is to present an overview of the benefits and drawbacks of each category to enable you to make more intelligent and informed decisions when considering the possibilities open to you on the international scene.

Table 13-1. *Comparison of Entry Strategies for International Markets.*

Strategy	Definition	Intensity of Commitment	Amount of Investment	Extent of Control	Degree of Profitability
Exporting	Marketing in one country goods produced in another	Typically very limited	Possible investment in inventory	Rather limited, except in the case of exclusive distribution	Moderate, due to transportation cost, import duties, middlemen cost
Licensing	Licensor grants licensee right to use patent, know-how, etc.	Own marketing effort precluded until expiration of license	Virtually none	Very restricted; spelled out in license agreement	Fixed royalties dependent on licensee effort
Joint venture	Sharing ownership and control of foreign operation with at least one partner	Generally provide know-how and equity capital portion	Dependent on equity share	Dependent on ownership ratio and power play	Varies according to circumstances
Wholly owned subsidiary	Firm abroad 100% owned by U.S. company	Strong commitment of all kinds of resources	Substantial investment in plant, etc.	Complete control over all phases of operation	Can be highly profitable
Management contract	Managing a foreign facility under contract	Only human resources	Facility not owned by managing firm	Restricted by contract; typically quite limited	Moderate, due to its fee character

Exporting—Pros and Cons

Exporting, the most frequently used strategy for entering international markets, is virtually as old as mankind. The earliest tribes and nations traded with one another because each had resources or skills desired or needed by the others. Essentially the same reasons for exporting prevail today. Your company may want to export to take best advantage of its resources and capabilities by selling in markets that may be more responsive than domestic ones. If your productive capacity is not fully utilized, international markets can provide outlets that enable you to get extra mileage out of your plant. Many firms consider revenues produced by exporting as "found money," because the plant's fixed costs have already been covered by domestic sales and the profit margin earned on international sales can thus be substantially higher.

Many firms stumble onto the international scene because they have excess productive capacity and are looking for stopgap measures to bring utilization up to a more desirable level. These newcomers are often not serious about continuing their export activities, but are attracted by the ratio of considerable sales potential to limited commitment and risk.

At the outset, for instance, a firm might not be inclined to invest in inventories abroad. Rather, it would want to minimize its exposure by initially restricting itself to representation or distribution arrangements in a given country without committing funds for inventory, advertising, and so forth. There is a price to pay, of course, for this lack of initial commitment. If it leaves everything to its agents or distributors, a firm will have very little control over what happens. And with inexperience, costs tend to be somewhat higher than they otherwise would be, thus cutting into profit potential. In international trade, cost categories include transportation, import duties, and middleman expenses. The paperwork involved in exporting should not be underestimated, either.

With the exception of a few strategic industries, the U.S. government generally looks with favor on the exporting activities of domestic firms. After all, they provide employment opportunities at home and reduce the balance of payments (monetary inflows and outflows) deficit. At one time, the federal government even supported these activities by providing insurance against commercial and political risks arising from export transactions. Although the government no longer provides such insurance, it still provides assistance to exporters by supplying relevant information to marketing decision makers and by assisting in setting up offices or locating distributors abroad.

Licensing—Reaping Fruit Without Sowing

In a sense, the simplest way to enter international markets is through licensing. In this setup, a licensor grants the right to exploit patents, trademarks, or proprietary technological know-how to a licensee (usually one per country) on an exclusive basis. Thus, without additional investment, your company could benefit from the efforts of others, based on its specialized knowledge and proprietary rights. Its relationship with individual licensees is codified in licensing agreements. Such agreements generally stipulate the responsibilities of each party, the rights transferred, markets to be served, payments to be made, and control procedures. Protective clauses relate to the maintenance of proprietary rights, to protection against disclosure of information, and to arbitration or litigation procedures. Termination clauses state the length of the contract and the circumstances under which either party may end the relationship.

On the surface, licensing looks like the ideal way for reaping effortless rewards. You can penetrate overseas markets with virtually no investment. There is no need to make capital outlays and send key personnel abroad, as in other entry strategies. Your licensee is likely to be a firm that is well established in the field and can give maximum support and exposure to your product.

Licensing offers you a source of additional earnings with little risk and minor demands on executive time. It gives you a chance to meet the needs of foreign prospects, overcome trade barriers, build up goodwill, and protect your patents and trademarks through usage. Sometimes, licensor and licensee cross-license each other, thus mutually benefiting from present and future know-how in a field.

Licensors are compensated for granting the license in the form of royalties. The royalty rate depends on the value of the rights being made available, the bargaining power of each party, and the prevailing rate level. The amount of these royalties is, naturally, the direct outcome of the level of effort expended by the licensee. And this is the crux of the matter—once you have gained a license, you are at the mercy of your licensee. Though your agreement may provide for quality inspections and audits, you really cannot control the day-to-day operations of your licensee and the extent of market development.

The scenario is all too familiar. A firm that has valuable know-how in a specific area, but has no current intention of exploiting it in overseas markets, is approached by a prospective foreign licensee with a request to grant a license. In the euphoria surrounding this opportunity to take advantage of "found money," the firm is generous about the duration and geographic coverage of the license and lax as to performance requirements and termination provisions. As the licensee's efforts prove unsatisfactory or the licensed property's international potential grows, a license agreement can turn out to be a stranglehold, effectively restricting you from using your own property and quite possibly creating a strong international competitor. (So, look before you leap!)

Joint Venture—Often the Way to Go

If you want an active manufacturing presence in a host country transcending the amount of involvement and impact that you can have with exporting or licensing, a joint venture can be an attractive possibility. In essence, a joint venture means that your firm establishes a subsidiary abroad that is jointly owned with at least one individual or company native to the country in question. This approach may be advisable for a number of reasons:

- A joint venture may provide valuable help in gaining a foothold in a host country.
- It may reduce the risk of failure or expropriation.
- It provides additional capital or personnel you may lack to expand into this market on your own.
- It provides access to a local partner's distribution system or know-how.
- The law of the land may prevent setting up wholly owned subsidiaries.

In co-owning and co-controlling your common subsidiary, your firm and its overseas partner may share patents, trademarks, and control over manufacturing or marketing. Joint ventures prove to be an excellent vehicle for entering international markets if the local partner has the marketing expertise to complement your firm's technological know-how. A well-established local partner can provide your firm with physical facilities, a labor force, and contacts with businesses and officials, while your company may offer capital, technology, and managerial talent.

An example of such an operation in the United States is Dow Badische Company, a 50-50 joint venture between The Dow Chemical Company and BASF, the German chemical giant. While such arrangements are typical in developed countries, joint ventures in developing countries are somewhat different. For one thing, they are usually mandatory. Most Third World governments do not allow any new wholly owned subsidiaries to be formed; they often force established ones to be converted to joint ownership.

The most obvious disadvantage of joint ventures is the reduced control of the foreign co-owner. Points of view may differ as to the policies and practices of the joint venture operation. Differences in culture, language, and business philosophy may be difficult to overcome. While the potential for conflict is substantial, however, a well-chosen, well-motivated partner can be of great value.

Wholly Owned Subsidiaries—A Mixed Blessing

The greatest form of commitment abroad is a subsidiary that is wholly owned by your firm. The underlying idea is that ownership equals control and that complete control is necessary to meet corporate objectives. When demand and the competitive situation justify the substantial investment involved, this strategy can provide substantial benefits to the parent company. Your company may want to manufacture abroad in order to:

- Capitalize on low-cost labor.
- Avoid high import taxes or quotas.
- Reduce transportation cost.
- Gain access to raw materials.
- Export preferentially to related markets.

If your products are labor-intensive, you may want to locate plants in low-wage nations or areas, subsequently exporting the finished goods to more developed countries. Some countries and markets have erected high, even prohibitive, import duty barriers in an effort to preserve precious hard currency and foster local industry. In Brazil, for example, importation of anything not considered essential by the government is sharply restricted. In such instances, it pays to set up shop within the country to avoid the restrictions imposed on international trade.

In the past, the overwhelming majority of U.S. foreign investments were made in wholly owned subsidiaries, but this type of investment appears doomed, at least in the Third World countries. Developed countries, as a rule, are less concerned about such foreign usurpation of power, and permit U.S. subsidiaries to function on a more or less equal footing with native companies as long as reciprocity exists.

Less developed countries are concerned about possible exploitation of local resources if foreign firms within their borders do not have local partners. Thus, almost without exception, they require joint ownership and no longer permit wholly owned subsidiaries. Increasingly, even in developed nations, firms may insist on taking local partners into their overseas subsidiaries in order to avoid criticism and improve their ability to cope with union demands and the complex requirements of the host government.

Management Contract—Often a Last Resort

A management contract involves managing an overseas facility for its owner. It is entered into when the local owner does not possess, and cannot obtain, sufficient management expertise locally to run the facility efficiently. Such a contract may be connected with the building of a sophisticated new facility, such as an airport or an oil refinery in a less developed country. The general contractor of such a turnkey facility then often provides the talent to run it under a management contract.

But management by contract can represent the ultimate humiliation for the contractee when developing countries expropriate major industrial complexes and then ask the former owners to run these facilities under contract. This happened in the "friendly" takeover of oil-producing facilities by the Venezuelan government in 1976. Being pragmatic, U.S. firms agreed to manage their former properties in return for special considerations in addition to their management fees.

Summary You can feel out a chosen market through exporting. If you are successful, the need may arise for local production. If you are not ready for direct investment, licensing provides a reasonable substitute. In order not to have to go it alone from the financial and marketing angles, you may instead (or subsequently) choose a joint venture arrangement. Where permitted, wholly owned subsidiaries put you fully in charge. Management contracts offer a solution when a host country seeks your company's expertise, without allowing it to acquire ownership of the managed properties.

Whichever entry strategy your firm chooses to penetrate a foreign market, "going abroad" will increase potential for growth and profit.

The Team Approach—Thinking Like a Strategist

This section concerns the people interaction: the mind of the strategist and the human will. The human factors intensify whenever there is a conflict of human wills, whenever there is an effort to grow, expand, or achieve an objective.

The purpose is to show how the diverse talents of individuals can be coordinated into a cohesive force for developing competitive strategies. Therefore, the focus will be on (1) the role of strategy teams in developing competitive strategies; (2) broadening the perspective of teams to look at new developments that can be incorporated into competitive strategies; and (3) guidelines to thinking like strategists.

The Roles and Responsibilities of Strategy Teams

As mentioned in Chapter 1, the mind of the manager, the human factors, the people interactions are all key ingredients in utilizing the techniques of market and competitive analyses to organize input into a strategic marketing plan. Now let's overlay that concept with a repeat of the definition of marketing as *a total system of interacting business activities designed to plan, price, promote, and distribute want-satisfying products and services to household and organizational users at a profit in a competitive environment.*

The bending of people interaction and the marketing concept can be achieved most effectively through strategy teams consisting of individuals from all functional areas of the organization (for example, manufacturing, product development, R&D, finance, distribution, and sales/marketing). These functions may vary in some organizations but the key idea is that representation from the major interacting activities be present on a strategy team to fulfill the aim of marketing in a competitive environment.

One of the most notable users of strategy teams is Dow Chemical. It has had an organizational structure for over 20 years that permits strategy teams to operate for individual products and markets, and at various levels throughout its worldwide operations. At any given time there may be as many as 40 strategy teams at work within Dow. These teams have the various designations of Product Management Team (PMT), operating at a product manager level for a product line; Business Management Team (BMT) at the next higher level, dealing with a business unit or major market; and Industry Management Team (IMT), operating on a still broader dimension.

Looking, for example, at the PMT, the team is usually chaired by a product/marketing manager and staffed by individuals representing such functional activities as manufacturing, finance, and technical management. This arrangement not only allows for the dynamics of team members working together, but often defuses traditional adversarial relationships—for example, between marketing and manufacturing. Team members may change from time to time, and the frequency of meetings may vary with teams, but the key element is that the permanency of the team as part of the organizational structure exists and can be called into action at any time.

In establishing a strategy team in your organization, it is important to educate the members to the various concepts, planning requirements, and strategy techniques illustrated in the preceding chapters. Also brief the members, with the concurrence of senior management, on the team's roles and responsibilities, which follow. The strategy team, business management team, or product management team— whichever designation you wish to use—is one of the most successful organizational formats for encouraging and delivering innovative and entrepreneurial thinking. Such a team should be initiated at every operational level by using role and responsibility guidelines. For our purposes, let's designate the team as a **Business Management Team**.

Roles The Business Management Team serves as a significant functional contributor to the strategic marketing planning process with leadership roles in:

- Defining the business or product strategic direction.
- Analyzing the environmental, industry, customer, and competitor situations.
- Developing long- and short-term objectives and strategies.
- Defining product, market, distribution, and quality plans to implement competitive strategies.

Responsibilities
- Creating and recommending new or additional products.
- Approving all alterations or modifications of a major nature.
- Acting as a formal communications channel for field product needs.
- Planning and implementing strategies throughout the product life cycle.
- Developing programs to improve market position and profitability.
- Identifying market or product opportunities in light of changing consumer demands.
- Coordinating efforts with various functions to achieve short- and long-term objectives.
- Coordinating efforts for the interdivisional exchanges of new market or product opportunities.
- Developing a strategic marketing plan.

Identifying Opportunities

A team can be created rapidly and provided with a clear-cut mandate to create marketing opportunities or to tackle competitive threats. More specifically, the team should actively look for *opportunities* to create action. The following opportunities are presented as examples.

Opportunity 1: Search for opportunities in unserved, poorly served, or emerging market segments.

Actions: (a) penetrate and expand niches; (b) improve products and services; (c) stretch product lines; (d) position products to the needs of customers and against competitors.

Case Example

Curtice-Burns, Inc. This form of opportunity was demonstrated by Curtice-Burns Inc., a medium-size food processor that successfully attacked marketing niches largely ignored by the giants. Its strategy of trying to dominate small markets as diverse as canned sauerkraut and pie fillings produced big gains. Profits shot up 18 percent annually during 1981–86, about twice the industry average. In 1984 alone, earnings jumped 22.4 percent to $10 million, while sales climbed 18 percent to $600 million.

Curtice-Burns is continuing its niche strategy by looking for segments of the market in its traditional lines, but is also moving quickly to capture new, low-profile markets. For example, it spotted the Mexican food trend early and introduced its La Suprema Tortilla Chips, which now account for 6 percent of its sales in the northwestern United States. The company has also expanded its canned sauerkraut sales by introducing a crispier version to appeal to a younger segment of the market.

While pursuing all these market niche and product development strategies, Curtice-Burns has also shown remarkable capabilities in the area of promotion as a means of positioning itself to the needs of customers and against competitors. The best example of its capabilities was explained by President McDonald, who stated, "Our people go into a grocery and say, 'I can help you sell your private label baking ingredients' instead of saying 'I've got a great deal on our pie fillings this week.' "

Not only does the company display sound customer (grocery) relationships; it also displays an ability to develop sound consumer relations. For example, several years ago the company offered to donate a percentage of its profits from Blue Boy vegetables to charities selected by customers. This offer turned out to be a trend-setting promotion that achieved extraordinary results.

Opportunity 2: Identify ways to create new opportunities.

Actions: (a) seek new product or market niches; (b) participate in new technology, innovations, and manufacturing; (c) pioneer something new or unique.

Case Example

Seminole Mfg. Co. Actions (b) and (c) are demonstrated by Seminole Mfg. Co., a garment maker, and Wal-Mart Stores, Inc., the large discount chain. These two organizations have formed a successful supplier–customer relationship that innovates with technology to achieve one of the key factors of strategy: *speed.* More precisely, Seminole was able to cut in half its delivery time of men's slacks. Now Wal-Mart is better stocked in all 64 size and color combinations of Seminole's slacks and those sales went up 31 percent over a nine-month period.

What makes speed a marketing reality is *electronic data interchange* (EDI). In brief, EDI permits documents such as purchase orders to be sent from one company's computer to another's. The advantages of EDI all complement speed. For example:

It uses fewer data entry employees, thereby reducing human error and avoiding delays of days or weeks.

It replenishes inventory levels rapidly.

It eliminates lost invoices and improves customer service, since a company can respond faster to customer needs.

EDI provides long-term opportunity in that it can be used as strategy to gain a competitive advantage over rival companies. There are many new technologies available that can serve to create such an advantage. The new inroads of affordable computerized systems that work off small personal computers can provide *just-in-time* (JIT) delivery to customers; or *computer-aided-design* (CAD) systems can offer customers a range of custom-designed products in short periods of time.

Opportunity 3: Look for opportunities through marketing creativity. *Actions:* (a) promote image through quality, performance, and training; and (b) promote creativity in sales promotion, advertising, personal selling, and telemarketing.

Marketing creativity is also linked to new technologies. For example, the new inroads in interactive video seem almost boundless. Hotel chains are experimenting with check-in interactive video systems. Travel agencies are installing kiosks where customers can preview potential vacation spots and make airline reservations. Even the U.S. Postal Service is developing an automated system that will do practically everything a human clerk can. Such systems are used to promote image and to assist in personal selling. For example, Florsheim Shoe Company uses interactive video to prevent losing sales. If customers can't carry out a pair of shoes they want because of an out-of-stock situation, the salesperson can make a promise that the shoes will be delivered to their home within a week. The extra service is provided by the interactive system. It helps the shopper select any of Florsheim's 300 styles; then it places an order directly with the company's warehouse. Large retailers can provide greater selection. Sears, Roebuck, and Co., for example, offers 11,000 types and sizes of curtains, blinds, and shutters, but each store can stock only a tiny fraction of the items. So, Sears uses interactive video to allow customers to browse through the entire range, receive optional decorating tips, and get a printout of the item they decide to order.

The strategy team serves as a forum to explore the extraordinary marketing creativity that is available today to create the competitive advantage.

Opportunity 4: Monitor changing behavioral patterns and preferences.

Actions: (a) practice segmenting markets according to behavioral patterns and (b) identify clusters of customers who might buy or utilize different services for different reasons.

The opportunity for monitoring change has been demonstrated by General Electric and the Whirlpool Corporation, companies that have elevated the service function to full marketing status as a means of monitoring complaints, behavioral patterns, and preferences. What used to be a complaint section staffed by indifferent, low-paid clerks is now a potent marketing tool to identify opportunities. For example, in just three years General Electric built, almost from scratch, one of the most sophisticated service centers in the country. GE found that 25 percent of callers asked prepurchase questions about products. Considering that there were 2.4 million calls in 1985, there was a potential for 500,000 purchases. At Whirlpool, 20 percent of the calls came from do-it-yourselfers. Such valuable feedback identified which parts failed in older models—information that could then be communicated to product development and manufacturing units.

Those companies, as well as a growing number of smaller firms, are finding that service makes marketing less expensive and provides information on a range of opportunities, such as:

- Updating demographic and geographic information
- Directing advertising to target audiences
- Utilizing market intelligence for deploying sales forces and managing territories
- Identifying problem products by model, type of defect, and area of distribution
- Providing clues to customer concerns or product applications
- Providing analysis of life expectancy of products
- Generating ideas for new products and services

Opportunity 5: Learn from competitors—adapt strategies from other industries.

Action: Understand competitors:

- How they conduct business
- What products they sell
- What strategies they pursue
- How they manufacture, distribute, promote, and price
- What their weaknesses, limitations, and possible vulnerabilities are

Case Example

Black & Decker Corp. Black & Decker Corp. continues to successfully challenge Japanese competition. Where Black & Decker factories were once operating at half capacity, they are now churning out an impressive array of power tools, home appliances, and other products. The turnaround has been slow and painful, though, for the once dynamic company. Complacency, the strong U.S. dollar, and dismal marketing let Japan's Makita Electric Works, Ltd. carve out a giant position in U.S. markets. However, Black & Decker learned from its competitor and took positive actions, such as introducing the successful Dustbuster cordless vacuum, purchasing GE's small appliance line, and streamlining operations by closing 7 out of 25 plants.

Management reorganized operations and pared the unwieldy number of product lines to a group that matched corresponding market niches. It filled product gaps in the mid-priced tool segment—the market niche that Makita used to enter indirectly against Black & Decker with virtually no opposition.

Most significantly, there has been a transformation from a product-driven orientation to a market-driven mentality, with a new focus on identifying and satisfying customers' needs and wants. Within that framework, management wants the tool division to come up with at least 12 new products each year—more than it introduced in a previous five-year span. Further, the application of the market-driven orientation is demonstrated by the sources of new product ideas from previously untapped groups: distributors and customers. One of the vehicles through which the ideas emerge are ten advisory panels created by management consisting of distributors or customers.

Appendix

Checklists for Developing Competitive Strategies

The potential for you to strategize, to innovate, to be entrepreneurial, is truly in your hands, regardless of your position in an organization. To round out your exposure to the principles for developing competitive strategies, here are two final examples of those principles at work.

Case Examples

Digital Equipment Corp. Digital Equipment Corp. (DEC), the third largest computer maker in the world, started a massive overhaul in 1983. The company had been suffering from the following afflictions:

- Lack of strategic direction
- A myopic product orientation rather than an expansive customer orientation
- An unresponsive organization divided into numerous fiefdoms that prevented quick reactions to market needs as well as to competitive inroads
- A product strategy that was slow to react to changing buying patterns
- A competitive posture aimed at coexisting with competitors rather than challenging them for market share
- An inability to attack new markets and defend existing ones
- An inability to coordinate all parts of the marketing mix into a well-honed strategy

Fortunately for DEC, the ailments were identified by the founder and CEO, Kenneth Olsen, in time to take action. As he indicated: "The issues that led to the overall situation are not technical but have to do with products and marketing." With some urgency, Olsen began the rehabilitation by taking the following steps:

1. The engineering mentality was transformed into a marketing-driven one in which managers listened to what customers were asking for in terms of product, service, training, and software applications.
2. The corporate bureaucracy was trimmed, decision making was decentralized, and the lines of communication from the field to the home office were shortened.
3. A broad-based market strategy was developed to compete aggressively with IBM, Wang Laboratories, Inc., AT&T, and the Japanese.
4. Product development was speeded up by consolidating 12 U.S. product groups into three regional management centers, engineering and manufacturing operations were combined, and product managers were given bottom-line marketing responsibilities.
5. The sales force focused on managing accounts rather than specific markets. The aim was to eliminate the wasteful practice of as many as six sales reps, each from a different product line, calling on one large account.
6. A product strategy was formed that made DEC's low-end desktop products work together with its established minicomputer line so that they could be sold together as a system.
7. Marketing skills were improved for aggressive movement of the company into explosive markets for education and training, as well as for expansion into the growing small business market.

Echlin Inc.   Echlin Inc., a Connecticut-based producer of auto and truck parts, is displaying a unique characteristic. It is competing aggressively and *successfully* against equally aggressive competitors from Taiwan, Japan, and South Korea.

Echlin's strategy is beginning to appear as a pattern among those organizations that are competing successfully within their own marketing battleground. Two of the visible aspects of the pattern are the development of manufacturing efficiency and the recognition that service and quality are integral components of a marketing mix strategy.

Going beyond the buzzwords of service and quality are distinctive competencies that lead to competitive advantage. Those competencies can be considered in the form of competitive strategies displayed by Echlin:

1. *Product:* Nearly 150,000 different parts for every car from the Model T to a Rolls-Royce are produced by Echlin. The competitive advantage is that no Far East company offers any *single source* of supply for the number of parts deliverable from Echlin.
2. *Delivery:* Speed is essential for a repair shop that can't afford the time or the irritation to the customer of tying up

a car for one day longer than necessary. Echlin puts managers on rigid performance standards requiring, for example, that 95 percent of all orders be filled within 48 hours. Every percentage point above or below 95 percent is valued at 5 percent of pay in bonus or bonus debit.

3. *Service:* Counter people at jobbers' locations are taught how to look efficiently in a catalog to locate the appropriate (Echlin) part. Echlin personnel also work with mechanics, which results in pulling through extra sales. The service, plus the speed of delivery, often overcomes the price differential from Far East competitors.

4. *Customer satisfaction:* Echlin recognized a changing behavioral pattern in one segment of its market. Foreign cars were aging and foreign-car dealers were swamped with warranty work. Managers observed that those car owners were heading to local garages for their repairs. With half of its sales from neighborhood mechanics, Echlin was ready to meet the specific demands of that customer group.

Thus, you can see in the Echlin example that the name of the strategy game is *competitive advantage*. It is an urgency at all managerial levels, particularly among middle managers who face a day-to-day confrontation with competing products. The Digital Equipment example focuses on a wide range of activities, including transforming an engineering mentality to a marketing-driven one, trimming the bureaucracy, developing broad-based market strategies, and coordinating all parts of the marketing mix into a well-honed strategy.

You, too, can gain competitive advantage by developing your own competitive strategy. Use the forms that follow, along with what you've learned from the various chapters, to become a successful strategist.

Part I: Competitive Advantage Analysis
(by market or product 1–10 rating, 10 = best)
Product

Product: _____	*Your Firm/Product*	*Competitor A*	*Competitor B*	*Competitor C*	*List Advantage and Define Strategy*
Quality					
Features					
Options					
Style					
Brand Name					
Packaging					
Sizes					
Services					
Warranties					
Returns					
Versatility					
Uniqueness					
Utility					
Reliability					
Durability					
Patent Protection					
Guarantees					

Price and Distribution

Price: _____	Your Firm/Product	Competitor A	Competitor B	Competitor C	List Advantage and Define Strategy
List Price					
Discounts					
Allowances					
Payment Period					
Credit Terms					
Distribution: ___ Channels					
Warranties					
Direct Sales Force					
Distributors					
Dealers					
Market Coverage					
Warehouse Locations					
Inventory Control Systems					
Physical Transport					

(*continued*)

Part I: Continued

Promotion

Promotion: _____	*Your Firm/Product*	*Competitor A*	*Competitor B*	*Competitor C*	*List Advantage and Define Strategy*
Advertising					
Customer					
Trade					
Personal Selling					
Incentives					
Sales Aids					
Samples					
Training					
Sales Promotions					
Demonstrations					
Contests					
Premiums					
Coupons					
Manuals					
Telemarketing					
Publicity					
TOTAL SCORE					

Part II: Competitors' Strategies Analysis
(by market, 1–10 rating, 10 = best)
Market Segments by Size, Location, or Product Applications

A. MARKET DIMENSION (List product/market segments)								Current $	Potential $
TOTAL									

TOTAL

(*continued*)

Market Segments by Size, Location, or Product Applications (continued)

B. MARKET ENTRY How do competitors usually enter a market? Is there a market leader among the competitors? Who are the followers? Identify by:						
First-in Strategy	Price					
	Product					
	Promotion					
	Distribution					
Follow-the-Leader Strategy	Price					
	Product					
	Promotion					
	Distribution					
Last-in Strategy	Price					
	Product					
	Promotion					
	Distribution					
C. MARKET COMMITMENT How much commitment do competitors give to a specific market in terms of people, dollars, research, products? Commitment						

Market Segments by Size, Location, or Product Applications

D. MARKET DEMAND How flexible are competitors in changing strategies for different market situations?					
Prune markets when demand slackens					
Concentrate on key markets when demand increase					
Harvest profits when sales plateau					
E. MARKET DIVERSIFICATION How have competitors responded to diversification opportunities?					
Specialized resources by segment					
Added another stage of distribution					

(*continued*)

Part II: Continued
Product

A. POSITIONING How efficient are competitors in monitoring customer perceptions and identifying customer niches as related to:				
Positioning a single brand				
Positioning a multiple brand				
Repositioning older products				
B. PRODUCT LIFE CYCLE How efficient are competitors in extending the life cycle of their products as related to:				
Promoting more frequent usage				
Finding new users				
Finding more uses for products				

Product

C. PRODUCT COMPETITION To what extent do competitors attempt to gain a larger share of a market by introducing:					
Packaging					
Competing brand					
Private label					
Generic product					
D. PRODUCT MIX Where do competitors stand as related to width and depth of product lines?					
Single product					
Multiple products					
Product systems					

(continued)

Part II: Continued
Product (continued)

E. PRODUCT APPLICATION How much manufacturing and application flexibility do competitors display as related to:					
Standard products					
Private label products					
Standard product, modified					
F. NEW PRODUCTS What has been the pattern of competitors related to the following areas of new product development?					
Innovation					
Modification					
Line extension					
Diversification					
Remerchandising or reformulating existing products					

Product

F. NEW PRODUCTS (*Continued*)					
Market extending (existing products)					
G. PRODUCT AUDIT How flexible have competitors been in managing their product lines as displayed by:					
Line reduction					
Line elimination					

(continued)

Part II: Continued
Price

A. NEW PRODUCTS What has been the pattern of competitors in pricing new products? Do they tend to use:					
Skim (high) pricing					
Penetration (low) pricing					
Follow-the-leader pricing					
Cost-plus pricing					
B. ESTABLISHED PRODUCTS What has been the pattern of competitors in pricing established products? Do they tend to use:					
Slide-down (gradual reduction) pricing					
Segment pricing					

Price

B. ESTABLISHED PRODUCTS (*Continued*)					
Flexible pricing					
Preemptive (reacting to competitors') pricing					
Loss-leader pricing					

(continued)

Part II: Continued
Promotion

A. ADVERTISING To what extent do competitors use advertising to do the following:					
Support personal selling					
Inform target audience about availability of product					
Persuade prospects to buy directly from advertising					
B. SALES FORCE What is the profile of competitors' sales forces related to:					
Sales force size					
Sales force territorial design					
Compensation systems					

Promotion

B. SALES FORCE (*Continued*)					
Training					
Technical or service backup					
C. SALES PROMOTION How well do competitors integrate sales promotion with their advertising and sales force strategies? Is sales promotion used to:					
Encourage more product usage					
Induce distributor and dealer involvement					
Stimulate greater sales force efforts					

(*continued*)

Part II: Continued
Distribution

A. CHANNEL STRUCTURE What has been the distribution strategy of competitors in reaching customer markets?					
Direct distribution to the end user					
Indirect distribution through intermediaries (distributors, dealers)					
Direct sale to end user					
B. CHANNEL DIMENSION Are competitors displaying any strategies that could alter their distribution methods? Are they looking at:					
Exclusive (restricted) distribution					
Intensive (widespread) distribution					

Index